THE MONARCHY OF BRITAIN

ABOVE William the Conqueror and his barons,
from a 14th-century manuscript.

OVERLEAF Charles II, from the Plea Rolls.

THE MONARCHY OF BRITAIN

Josephine Ross

William Morrow and Company, Inc.
New York 1982

CONTENTS

ACKNOWLEDGMENTS   6
MAP   7

Copyright © 1982 by Josephine Ross

First published in the United States of America in 1982 by William Morrow and Company, Inc.

First published in Great Britain in 1982 by George Weidenfeld & Nicolson, Ltd, London, under the title *The Monarchs of Britain*.

All rights reserved. No part of this book may be reproduced or utilized in any form or by any means, electronic or mechanical, including photocopying, recording or by any information storage and retrieval system, without permission in writing from the Publisher. Inquiries should be addressed to William Morrow and Company, Inc., 105 Madison Avenue, New York, N.Y. 10016.

Library of Congress Catalog Card Number: 82-81952

ISBN: 0-688-00949-2

Art editor Allison Waterhouse
Designer Sandra Buchanan
Filmset by Keyspools Ltd, Golborne, Lancs
Colour separations by Newsele Litho Ltd
Printed and bound by L.E.G.O., Vicenza

First Edition

1 2 3 4 5 6 7 8 9 10

Chapter four
THE HOUSE OF LANCASTER   56

Henry IV   1399–1413   57
Henry V   1413–22   59
Henry VI   1422–71   62

Chapter five
THE HOUSE OF YORK   66

Edward IV   1461–83   66
Edward V   1483   69
Richard III   1483–85   72

Chapter one
THE NORMANS   8

William I   1066–87   8
William II   1087–1100   13
Henry I   1100–35   15
Stephen   1135–54   17

Chapter two
THE ANGEVINS   24

Henry II   1154–89   24
Richard I   1189–99   27
John   1199–1216   31

Chapter three
THE PLANTAGENETS   36

Henry III   1216–72   36
Edward I   1272–1307   38
Edward II   1307–27   42
Edward III   1327–77   46
Richard II   1377–99   49

Chapter six
THE TUDORS   76

Henry VII   1485–1509   76
Henry VIII   1509–47   79
Edward VI   1547–53   84
Mary I   1553–58   87
Elizabeth I   1558–1603   89

Acknowledgments

The photographs in this book are reproduced by kind permission of the following (numbers refer to pages):

By gracious permission of Her Majesty the Queen: 69, 85, 95 right (by permission of the Controller of Her Majesty's Stationery Office), 113, 118 bottom right, 124 right, 130, 144 bottom, 147, 151, 152, 154–5, 156 top, 157 top, 157 bottom, 158 right (Royal Archives, Windsor Castle), 162 bottom, 164, 165 (Royal Library, Windsor), 168, 174 top
Aerofilms: 64 top left
John Bethell: 23 top and bottom, 41 right and bottom, 44 bottom, 58, 61
Bibliothèque Nationale, Paris: 42
Bodleian Library, Oxford: 16, 13 bottom, 30 bottom, 34
Bridgeman Art Library: 142, 169 left, 177
British Library: 12, 13 top, 14, 15, 18, 28, 36, 47 top, 49 right, 50–1, 56, 59, 88
British Museum: 64 top right, 112, 120, 156 bottom
British Tourist Authority: 44 top
Cambridgeshire Libraries: 118 top right
Cambridge University Library: 9 top
Camera Club (Marcus Adams): 172
Dean and Chapter, Canterbury Cathedral: 70–1, 82 bottom left
Cooper-Bridgeman Library: 31 (British Library), 119, 125, 126 bottom (Victoria & Albert Museum), 131 right, 137 (Royal Naval College, Greenwich), 140 top
Corpus Christi College, Oxford: 45
Department of the Environment Library: 54
E.T.Archive: 63, 115 top (British Museum), 136 (Tate Gallery)
Tim Graham: 178, 180–1, 180 bottom
Her Majesty's Stationery Office: 32 bottom right, 162 top
Michael Holford: 8–9, 10–11, 20, 22, 26, 30 top, 48, 57, 88 left and right, 133, 141, 145 top and bottom (Science Museum), 148–9 top and bottom
Angelo Hornak: 10 top, 24, 43, 76–7, 114, 124 left, 131 left, 138
Huntingdon Library: 51 left, right and bottom
A.F.Kersting: 32 bottom left, 37 left, 78 top right and bottom right, 86
Lambeth Palace Library: 60–1
London Museum: 127 right
Mansell Collection: 81, 84 top, 128
National Army Museum: 139
National Film Archives: 160–1
National Gallery: 52–3
National Galleries of Scotland: 97, 99, 103, 104, 108 top
National Library of Scotland (Sir David Ogilvy): 95 left
National Maritime Museum: 90, 140 bottom
National Monuments Record: 37 right, 41 top left
National Portrait Gallery: 73, 79 right, 84 bottom, 91, 110, 123, 132, 150
National Trust: 105, 107, 127 left
National Trust for Scotland: 106 left and right
Pepys Library, Magdalene College, Cambridge: 126 top
Musée de Picardie, Amiens: 116–7
Pitkins Pictorials: 17, 49 left
Popperfoto: 166 top, 167 top, 169 right, 173, 175, 179 right
Public Record Office: 108 bottom
Royal Naval College, Greenwich: 129
The Royal Pavilion, Art Gallery and Museums, Brighton: 148 left
Scala: 25
Scottish Tourist Board: 96, 98, 109 left, 174 bottom
Snark: 46–7 top
Victoria & Albert Museum: 92 bottom
Andy Williams: 178–9
Woodmansterne: 176 bottom
Weidenfeld & Nicolson Archives: 21 (Aerofilms), 27 (British Museum), 29 (British Museum), 33, 39, 40, 46–7 bottom, 62, 66 (British Museum), 67 left, 75, 79 left, 80 (Thyssen Collection), 82 top, 101, 109 right, 115 bottom, 118, 122, 134, 135, 143, 146, 153 (Victoria & Albert Museum), 161 (Royal Photographic Society), 163, 166–7 bottom (Guildhall Art Gallery), 170 (Eileen Hose, Broadchalke), 171, 176 top (Eileen Hose)
Dean and Chapter, Worcester Cathedral: 32 top

GAZETTEER MAP

GREATER LONGON

Hammersmith, Kensington, Chelsea, Fulham, Richmond, Battersea, Westminster, Lambeth, Greenwich, River Thames

Key

1. Richmond Palace Gatehouse
2. Royal Botanic Gardens
3. Royal Hospital Chelsea
4. Kensington Palace
5. The Science Museum
6. Victoria and Albert Museum
7. Queen's Gallery
8. St. James's Palace
9. Horse Guard's Parade
10. Buckingham Palace
11. Westminster Abbey
12. Westminster Hall
13. Palace of Westminster
14. Museum of London
15. Guildhall
16. St. Paul's Cathedral
17. Tower of London
18. The Queens House
19. National Maritime Museum
20. Royal Naval College
21. Royal Observatory

SCOTLAND

Castle of Mey, Inverness, Battlefield of Culloden, Aberdeen, Balmoral Castle, Fort William, Glamis Castle, Perth, Dundee, Falkland Palace, Dunfermline Abbey, Battlefield of Bannockburn, Stirling Castle, Linlithgow Palace, Holyrood House, Glasgow, Edinburgh (castle), Craigmillar Castle, Battlefield of Flodden, Melrose Abbey, Bamburgh Castle, Traquair House, Kelso Abbey, Alnwick Castle, Newcastle-upon-Tyne, Durham (cathedral), Richmond Castle, Rievaulx Abbey, Pickering Castle, Fountains Abbey, York, The Railway Museum, Leeds, Hull, Manchester, Liverpool, Sheffield, Lincoln, Chester, Newark Castle, Caernarvon Castle, Stoke-on-Trent, Belton Park, Sandringham House (Museum), Harlech (castle), Boscobel House, Nottingham, Castle Rising, Shrewsbury, Tutbury Castle, King's Lynn (Guildhall), Birmingham, Coventry, Huntingdon, Cromwell Museum, Norwich, Worcester (cathedral), Kenilworth Castle, Ely Cathedral, Ludlow Castle, Warwick, Cambridge King's College, Framlingham Castle, Lord Leicester Hospital, Tewkesbury Abbey, The Eleanor Cross, Orford Castle, Sudeley Castle, Audley End, Monmouth Castle, Blenheim Palace, Hatfield House, Pembroke Castle, Swansea, Oxford (castle / Martyr's Memorial), Gloucester, The Royal Mausoleum, London, Berkeley Castle, Runnymede, Windsor (castle), Eltham Palace, Rochester Castle, Cardiff (castle), Hampton Court, Knole, Canterbury (cathedral), Battlefield of Sedgemoor, Winchester (cathedral/castle), Eton College, Battle Abbey, Dover (castle), Taunton Castle, Broadlands House, Southampton, Lewes Battlefield, Hastings, Arundel Castle, Eastbourne, Exeter, Porchester Castle, Brighton, The Royal Pavilion, Osborne House, Carisbrooke Castle, Plymouth, Penzance

7

Chapter one
THE NORMANS

William I
1066-87

THE YEAR 1066 saw two coronations in England. Early in January, in the splendid setting of the newly built and consecrated Abbey at Westminster, the last of the Anglo-Saxon kings, Harold Godwine, was crowned. But within 12 months he was dead, and a foreigner ruled his kingdom; for in 1066, the most famous date in English history, William the Conqueror invaded to claim the throne and the monarchy of England passed to the Normans.

The invasion from across the Channel by William, the Duke of Normandy, had been expected throughout King Harold's brief reign. Though Harold was the rightful ruler – elected, according to Anglo-Saxon custom, by the council of elders called the Witenagemot and anointed before God – Duke William claimed that he himself had been promised the throne by the late king, his cousin Edward the Confessor; and this claim the warlike William was determined to enforce.

Throughout the spring and summer of 1066 William prepared his invasion fleet. The masterpiece of Norman needlework known as the Bayeux Tapestry, recording in exquisite detail the events of the Conquest, shows boats being built and mail-coated soldiers mustering, while overhead Halley's Comet appears, as it did about Easter of that year, as a portent for the English. By the end of August the invasion was ready, and only the lack of a favourable wind prevented Duke William from embarking.

The apparent setback of the weather

RIGHT King Harald Hardrada of Norway fights the northern army at Fulford on 20 September 1066, from a French manuscript.

The Norman fleet heading for Pevensey, from the Bayeux tapestry.

8

ET VENIT AD PEVENESÆ:·

played a crucial part in the Norman Conquest of England. While William was delayed in Normandy, King Harold's army fought a great battle at Stamford Bridge near York, against a yet more threatening claimant to the English throne, the powerful Harald Hardrada, King of Norway. Though King Harold of England won a resounding victory and the Viking invader was killed, it was a depleted and battle-weary English army which finally faced the Normans under Duke William, on 14 October, near Hastings. By nightfall the luckless Harold lay dead, not with an arrow in the eye but felled by a sword, and, in the words of the Anglo-Saxon Chronicle, 'the French had possession of the place of slaughter'.

The second coronation of 1066 took place on Christmas Day, when the Norman Conqueror became King William I of England. He was then about 38 years old, an imposing figure, six feet tall and heavily built. Born out of wedlock, the son of Duke Robert I and a tanner's daughter named Herleva, or Arlette, he had grown up with the nickname

RIGHT Norman columns in St John's Chapel, in the Tower of London.

The death of Harold at the battle of Hastings (he is the figure being cut down under the words *Interfectus est*).

of William the Bastard. But despite his illegitimacy, in 1035 he had succeeded to his father's rich and powerful little duchy, while still a child; and in the dangerous years that followed he learned the skills of war and strong government. As King of England he was to rule with ruthless efficiency, taxing his conquered subjects heavily, enforcing law and order, and, in the process, reshaping Anglo-Saxon society along the lines of feudal Normandy. The great stone keep of the Tower of London, begun by William in 1078, was an impressive symbol of the power of the Norman conquerors.

In the early years of William I's reign there were scattered risings against the Norman occupation. The most serious came in 1069, when a Danish invasion party sailed up the Humber and joined forces with local inhabitants and English leaders, seizing the city of York. William's response provided a brutal warning to other rebels: he laid waste the north, killing and burning without mercy. Almost the last pocket of English resistance disappeared in 1071, when the Saxon folk-hero Hereward the Wake, who had held out in the Fen country after briefly taking Peterborough, eluded the Normans and

passed into history. William confiscated the estates of rebel earls and thanes and gave them out as rewards to his Norman followers, thus strengthening his hold on England. The native ruling class almost vanished from the wooden halls, to be replaced by the new foreign overlords, who built themselves stout castles, first of wood, later of stone; by 1085 only two English landowners of any importance were left.

Under the feudal system, each man had a lord directly above him to whom he owed service in return for tenure of land. At the top of the social hierarchy, the king was overlord of all. The Norman barons whom William rewarded with estates enjoyed their lands as tenants of the king; in return, they were bound to provide him with a yearly quota of knights for his military service. Many of these knights found themselves fighting on the Continent in Normandy's wars, which English taxes helped to finance. Even after he became King of England, William I remained entirely Norman, and he spent much of his time out of the kingdom in France, governing his duchy and conducting its constant wars in person.

The changes which came about in

England after the Conquest arose through William's need to enforce law and order, rather than as a matter of policy. The Conqueror was conservative by temperament, and where possible the existing Anglo-Saxon law and institutions were left intact or adapted. Though the former English ruling class disappeared and the native culture was submerged beneath the speech and customs, manners and fashions, art and architecture of the Norman masters, this forcible exposure to Continental influence was eventually to revitalise the society of England, just as the French language enriched the English tongue.

The Norman genius for efficient administration was well displayed in the making of the national survey known as the 'Doomsday Book', which William I commissioned in 1085, shortly before his death. To gain precise records of all his subjects' possessions for taxation purposes, King William sent royal commissioners into every part of England, compiling information, until there was 'not an ox, cow or swine that was not set down in the writ'. Though some contemporary chroniclers thought it an example of the king's greed and 'shameful to tell', the

haraldo triumphatoi magnificus potent adquisita subiugau / Abbaciã de bello ubi tumpharat fundau. Regnau anis xxi. 7 aplius

trem ei receper? rfim tauer? mltiplir fatigar? repuls / aulã Westm gstrur. tande sagr̃ta pûr p̃m regnaui? ar̃ / xiii

Willelm rex anglie pmi p co quisiconem ei

Will rex Ruf

Henricus se nior Rex tci

Ste rex Bl

Iste henricus vir potens 7 sapiens iurau leges sci edwardi iui / clabis? tene. s; p̃m uicat frem suu: noluit. Nobile cenobiu de / Radigto ubi sepult̃ iace; fundaui 7 repaui gstitur kr̃r. Regnau au / annis xxxv. 7 circiter dimidiu.

Iste Stephanus miles strenuissim? omnib; dieb, / dubiis casib; bellorum intfuit. Iste Abbaciam de feurcha / fundauit. In qua ip̃e 7 Eustachii sihus ei 7 Matildis reg / uxor ei iacent sepulti. Iste Regnauit Ann. s xix.

Doomsday Book was a remarkable achievement, and bears lasting witness to the Conqueror's strength of purpose.

Calculating, even brutal, as William I could be, in private he showed a more sympathetic side to his character. He was almost illiterate, yet he valued learning, and his dearest friend was the great Italian scholar Lanfranc, whom he made his Archbishop of Canterbury in 1070 and who undertook a major reorganisation of the English Church with William's approval. To his wife, Queen Matilda, William I showed a devotion and faithfulness unusual for the time; perhaps in reaction to the circumstances of his own illegitimate birth, he was a highly moral man.

Three of William's four sons – Robert, William and Henry – were to outlive him. In his will, in accordance with Norman custom, the Conqueror left his patrimony, the Duchy of Normandy, to Robert, the eldest son, and the newer possession of England to William. To Henry, the youngest, he left a fortune in silver. Like many great men of history, William the Conqueror had troublesome sons; and although William, his favourite, was at his bedside when he died, Robert had taken up arms against him and was at the court of his enemy, the King of France.

In the summer of 1087, while campaigning in France, William I was fatally injured by his horse rearing under him, and on 9 September he died. It was fitting that a King of England who spoke only French, and who was to be described by the English for nine centuries as 'the Conqueror', should have been buried in his native land, at Caen.

William II 1087-1100

T HE SECOND Norman king of England was stout, like his father, with auburn hair and a florid face that earned him the nickname of 'Rufus', meaning 'the Red'. He had the Conqueror's love of hunting and his fondness for money, but the greater qualities of William I were not passed on to William II. Contemporary chroniclers were shocked by Rufus's debaucheries; and Archbishop Lanfranc was at first reluctant to perform the sacred ceremony of coronation

ABOVE   William Rufus is killed in the New Forest; Henry is told of the event.

for so unworthy a king. Eventually, however, the Conqueror's will was carried out, and on 26 September 1087 King William II was crowned in Westminster Abbey.

He soon became unpopular with almost every section of English society, including the Norman barons. Many of them now had estates on both sides of the Channel, and were thus bound to two different overlords – Duke Robert in Normandy, and his brother and rival King William in England. Some attempted to resolve this conflict of interests by rebelling against William, in the hope of uniting duchy and kingdom under Robert; but they had given their support to the weaker brother. For all his faults, William Rufus did not lack skill in war-making. He put down rebellion with a firm hand, and in his turn manoeuvred to oust Duke Robert from Normandy. By 1096 he had obtained virtual control of the duchy. In return for a payment of 10,000 marks Duke Robert agreed to go far away, on a crusade to the Holy Land, in support of Pope Urban II.

For his own expenses, as well as for this kind of diplomatic bribery, William was in constant need of money. His court lived luxuriously; where once his father had 'kept a great state', with stern dignity, Rufus now

St Anselm, Archbishop of Canterbury under William Rufus.

enjoyed a round of bawdy, drunken merry-making. He may have been homosexual; certainly he never married, showed scant interest in mistresses and had no acknowledged bastards, yet was castigated for possessing unspeakable vices. To the monks who wrote the records of the time, Rufus was a lecherous, blasphemous tyrant, who gave

The four Norman kings.

13

William Rufus and
Henry I, from a
14th-century
manuscript.

free reign to 'everything that was hateful to God and to righteous men'.

With Rufus's loose living went an open contempt for the Church. He made a profitable practice of failing to appoint new bishops and abbots, so that he could take the Church funds due to them for his own use. After the death of the good and wise Lanfranc, in 1089, the English had no Archbishop of Canterbury for four years. William did, however, fill the position of Bishop of Durham – he gave it as a reward to the man who helped him in his unscrupulous financial dealings, an ambitious cleric named Ranulf Flambard.

Ungodly as he was, William Rufus experienced a brief religious conversion early in 1093, when a sudden bad illness brought him close to death. Among other penitent measures, he at last appointed an Archbishop of Canterbury, Anselm of Bec, who was later canonised. The king's fit of faith passed with the illness, however, and eventually William succeeded in driving Anselm into exile, leaving the English Church leaderless once more.

In a superstitious age, when an earthquake or the appearance of a comet in the sky was sure to be greeted as an omen, the manner of William Rufus's sudden, violent death was seen by many as a punishment for his life. On the morning of 2 August 1100, while out hunting deer in the New Forest, Rufus received an arrow in his heart and died, 'in the midst of his sins, without repentance'. His body, having lain neglected for several hours, was carried to Winchester in a humble charcoal-burner's cart, and buried beneath the cathedral tower.

Who shot William Rufus has never been proved. One account suggested at the time that the King had accidentally killed himself, while others stated that a Norman lord named Walter Tirel loosed the fatal arrow. Tirel fled the country, yet he always maintained his innocence, and the evidence points to another's guilt: as soon as Rufus was dead, the youngest of the Conqueror's three surviving sons, Henry, seized power with suspicious ease and swiftness. If there was a plot to murder William Rufus, it would seem that Henry I was behind it.

Few mourned William Rufus. His most enduring foundation, which still stands today, was Westminster Hall, used by English monarchs ever since for ceremonial occasions such as coronation banquets and lyings-in-state. A successful soldier, he recovered for Normandy the disputed territories of Maine and the Vexin, which Duke Robert had lost, and he led English troops into Scotland and Wales with some success.

But his evil reputation largely overshadowed his achievements – and it was another sign for the superstitious when, a year after his burial at Winchester, the tower above his remains tumbled down.

Henry I 1100-35

AT THE TIME of William Rufus's sudden death, his younger brother Henry was 32 years old. Nicknamed 'Beauclerk', or 'fine scholar', by later generations, Henry enjoyed a reputation for learning which was flatteringly exaggerated during his lifetime. However, he could certainly read and write and speak some English, unlike his father and brothers, and his interest in Saxon law and judicial reforms earned him the name of 'the Lion of Justice' from contemporary writers.

The means by which Henry became King of England in the summer of 1100 revealed his devious intelligence. Under an agreement between the Conqueror's two elder sons, Robert of Normandy and William Rufus of England, each was the other's heir. When Rufus set out on his last, fatal hunting-party Duke Robert was known to be on his way home from the Crusades, having acquired not only a reputation for chivalry but a fair young wife, who might be expected to bear him sons. With Rufus lying dead and Robert still some distance from Normandy and England, Henry acted swiftly. He took possession of the Treasury at Winchester and then galloped to London to have himself proclaimed King of England instead of Robert.

The basis of Henry's claim was that he had been 'born in the purple': his birth had taken place in England, after the Conquest, when his father was the reigning king, instead of merely Duke of Normandy. According to the custom of some parts of feudal Europe, this would give Henry the right to inherit the throne, rather than his elder brothers. It was thus as the Conqueror's heir, and not William Rufus's, that he was crowned King Henry in Westminster Abbey on 5 August 1100.

To support his uncertain claim, Henry took care to present himself at the beginning of his reign as a good and just king. He issued

King Henry I mourns the death of his son William, who drowned in the wreck of the White Ship.

15

King Henry I crossing to England from France, from a 12th-century manuscript.

a charter of liberties, to be read in every shire of the realm, in which he promised to restore the laws of William I and Edward the Confessor, and right the wrongs done by his brother. As proof of his good faith, he imprisoned the unpopular Ranulf Flambard and began to restore the power of the Church, inviting Anselm, the Archbishop of Canterbury, to return from exile, and appointing new abbots and bishops to the offices which had been left vacant by Rufus. In November 1100 he took a major political and dynastic step: he married Edith, the sister of King Edgar of Scotland, and a descendant of Alfred the Great. Many of the Norman barons sneered at their king for allying himself with a princess of Saxon descent, but Henry understood the value of diplomatic marriages. By his own, he brought together the royal and ducal blood of England, Scotland and Normandy in his descendants, secured a period of peace with Scotland, and gratified his English subjects.

Within a year of Henry's coronation, as expected, Duke Robert of Normandy invaded England in an attempt to claim the throne. He had considerable support among King Henry's Norman subjects, and he brought with him a powerful fighting force; but the younger brother had the advantage of the sharper wits. In a confrontation on the road to London, with their armies drawn up in readiness to fight, King Henry offered Duke Robert terms which included an amnesty for his followers in England, a yearly payment of 3,000 marks for himself and help with his territorial ambitions on the Continent. Swayed by these promises, Robert foolishly chose to concede, and returned in peace to his duchy. Henry proceeded to punish the pardoned barons by falsely accusing them of other crimes, and subjecting them to ruinous fines. The greatest of them, Robert of Bellême, Earl of Shrewsbury, was eventually banished from the kingdom, but he continued to work against Henry from the shelter of his estates in Normandy.

The conflict between the two brothers continued to simmer, fuelled by the activities of interested parties such as Robert of Bellême, until it was finally resolved in 1106, in battle near Tinchebrai. This decisive confrontation on Norman soil, between the sons of William the Conqueror, took place just 40 years after Hastings. At Tinchebrai, however, the Duke of Normandy was beaten and taken prisoner by the King of England. The duchy and the kingdom were united under one ruler again, and for the rest of his life Robert was Henry's captive in England.

For all his literacy and intelligence, Henry I was in some ways the least admirable of the Conqueror's sons. Robert was weak and ineffectual, Rufus had been gross, but Henry was capable of deliberate cruelty. In 1090, a prisoner who had betrayed an oath of allegiance was pushed off the ramparts at Rouen, not merely on Henry's orders, but by his own hand. Later in the reign, as a reprisal for the blinding of a young hostage by one of his sons-in-law, Henry gave permission for his own little grandaughters to be hideously mutilated by the dead youth's vengeful father. Even by the standards of a brutal age, Henry I was a king to be feared.

Once his position on the throne was secure, he departed from some of the promises which he had made at the time of his coronation. Rather than restoring old laws he revised the legal system of the realm to extend his power, curb the growing might of the unruly barons, and make the administration of justice and taxation more efficient. He chose his servants well, finding careful, trustworthy men such as Bishop Roger of Salisbury, who rose from humble beginnings to become Chancellor, Treasurer and the King's right-hand man. It was Bishop Roger who built up the new court at

16

Winchester for the collection of royal revenues; calculations were made there by means of counters on a large chequered cloth, and so the term 'Court of the Exchequer' came into being. To the king's council, or Curia Regis, Henry gave new strength and centralised authority. From this governing body, made up of leading dignitaries such as barons, tenants-in-chief and bishops, the institutions of Parliament, the King's Bench and the Privy Council were ultimately to develop. The laws enforced by the Curia Regis often carried dire penalties, from heavy fines to hanging; but if the administration of justice was harsh under King Henry I, it was at least meted out even-handedly to Norman and Saxon alike, and gave some protection to the humblest of his subjects.

Henry's early undertaking 'to make the holy Church of God free' was not fulfilled. Having invited Anselm back from exile in 1100, he found himself in conflict with his Archbishop over the issue of lay investiture. While Henry was determined to maintain his right to appoint and invest bishops, installing them in office himself, as a necessary aspect of royal power, Anselm insisted that he must abide by recent papal rulings which denied such spiritual authority to the king. In 1107, under threat of excommunication, Henry agreed to compromise: he renounced his right of investiture, but retained his claim to the bishops' homage for the lands which went with their offices. Officially, at least, something of the mystic power had gone out of monarchy. The dispute had been conducted without anger between the King and the Archbishop, and Henry always maintained an outward show of respect for the Church, but on Anselm's death in 1109 Henry reverted to one of Rufus's practices – he left the Archbishopric of Canterbury vacant for the next five years.

It was a sad irony that Henry I, who fathered some 20 bastard children, should have ended his life without a legitimate male heir, and so left England a legacy of uncertainty over the succession. In November 1120, while crossing to England from Normandy in the White Ship, his only legitimate son, William, was drowned. Henry was a widower at the time; but though he quickly remarried, his new Queen, Adelaide of Louvain, bore him no children. It was thus to his only daughter, Matilda, that Henry arranged to leave his kingdom and his duchy; and to this end he married her in 1128 to Geoffrey, the 16-year-old son of the Count of Anjou.

By securing this alliance with Normandy's traditional enemy he hoped to strengthen Matilda's hold over the troubled duchy; in the event, it weakened her position as ruler of England, where the Norman barons had no wish to become the subjects of a queen with a husband of the hated house of Anjou. By the summer of 1135, the long period of stability which Henry I had brought to England was at an end and fighting had already broken out. While out hunting in Normandy, Henry fell ill – the result, it was decided, of eating too many of the small eels called lampreys. On 1 December 1135 he died, and soon all England was in the grip of civil war.

Stephen 1135-54

ALTHOUGH THEY had sworn to support Henry I's daughter Matilda as their ruler if the King should die without an heir, few of the barons in England and Normandy were prepared to stand by their oath. Not only was she a woman, she was also arrogant and unpopular, and above all she was married to the Count of Anjou, ruler of England and Normandy's traditional enemy. When Henry I died, at the end of 1135, the barons assembled to debate the succession, and from several possible candidates – including Matilda's infant son, Henry – they chose Count Theobald of Blois, the elder son of William the Conqueror's daughter, Adela. The throne was offered to Theobald, and negotiations were in progress when startling news arrived – another candidate, Theobald's younger brother Stephen, Count of Mortain and Boulogne, had already made himself King of England.

Stephen had been a particular favourite with his uncle Henry I. The King had virtually brought him up, arranged his marriage with an heiress and endowed him with the Norman county of Mortain and so many English estates that he was one of the wealthiest men in England. It had seemed as though Henry might be grooming him for future kingship, and such was the basis of Stephen's claim. As soon as he heard that the King was dead, he sailed for England, where he declared that Henry had named him as his heir on his deathbed. With the support of his brother Henry, whom the king had created

Archbishop Thurstan of York, who constructed the standard after which the famous battle of 22 August 1138 against the Scots was named.

17

King Stephen holding a hawk.

Bishop of Winchester, and the citizens of London, he persuaded the clergy to acknowledge him, and the Archbishop of Canterbury crowned him on 22 December 1135.

Stephen had been popular at King Henry's court. He was charming, he was courageous in battle, he was a generous patron of the Church, and he was, in general, chivalrous –

he later became the first English king to permit jousting. 'When he was a Count', wrote a contemporary chronicler, 'by his good nature, and by the way that he sat and ate in the company of even the humblest, he had earned an affection that can hardly be imagined.'

The barons were willing at first to accept

Stephen's rule. At a prolonged Easter court in 1136 nearly all of them, including the late King's favourite illegitimate son, Earl Robert of Gloucester, swore allegiance to him.

It was not long before they became disillusioned. Though Stephen was a fine courtier and soldier, he was a failure as a king and a commander. He quickly lost the support of the Norman barons through his incompetence; and in the spring of 1138 the powerful Earl Robert of Gloucester transferred his allegiance to his half-sister, Matilda.

When the news became known, Robert's English vassals and friends fortified their castles in open rebellion, and while Stephen continued to make mistakes, the opposition mounted. Instead of attacking the rebel headquarters at Bristol, he wasted his time attacking smaller, insignificant castles; when his loyal northern barons defeated a Scots invasion at the Battle of the Standard (so called because the Archbishop of York had constructed an enormous standard with the banners of the patron saints of York, Ripon and Beverley flying from it), he squandered the victory by ceding the earldom of Northumbria to the son of the King of Scots in return for no more than a token contingent of Scots for his army. In order to weaken the power of the bureaucracy built up by King Henry, which might be expected to support his daughter, he arrested the Bishop of Salisbury and other bishops and councillors who were members of his family, thereby losing himself the vital support of the Church; and when Matilda landed in England with Earl Robert, in the autumn of 1139, he was persuaded to abandon his plans to besiege the castle of Arundel where Matilda had taken up residence, and, most foolish of all, to grant her safe passage to join Earl Robert in Bristol.

With the last chivalrous but fatal gesture, the rebellion became a full-scale civil war. Barons bargained with Stephen and Matilda, selling their support to the highest bidder and then changing sides as it suited them. In some areas they fought their own private wars, in others they raided and pillaged like bandits, until it seemed, in the words of the Anglo-Saxon Chronicle, that 'Christ and his saints slept'.

On 2 February 1141, Stephen was besieging the rebel castle of Lincoln when Earl Robert appeared in his rear with an army. Although he was outnumbered, Stephen gave battle. Even after he had been surrounded he fought on, swinging a sword until the blade broke and then an axe till the shaft shattered, and he was finally stunned by a stone thrown from behind.

King Stephen was held as a prisoner in chains at Bristol, and in the summer of 1141 Matilda entered London. But she was never crowned. Enraged by her heavy taxes, the citizens drove her out, and when Earl Robert was captured by the King's supporters in September, she was forced to release the King in return for her most valuable ally.

After his release, Stephen was reconciled with the disenchanted clergy. With her supporters under threat of excommunication, Matilda sent Earl Robert to Anjou to plead for help from her husband, but Count Geoffrey was engaged in a successful invasion of Normandy, and could offer nothing. While Robert was away, Stephen laid siege to Matilda in Oxford Castle, but on a December night, shortly before the castle surrendered, when the river was frozen and the fields covered in snow, Matilda and four knights, dressed all in white, climbed down from a tower and slipped unnoticed through Stephen's lines.

For the next five years the war was a miserable stalemate. With the death of Earl Robert in October 1147, Matilda finally lost heart, and early in the following year she departed for Anjou. She never saw England again.

The civil war did not end with her departure, however. By 1145 her husband had conquered the whole of Normandy, and since it seemed unlikely that the incompetent Stephen would reconquer the duchy, some of the English barons who owned Norman estates concluded that their only hope of retaining their possessions on both sides of the Channel lay in continuing to fight for an Angevin victory in England. Since Matilda had forsaken them, they turned to her son Henry – the heir to the House of Anjou.

It seemed that the struggle between Stephen and Matilda was to be carried on into the next generation. To counter the threat from Henry, Stephen attempted to ensure the succession for his own elder son, Eustace, by having his heir crowned in his own lifetime. But the Archbishop of Canterbury, backed by the Pope, refused to perform the coronation.

By the time Henry returned to England, in 1153, he had become the most powerful feudal prince in Europe; through inheritance and marriage, the hereditary Count of Anjou was now Duke of Normandy and Aquitaine as well. When he landed with a small army, barons flocked to join him, and the issue might, it seemed, be decided in a single battle. Realising this, the barons on both sides began to fear that an outright victory might end in reprisals, and they attempted to conclude a peace. For a time Stephen was adamant that his son should succeed, but when Eustace died, in August 1153, the King lost interest in the succession, and on 6 November the civil war was ended by the Treaty of Winchester. It was agreed that Stephen should rule for the rest of his life, while Henry was acknowledged as his heir.

Stephen did not enjoy the peace for long. He died on 25 October 1154.

Chronology
THE NORMANS

1066	*5 Jan* Death of Edward the Confessor *6 Jan* Coronation of Harold Godwine *25 Sep* Battle of Stamford Bridge *14 Oct* Battle of Hastings *25 Dec* Coronation of William I
1069	Danish invasion; York seized
1070	Norman rule established in England. Lanfranc becomes Archbishop of Canterbury
1086	Doomsday Book compiled
1087	*9 Sep* Death of William I *26 Sep* Coronation of William II
1092	William II invades Scotland and regains Cumbria
1093	Anselm of Bec becomes Archbishop of Canterbury
1100	*2 Aug* William II killed by an arrow *5 Aug* Coronation of Henry I *5 Nov* Marriage of Henry I to Edith, who took the name Matilda.
1101	Duke Robert of Normandy invades England
1106	*28 Sep* Battle of Tinchebrai
1118	Death of Queen Matilda
1120	*Nov* Henry I's son William drowned in the White Ship
1121	Marriage of Henry I to Adelaide of Louvain
1128	Marriage of Henry I's daughter Matilda to Geoffrey of Anjou
1135	*1 Dec* Death of Henry I Stephen of Mortain and Boulogne (son of William I's daughter Adela) claims throne of England. *22 Dec* Coronation of King Stephen
1136	Easter Court – barons swear allegiance to King Stephen
1138	Battle of the Standard; Northern barons defeat Scots
1139	Matilda lands in England
1141	*2 Feb* Stephen captured Matilda enters London *Sep* Stephen released
1147	Matilda leaves England
1153	Henry of Anjou comes to England *Aug* Death of Eustace, Stephen's son *6 Nov* Treaty of Winchester; end of Civil War
1154	*25 Oct* Death of Stephen

IN NORMAN BRITAIN

Rochester Castle, Kent
(below)
This is one of the earliest and finest examples of Norman military architecture. It was built at the end of the 11th century by Bishop Gundulf; the massive keep was added under Henry I.

Durham Cathedral, Durham
(Opposite)
Much of this cathedral was built during the period 1070–1140; the nave dates from the time of William Rufus's friend Ranulf Flambard, to whom he gave the Bishopric of Durham.

Ely Cathedral, Cambridgeshire
(Opposite)
The cathedral's Norman tower collapsed in the 14th century, but its Norman nave has endured, amid the splendid additions of later periods.

Battle Abbey, Hastings, Sussex
(Right)
The abbey built in thanksgiving for his victory by William the Conqueror is now a ruin. According to tradition, the high altar stood on the spot where King Harold fell; the gateway is shown here.

The Tower of London, London E1
(Below)
Here, on the site of former strongholds, William I build a Norman castle, first of wood, later of stone – and today the massive keep known as the White Tower still dominates its surroundings. It was begun in the late 1070s, by King William's architect Bishop Gundulf.

Richmond Castle, Yorkshire
One of the stoutest of the Norman castles, Richmond was virtually unassailable, and was never attacked. Today its keep gives the visitor a commanding view over the town.

Westminster Hall, Parliament Square, London SW1
One of the few parts of the early Westminster Palace to escape destruction by the 19th-century fire, Westminster Hall was begun by William Rufus during the 1090s. At the time it was the largest hall in England. Today, only the lower part of the walls would be recognisable to King William.

Winchester Cathedral, Hampshire
When William II's body was brought here for burial, there was a tower beneath which he was laid; a year later the tower collapsed. The superstitious took this to be a sign of God's displeasure at the king's corrupt life.

Cardiff Castle, South Glamorgan, Wales
At Cardiff Castle Henry I kept his brother Robert of Normandy a prisoner for 28 years.

Oxford Castle, Oxfordshire
From a window of the castle Queen Matilda and her companions escaped, dressed all in white, across the snow, and slipped unnoticed through Stephen's soldiers to rejoin Earl Robert.

23

Chapter two
THE ANGEVINS

Henry II
1154-89

ACCORDING TO legend, a daughter of the Devil once married a Count of Anjou; and ever afterwards the Angevins revealed their ancestry in the fiendishness of their temper. Henry II, eldest of the three sons of Matilda and Count Geoffrey of Anjou, inherited the family temper in full measure, along with the vast possessions of both his parents. Soon after he was crowned King of England in Westminster Abbey on 19 December 1154, he also claimed Brittany, and so by the time he was 25 years old he was master of an empire which stretched from Scotland's border to the Pyrenees. Henry II had, indeed, the devil's own luck.

In 1151, at the age of 19, he had added to his domains by marrying the greatest prize in Europe – Eleanor of Aquitaine, richly-endowed former wife of the King of France. Ten years his senior, Eleanor was beautiful, spirited and clever, and despite the difference in their ages Henry and Eleanor were well matched. Her dissolved marriage to the French king had been childless, but she proceeded to complete her new young husband's happiness by bearing him eight children, five of them sons. These Angevins were later known in England by a new name, 'Plantagenets' – either in reference to Henry's father's habit of planting 'genêt', or broom, where he wished game to thrive, to improve his hunting-grounds, or because he habitually wore a sprig of broom in his cap. But as the sons of Henry II grew older and fell to feuding with one another, they were to acquire another nickname: 'The Devil's Brood'.

In Henry II the English had a king of outstanding abilities. Short and strongly built, with bright grey eyes and an unusual, harsh-sounding voice, he was famous for his phenomenal energy, both of body and mind. His secretaries complained of overwork, his household was kept constantly on the move between England and France, and his companions found it hard to keep pace with a king who expected them to sit up half the night making merry after an exhausting day's work or travelling. Henry was a man of wide interests: well educated and scholarly, he also loved the pleasures of hunting, feasting and womanising. As his once-passionate relationship with Queen Eleanor cooled into estrangement and even enmity, after the birth of their last child, John, in 1167, he turned to one of the most celebrated of all royal mistresses, the 'Fair Rosamond', whom he kept out at Woodstock. Rosamond de Clifford's sudden death in 1176 later attracted legends and the story grew up, falsely, that she had been poisoned by the jealous Queen; but as Eleanor was at that time imprisoned in Touraine, on her husband's orders, such a feat would have been impossible, even for her.

Only a man of Henry's talents could have administered so large an empire with any degree of success. England, though a rich kingdom, was only one part of the Angevin domains, and during the 34 years of his reign, Henry II spent two-thirds of his time

ABOVE A window in Canterbury Cathedral shows Henry II at Becket's tomb.

RIGHT The murder of Becket, a fresco in a church in Spoleto, Italy.

24

IN HENRY II's ENGLAND

Orford Castle, near Woodbridge, Suffolk
(*Below*)

King Henry built Orford between 1166 and 1172, at the huge cost of £1,400, as a stout royal bastion in the eastern part of the kingdom. Today only the elaborate and unusual keep remains.

Canterbury Cathedral, Kent

Before the High Altar in Canterbury Cathedral, Henry II's Archbishop of Canterbury, Thomas à Becket, was sacrilegiously struck down and murdered by four knights, on 29 December 1170. Becket was canonised, and his shrine in Canterbury Cathedral became a centre of pilgrimage. One of the earliest pilgrims was Henry II himself, who came to do penance at his tomb; in a later age, Chaucer's famous fictional Canterbury Pilgrims were on a journey to the same shrine.

on the Continent, where his possessions were under constant danger of attack, in particular from the King of France. In his absence, Henry had to ensure the smooth running of his English kingdom, and to do this he made far-reaching provisions for administering royal justice and restraining the power of the ambitious barons. One of his first acts on coming to the throne was to order the removal of castles which had been illegally built, without royal permission, during the years of the civil disorder under Stephen. In demolishing such castles, Henry both weakened the lords who owned them and asserted his own central authority.

As the reign progressed, he set about reforming the law. Under Henry II, the Curia Regis became a regular court of qualified lawyers and administrators. A system of royal courts was established throughout the kingdom, held by King's Justices who travelled between them, and the foundations of English Common Law were laid down. It was a far more popular system than the old, hit-and-miss feudal courts, from which local barons had profited; and such ancient barbarities as trial by combat were done away with, to be replaced by the beginnings of the modern jury system. The reforms benefited the monarch as well as the people by making the king's presence felt all over the realm in his subjects' legal dealings, and the power of the barons was reduced.

One of Henry II's great strengths lay in his ability to choose good and loyal servants to whom he could safely delegate responsibility. In 1162, however, he made a choice which he was to regret bitterly. He appointed his close friend and Chancellor, Thomas à Becket, as Archbishop of Canterbury.

Henry's mistake was that he had chosen too good a man for his purpose. When Becket became Archbishop he underwent a profound change of loyalty – he could no longer obey the King's will where it conflicted with his duty to God. The disagreement between them came to a head in 1164 when Henry proposed, among other measures, to send convicted clergymen for sentencing in the ordinary courts, instead of in special Church courts, where they would be exempt from the death penalty for murder. Becket opposed the King vehemently, and finally fled into exile. By 1170 he was back in England, but the uneasy reconciliation between the former friends did not last. In December of that year, Henry flew into one of his legendary Angevin tempers. Almost mad with rage, he roared, 'Will no one rid me of this turbulent priest?' and tragically, four listening knights took him literally. On 29 December 1170, the knights burst into Canterbury Cathedral and murdered the Archbishop before the altar, in one of the most dramatic scenes in mediaeval history. The martyred Becket was canonised only two years later, and his tomb in Canterbury Cathedral became a shrine for pilgrims from all over Christendom. One of the earliest was King Henry himself, who did penance by making a pilgrimage to the tomb, and having himself scourged.

There was greater punishment in store for Henry II, however, in the bitter feuding which broke out amongst his own family in the later years of his reign. King Henry sought to avoid discord with his heir, Prince Henry, by a singular method: he had the young man crowned King of England, in 1170, while he himself still lived and ruled. It was the only occasion when two kings have ruled England at once – but the 'Young King' was dissatisfied with the emptiness of his title and, abetted by his mother and her former husband, the King of France, he rebelled against his own father. It was the first of a series of armed disputes between Henry II and his troublesome sons; even when Queen Eleanor was put into honourable captivity for her part in them, there was a King of France eager to foster rebellion against the English ruler. Even the deaths of Henry II's elder sons, the 'Young King' Henry in 1183 and Geoffrey in 1186, did not end the hostilities, as Richard, now the heir, knew his younger brother John to be their father's favourite and feared dispossession.

Richard, in alliance with the new King of France, Philip II, was fighting against his now aged father in the summer of 1189. When old King Henry II learned that his much-loved youngest, Prince John, had joined the rebel cause, he lost the will to live.

On 6 July Henry II died at Chinon, aged 56. He had been one of England's greatest monarchs, and a founder of the nation's common law.

Richard I
1189-99

RICHARD THE LIONHEART, the crusader-king, has held a unique place in English folklore since the Middle Ages; in some myths and ballads, written after his time, he is even linked with another mediaeval hero, Robin Hood, who is credited with guarding the Lionheart's subjects against the wicked Prince John during his absence. In fact, Richard I hardly knew his English kingdom, and during a ten-year-long reign he spent less than six months there. He was born in England, on 8 September 1157, but he looked on Aquitaine, where he grew up, as his home, and he never even learned the English language.

He was brought up and educated in the sophisticated surroundings of Queen Eleanor's court. The elaborate cult of the troubadours, with their songs and romances of unrequited love, was then at its height, and along with such subjects as Latin, music and French, the young Prince Richard learned the stylised traditions of chivalry and courtly love. Most important of all, he was trained in the arts of warfare, so that by the time he was 16 he was commanding soldiers in the field against his father, and before he was 20 he had begun to earn himself a formidable military reputation. With his tall build, warlike temperament and mane of red-gold hair, Richard had the looks as well as the courage of a lion, and he may have acquired the famous nickname of 'Coeur-de-Lion' or 'Lionheart', during his own lifetime.

Richard's early experience of warfare was gained in the constant quarrels within his own family and in subduing the troublesome nobles in his homeland of Aquitaine, which was to be his inheritance, before the deaths of his elder brothers made him heir to all the Angevin empire. In 1187, however, a more glorious military opportunity presented itself, when news reached Europe that the great Saracen leader, Saladin, had captured Jerusalem. Richard did not hesitate: he

Richard attacks the French king Philip Augustus at Gisors, in 1198.

27

The coronation procession of Richard I.

immediately 'took the cross', making a vow to go on a Crusade to free the Holy City from the infidels. For two years family affairs kept him at home, but his father's death made him his own master at last, and in 1189 he set out on the Third Crusade, in the company of his old companion-in-arms, King Philip II of France.

Before departing, Richard made one of his rare visits to England, so that his coronation could take place, on 3 September 1189, in Westminster Abbey. While he was in his rich kingdom he raised as much money as he could, to pay for the costly Crusade. 'I would sell London itself if I could find anyone to buy it', he was reported to have said. To govern England while he was away he appointed one of his closest friends and advisers from Aquitaine, William Longchamp; and he

sought to remove one likely source of trouble during his absence by presenting his brother John with great estates and a large income, and then banishing him from the kingdom. In December 1189, Richard I left England, not to return for four years.

His journey to the Holy Land was plagued by difficulties. In Sicily, where he and King Philip had to pass their first winter, fighting broke out between the crusaders and the Sicilians, and eventually Richard stormed and took the city of Messina. Then the two kings quarrelled, and the upshot was that Philip set off in advance for the Holy Land, by himself. A major cause of their rift was Richard's failure to marry the French King's sister, Alice, after a courtship of many years. Richard the Lionheart was quite possibly a practising homosexual, but this was not his reason for not marrying Alice, for within weeks of leaving Sicily he married another woman, Berengaria of Navarre, whom his

mother, Queen Eleanor, brought out to Sicily as an alternative bride. Their wedding took place in May 1191, at Limassol, after Richard had captured Cyprus.

From Cyprus, Richard I went on to the town of Acre, on the Palestine coast, where a Christian force was besieging the Moslem garrison, whilst itself pressed by another Moslem force commanded by Saladin. Once the Lionheart had arrived, Acre fell to the Christians. But the victory was marred by the events that followed: King Richard and another eminent Crusader, Duke Leopold of Austria, quarrelled; Philip of France decided to leave for home, and the Lionheart unheroically, unchivalrously, massacred Acre's Moslem garrison.

The glorious recapture of Jerusalem for Christendom never materialised. Richard was a skilled warrior, and he won a measure of glory in his encounters with the legendary Saladin, but by the autumn of 1192 it was

Richard I: *left* in prison in Germany and *right* he is fatally wounded by an arrow at Chalus.

Apres Henry le secund regna Richard sun fiz .x. aunze
demy si entrepaytand de la tere seynt suist puis del duke
de Ostriz par eyde del Roy Phylippe de Fraunce. e suist reymt hors
de prison pur cent mil lyueres de argent. e pur cel tauncum su
rent les Chalix de Engletere puis. des Eglyses e vendiuz. Puis
suist tret de vn quarel de Alblast al Chastel de Chalezun. dunt
ceste vers su fet: Xpe tui calicis: predo sit preda calucis.

ABOVE Château-Gaillard, the castle in Normandy built by Richard to fill a gap in the Norman defences, towers above the Seine.

Saladin brandishes a sword at his cowering enemies.

clear that the Holy City could not, on this occasion, be reclaimed. To add to Richard's troubles, there was bad news from home: not only had his brother Prince John returned in 1191 to foment discontent, but William Longchamp had made himself so hated that he was obliged to flee the country in disguise. Longchamp was replaced by a new Justiciar, Walter of Coutances, and late in 1192, after concluding a truce with Saladin, Richard I sailed for England.

The hardships he met with on this voyage fostered the Lionheart legend. Forced by storms to travel overland, in December 1192 he was captured by his enemy Leopold of Austria, who imprisoned him in a fortress on the Danube, before handing him over to his Lord, the Emperor Henry VI, who demanded a ransom for his release. The story goes that Richard's favourite minstrel, Blondel, traced him, by singing beneath castle windows until one day he heard his master's familiar voice sing back at him. After more than a year in prison, while negotiations dragged on, King Richard was released for an enormous ransom, a large proportion of it to be found by the hard-pressed English.

In the spring of 1194 Richard I returned to England. Prince John's treachery was forgiven, and the barons reaffirmed their loyalty; within a month the Lionheart departed again, never to return. For the next five years he devoted his abilities to the affairs of his Continental territories, recovering lands lost in his absence, and strengthening his defences with new fortresses such as the magnificent Château-Gaillard, on the Seine. Ironically, the great warrior and far traveller met his death, not in a glorious battle, but in a minor skirmish on French soil. He was wounded by an arrow, in the shoulder; and in April 1199, the injury having turned gangrenous, he died, aged only 42.

John
1199–1216

THE INDOMITABLE Eleanor of Aquitaine was 45 years old when she gave birth to her last child, John, on Christmas Eve, 1167. As the youngest son, Prince John had no share in the division of the Angevin empire, and he was given the nickname 'John Lackland' in jesting reference to his lack of birthright. Though John grew up to be a weak and unscrupulous character, whom few people trusted, he evidently possessed a certain charm, and he was Henry II's favourite son.

King Henry made several attempts to provide an inheritance for John, without success. In 1185 he sent him, aged 18, to govern Ireland, but through his own irresponsibility and incompetence the young man succeeded only in alienating the Irish people, and he returned crestfallen to England before the year was out. King Henry died in 1189 in the knowledge that his

A 14th-century manuscript depiction of John out hunting.

31

IN KING JOHN'S ENGLAND

Worcester Cathedral, Hereford and Worcester
(*Right*)
King John was buried here, and his tomb and splendid effigy can still be seen.

Dover Castle, Kent (the keep)
(*Below*)
The battlements of this vital strategic fortress were completed by King John. It was put to the test in his reign when it was assailed – unsuccessfully – by the forces of Prince Louis of France.

The Coronation Spoon, Tower of London, London E1
(*Above*)
One of the earliest items among the Crown Jewels, the gold coronation spoon was almost certainly used at John's coronation in 1200. It is shown here with the later ampulla.

King John's Cup, Guildhall, King's Lynn, Norfolk
(*Opposite*)
This cup was found in the fen country where King John's baggage train, containing the Crown Jewels, was lost while crossing the Wash. Its magnificence makes its royal ownership seem more than probable.

Runnymede Meadows, near Staines, Surrey
The Thames-side meadow where King John was obliged to fix his seal to Magna Carta, the great charter of liberties, can still be seen. It is marked now by fine modern memorials, designed by Lutyens.

Newark Castle, Newark, Nottinghamshire
The castle where King John died in 1216, after losing his baggage train in the Wash, is now a romantic ruin.

John with Philip II of France.

beloved youngest son had turned traitor and fought against him, on the side of the King of France. Thereafter, John fulfilled the combined roles of heir and troublemaker to his brother, Richard I, conspiring with King Philip of France again and attempting to rouse England to rebellion while Richard was far away on Crusade. Even then John Lackland's personal charm saved him; when

Richard was released, and returned to England, he quickly pardoned his traitor brother, saying, 'Fear not, John. You are still a child. You have been in bad company, and it is those who have led you astray who will be punished.' John was then 27, but still an innocent youngster in King Richard's eyes.

When Richard I died in 1199 he named John as his heir, and in England and

34

Normandy his choice was accepted. Anjou, Maine and Touraine rejected it, however, choosing instead his dead brother Geoffrey's son, Arthur of Brittany, as their lord. Fortunately for John, Arthur was only 12 years old, a vulnerable opponent; by the spring of 1200 he had ousted the boy and made himself master of all the Angevin dominions. He did not hold them long.

In the autumn of 1200, having divorced his first wife, King John took the beautiful young heiress Isabella of Angoulême as his Queen. For this child-bride he showed such passion that some said she had bewitched him, and others jeered that he was chained to the marriage-bed. The marriage cost John dear in the end. Isabella had formerly been betrothed to Hugh of Lusignan; and he chose to appeal to King Philip of France for justice over the loss of his intended bride. Summoned to answer the charge by King Philip, John refused, with the result that the French king declared John's continental possessions forfeit. Once again, the Kings of France and England went to war.

In the ensuing struggle, King John occasionally showed that he could be a daring strategist; in one exploit he marched at speed from Le Mans to Mirabeau, where his 80-year-old mother was being besieged, and not only rescued Queen Eleanor but took a number of important prisoners, among them his nephew and rival, Arthur of Brittany. Such glory as he might have gained in this venture was tarnished, however, when it was put about that young Arthur had been brutally murdered in captivity – possibly by his uncle's own hand, certainly on his orders.

A king with John's reputation could inspire little confidence in his soldiers, and at the end of 1203 he left for England. The months that followed saw the break-up of the great Angevin empire, as stronghold after stronghold fell to King Philip. By the spring of 1205 Normandy and Anjou were lost, and the King of England had acquired a new nickname; the defeated John was mocked now as 'Softsword'.

For the rest of his reign King John dreamed of recovering his lost domains. He spent far more time than his predecessors in England; there he made use of the efficient administrative system built up by his father, to levy enormously heavy taxes to pay for his military preparations. A heavy financial burden was placed upon a people already faced with rising prices and monetary inflation. To add to his mounting unpopularity, King John proceeded to fall out with the Church, by disputing with the Papacy over the election of the Archbishop of

Canterbury. Pope Innocent III wanted the scholarly Stephen Langton to be the next Archbishop; John opposed him. Eventually England was put under a Papal interdict in 1208, whereby all religious rites, including baptism, marriage and burial, were suspended. When John took advantage of this situation to confiscate Church estates, he was excommunicated.

It was a dangerous predicament for a monarch in mediaeval Europe, and by the spring of 1213 King John could hold out no longer. Threatened by conspiracies among his own barons and invasion from Philip of France, he performed a cynical about-face. Not only did he accept Langton as his Archbishop, he made Pope Innocent England's overlord by giving him the kingdom 'in fief', and receiving it back from him in return for a yearly tribute. With Pope Innocent thus neatly secured as his ally and patron, John prepared to face his enemies at home and abroad.

The hardships which his rule had imposed on England during the past eight years could only have been justified by victory against the French king, but this was denied him. When news came, in 1214, that King Philip had won the decisive Battle of Bouvines, open rebellion followed in England. By the spring of 1215, the rebels had taken London, and John had no choice but to submit to their terms. Archbishop Langton did what he could to mediate; and a 'Great Treaty', the 'Magna Carta', was drawn up, setting out the discontented barons' demands. In June 1215, in a meadow at Runnymede, the document which in later centuries was to acquire the status of a guarantee of civil rights was sealed by a reluctant King John.

Even then the disputes between John and his barons were not over. The King continued to disregard his subjects' interests until finally the rebels took more drastic action: they invited the future King of France, Louis, to take over the kingdom of England. In May 1216 he arrived and, without difficulty, seized London. There could have been no greater proof of failure for King John.

He was not entirely devoid of virtues; he had encouraged the growth of municipal pride, granting civic charters and even founding the port of Liverpool, and he had helped to build up the English navy. He could be charming when he chose, though increasing stoutness in middle age must have reduced the attractions of his 5'6" person, and he never lost his fondness for food. With a foreign anti-king holding sway in his own capital city, John lost heart, and in October 1216, while civil war rent the kingdom, he died.

Chronology
THE ANGEVINS

HENRY II

1133	*25 Mar* Birth
1151	Marriage to Eleanor of Aquitaine
1154	*19 Dec* Coronation
1162	Thomas à Becket becomes Archbishop of Canterbury
1164	Becket in exile until 1170
1170	*29 Dec* Murder of Becket
1176	Death of Rosamund de Clifford
1183	Death of Prince Henry
1189	*6 Jul* Death of Henry II

RICHARD I

1157	*8 Sep* Birth
1187	Capture of Jerusalem by Saladin
1189	*3 Sep* Coronation *Dec* Joins Third Crusade England administered by Longchamp as Justiciar
1191	*May* Marriage to Berengaria of Navarre Longchamp replaced by Coutances
1192	*Dec* Richard captured, held prisoner by Leopold of Austria
1194	Returns to England
1199	*6 April* Death of Richard I from wound received in skirmish at Chalus

KING JOHN

1167	*24 Dec* Birth
1185	Governs Ireland briefly
1189	Marriage to Isabella of Gloucester
1199	Coronation
1200	Annuls previous marriage and marries Isabella of Angoulême
1205	Quarrel with Pope Innocent III over election of Archbishop of Canterbury
1209	John excommunicated
1213	Submits to papal wishes
1214	Battle of Bouvines: French victory
1215	Rebels seize London Magna Carta sealed at Runnymede
1216	*May* Louis of France becomes anti-king in London *19 Oct* Death of John

Chapter three
THE PLANTAGENETS

Henry III
1216-72

HENRY III was only nine years old when he succeeded to the Plantagenet throne in 1216. King John had left him an unenviable inheritance – a kingdom divided and disordered, with rebellious barons controlling much of the north, and London and the south-east in the hands of a foreign invader, the future Louis VIII of France. But fortunately for Henry he had the loyal support of two great men, William Marshall and Hubert de Burgh, and through their efforts the barons were subdued and Louis of France forced to depart.

For much of Henry III's minority Hubert de Burgh effectively ruled England, and by 1227, when the young king was 19 years old and declared to be of age, a semblance of order had been restored to the realm. It was dependant upon skilful government, however; and this King Henry III could not provide.

As a private individual Henry had many virtues. He was a cultured man, and his keen interest in the arts led to the rebuilding of the magnificent Gothic abbey of Westminster, intended as a shrine for St Edward the Confessor. He was also a good husband and father, and his marriage to Eleanor of Provence, which took place in 1236, was to prove a long and happy one. But as a King Henry III had major failings: he was weak, unreliable, extravagant and dangerously insensitive to the feelings of his subjects.

At a time when England had recently lost her possessions across the Channel and nationalism was rising, while French influence declined, Henry III showed a seemingly unpatriotic liking for all things French.

He relied heavily on a Poitevin, Peter des Roches, for advice, and he filled his court with foreigners, advancing them to high positions in Church and state, thereby arousing great resentment among many of his English subjects. In 1234, faced with mounting hostility from the great barons, Henry was obliged to dismiss his Poitevin favourites, including Peter des Roches. But

he had yet to find out how far his powers could be limited by his subjects.

Henry lacked authority over his barons. His generous patronage of foreigners infuriated them, and he had none of the ability for glorious warfare which would have rallied them to his service. Such military ventures as Henry III did undertake, in the hope of regaining the Continental pos-

Henry III.

36

sessions lost by his father, were unsuccessful, and by the Treaty of Paris, in 1259, he finally gave up all claim to Normandy, Maine and Anjou, keeping Gascony only in fief, with the French king as his overlord. A planned Crusade, by which he might have earned some glory, never materialised; and a project of obtaining the kingdom of Sicily for his younger son, Edmund, ended in expensive failure. By the late 1250s Henry's weakness, mismanagement and appalling extravagance were becoming intolerable to the

barons, and they decided to take matters into their own hands, demanding a programme of reforms.

Reluctantly King Henry agreed to his critics' demands for a new council, made up of members appointed by the barons as well as by himself, and he accepted that the assemblies of Church, state and legal dignitaries, which were becoming known as Parliaments, should meet regularly, three times a year. But these proved to be largely empty words: as soon as he could, Henry

sought absolution from his promises, with the backing of the Papacy and the King of France.

As the conflict between the King and the barons developed, a national leader emerged who was to become more famous than Henry himself – Simon de Montfort. A man of ambition and great abilities, de Montfort had come to England from France, in his 20s, to make his fortune like so many others at Henry's court. He successfully laid claim to the Earldom of Leicester and eventually

Battlefield of Lewes, Sussex
The scene of the historic battle between Henry III and Simon de Montfort, the early champion of Parliamentary democracy. In the battle, 'the King was much beaten with swords and maces', and he was defeated and taken prisoner for a time. Before the battle his son Prince Edward – later King Edward I – was quartered with his cavalry at Lewes Castle.

The shrine of Edward the Confessor, Westminster Abbey, London SW1 *(Above)*
Henry III rebuilt the old Westminster Abbey, traditional coronation place, and raised the present soaring Gothic structure, as a fitting burial place for Edward the Confessor and later kings, including himself. He based the plan on the French style of cathedrals, but used English architects, with magnificent results.

The Chapter House, Palace of Westminster, London SW1 *(Above)*
Another of Henry III's architectural triumphs, the Chapter House was begun in 1250 and completed three years later, probably under the supervision of an English mason.

named Master Alberic. Originally it was brightly decorated in blue, red and gold; when Simon de Montfort summoned the first meeting of the Commons there he declared it a symbol of shameful royal extravagance. The tiled floor has been preserved, as King Henry would have seen it.

IN HENRY III's ENGLAND

37

ABOVE   The Battle of Evesham.

The old Westminster Abbey.

married Henry III's sister, Eleanor, in secret. His close relationship with the king, and his foreign origins, did not initially endear him to the barons, despite his obvious abilities; but when Simon de Montfort finally fell out with King Henry, he won overwhelming popular support as the leader of national opposition. At the Battle of Lewes, in June 1264, Simon de Montfort set the seal on his power by defeating and capturing the king. He was now effectively master of England.

Later in that year, de Montfort's new régime demonstrated its political beliefs by holding an assembly to which not only knights but ordinary burgesses were summoned, from selected shires and boroughs throughout the kingdom. It was the first time the Commons had received Parliamentary representation.

But Simon de Montfort's success did not last. Henry's supporters made full use of the fact that the man representing English nationalism was himself a foreigner; and a rival popular leader emerged in the form of Henry's eldest son, the future Edward I, who also promised reform. Royalist support grew rapidly, and in the Battle of Evesham, on 4 August 1265, at which Henry, surrounded by his captors, was unwillingly present, Simon de Montfort was defeated and killed.

Henry III was king again, though the dominating force in the land was now Edward, his heir who had fought valiantly at Evesham. The ageing king was able to devote much of his time to his true interests, art and building, and he had the satisfaction of seeing the remains of St Edward the Confessor interred in the splendid setting of Westminster Abbey. Three years later, on 16 November 1272, Henry III died, aged 65. The ever-acid contemporary chronicler, Matthew Paris, described him as a king with a heart of wax; but the glorious Gothic Abbey bears witness to Henry's greater qualities.

Edward I
1272–1307

IN EDWARD I, the English found the king they sorely needed after the tribulations of Henry III's reign. Thirty-three years old at the time of his accession, Edward was an outstanding man, in physique as well as in character; fair-haired and handsome, he towered over most of his contemporaries, and his long legs earned him the nickname of 'Longshanks'. He had his father's droopy eyes, but in energy, efficiency and military skill he more resembled his earlier predecessors Henry II and Richard the Lionheart.

Born at Westminster, in 1239, Edward was married to Eleanor of Castile when he was 15 years old. It was a diplomatic alliance, arranged for the protection of English-owned Gascony, but it turned into a love-match. Queen Eleanor bore her hus-

band 16 children, seven of whom survived, and when she died in 1290, in Nottinghamshire, Edward mourned her bitterly. He vowed that he would build a cross in her memory at every town where her body rested on its way to Westminster; three still survive.

In his youth, Edward showed little promise. Despite his private happiness, in public life he was undisciplined and unreliable, and the chronicler Matthew Paris foretold a troubled future for England under his rule. As he grew older, however, Edward's image changed, and he began to acquire a reputation for courage and wisdom. He demonstrated his idealism by going on a Crusade in 1270; two years later, while he was away, his father died, and he succeeded unopposed to the English throne.

In the summer of 1274 Edward I landed at Dover to claim his kingdom, and almost immediately set about the task of governing a country whose monarchy had been weak-

This section of the painted sedilia by the high altar in Westminster Abbey is thought to represent Edward I.

38

The coronation chair made for Edward I to hold the Stone of Scone, in Westminster Abbey.

ened. Royal commissioners were sent out to visit every region and investigate the workings of the law and local administration; as the result of their findings, corrupt local officials were brought to heel and baronial powers defined and curbed. Extensive legal reforms were carried out, and under Edward separate Courts of the Exchequer, Common Pleas and King's Bench were established, with legal proceedings being recorded in full for the first time. It was an ambitious programme on which Edward embarked, but he gained the support of the people, and the sense of nationalism which had begun to emerge under Henry III, fostered by Simon de Montfort, gained ground.

In 1277 Edward I turned his attention to disaffected Wales. The Lord of Snowdonia, Llewellyn ap Gruffydd, had been acknowledged as Prince of Wales, and was seeking to consolidate his power, unchecked by the efforts of the Marcher Lords who controlled the border areas (or Marches), in return for considerable privileges from the English Crown. Llewellyn had for some time been refusing to pay homage to Edward; in 1277 Edward responded with an efficient campaign which ended in the Welsh leader's surrender. Terms were agreed, but five years later Wales rose again, and this time the King of England had a harder struggle on his hands. But eventually the death of Llewellyn turned the tide in England's favour, and Edward gained complete control of North Wales. The Statute of Wales, in 1284, gave him dominion over his valuable conquest, and an enduring monument to Edward I's occupation of Wales can still be seen in the circuit of grim castles which he built there, massive strongholds such as Conway, Caernarvon and Harlech. Despite his reorganisation of the Principality, revolts continued to erupt. According to tradition, in an attempt to win over the Welsh, the English king promised them that they should have a Prince who spoke no English – and produced his own baby son, Edward, who as yet spoke no words at all. Whatever the truth of that legend, in 1301, at the age of 16, this Edward – who had been born at Caernarvon – was proclaimed Prince of Wales, the first heir to an English monarch to bear the title.

The unification of Britain was Edward I's ambition, and having secured Wales he hoped for a time that Scotland might be peacefully annexed by means of a marriage between his heir and the infant Queen of Scots, Margaret. But the little Queen died in 1290, leaving the succession in dispute. Edward, who claimed overlordship of Scotland, stepped in to appoint the new ruler; and to his own benefit he chose John Balliol,

The Eleanor Cross, Hardingstone,
Northamptonshire
(*Below*)

Edward I's Queen, Eleanor, died at Harby,
Northamptonshire, on 28 November 1290.
Her body was taken to London for burial
and at each place where the bier rested for
the night the grieving King raised an
ornamental cross in her memory. Only three
of the original twelve now remain, at
Hardingstone, Geddington and
Waltham.

IN EDWARD I's BRITAIN

Caernarvon Castle, Gwynedd, Wales
(*Above*)

Edward I intended to make Caernarvon his
royal capital in subdued Wales. Caernarvon
Castle was one of the massive ring of
fortresses which he built, including Conway,
Harlech and Beaumaris; he modelled the
walls of Caernarvon on those of Byzantium,
the greatest stronghold in Christendom, and
the cost of the building works has been
estimated at over £10,000,000 in modern
money. His son was created the first Prince
of Wales; though the title has normally been
borne by the heir to the throne, none since
then has been born in Wales. The ceremony
of investiture at Caernarvon was revived in
1911, for the future Edward VIII, and the
present Prince of Wales was invested there
in 1969.

Harlech Castle, Gwynedd, Wales
(*Left*)

Built by Edward I in the late 1280s, Harlech
became crucial to the struggle between
Owen Glendower and the English Crown in
the early 1400s, when Glendower took the
castle, and made it his home.

a relatively weak candidate, and proceeded to assert his own interests in the northern kingdom. When the Scots found themselves a valuable ally in the King of France, with whom Edward was then at war, the English king marched on Scotland.

What followed was, from the Plantagenet king's standpoint, a dramatically successful campaign. He swept in triumph through Scotland, received homage from the Scots nobles and leaders, and returned to London with the prize of the great Stone of Destiny in his possession. Known in England as the Stone of Scone, since it had been taken from Scone Abbey, it was the object on which Kings of Scots had traditionally been crowned; its symbolic value to Edward was thus immense. He had it placed beneath a specially-built chair in Westminster Abbey, and monarchs of England and Great Britain have been crowned above it ever since.

The defeated Scots, in response to the English incursions, rallied round their own nationalist heroes. The first to emerge, William Wallace, was a master of guerrilla warfare. Helped by his knowledge of the terrain and the fierce loyalty of his followers, he won an impressive victory over the English commander Earl Warenne at Stirling Bridge in 1297. A year later, Edward himself appeared at the head of a huge army and defeated Wallace's force at Falkirk, though the Scots leader eluded capture until 1305. His place was soon filled by another celebrated figure, Robert Bruce, who had himself crowned King of Scots. Bruce did not share Wallace's success, but he remained a potent force in Scottish affairs. Despite his increasing age and ill-health, Edward was determined to crush the Scots finally.

He was on his way to the Scottish border to pursue his ambition when he died, on 7 July 1307. It was the last command of the king who was to be remembered as 'the Hammer of the Scots' that his heir should carry on his efforts until the last Scottish soldier had surrendered.

Edward I's concern for justice was deep-rooted; but he did not transcend the bigotries of his time. To add to his record in Scotland and Wales, in 1290 he had turned on the time-honoured scapegoats for a nation's ills, and expelled the Jews from England. It proved an unwise, as well as inhuman, action, as he had then to find other sources of credit for the Crown, and he ended his reign heavily in debt.

Nevertheless Edward was a respected ruler; and for his far-reaching legal reforms and his encouragement of the growth of Parliament in his reign, he could justly be called the greatest of the Plantagenets.

Edward II 1307-27

THE NAME of Edward II was to become a byword for bad kingship. In contrast to 'the Hammer of the Scots', his famous father, the second Edward was an ineffectual dilettante, and his rule brought little but defeat and disorder to England.

Edward II was 23 when he succeeded to the throne in July 1307. Tall, fair and attractive, he appeared to be a typical Plantagenet monarch, but to his contemporaries' disgust his interests were anything but kingly. He had no taste for combat; what he enjoyed was a curious mixture of the luxurious, such as dancing and finery, and the physical, such as swimming, rowing and digging. It had been Edward I's last wish that his son should pursue the war with Scotland unrelentingly, but the new king quickly abandoned the turbulent north and returned to the pleasures of his court in London. There he renewed his passionate friendship with a handsome young Gascon named Piers Gaveston – 'brother Perrot', as the King called him. Edward showered Gaveston with gifts, raised him to the title of Earl of Cornwall, normally reserved for royalty, and outraged the barons by leaving Gaveston as Regent while he went to France to marry the Princess Isabella, in 1308. Even the charms of his young bride could not distract King Edward from his male favourite for long; he handed over a selection of the richest wedding-gifts to Gaveston on his return.

If the King's behaviour towards his barons was foolish, Gaveston's was actively insulting. He ridiculed some of the most powerful

ABOVE   Queen Isabella enters Bristol, and is warmly greeted.

RIGHT   The monument to Edward II in Gloucester cathedral.

42

IN EDWARD II's ENGLAND

Berkeley Castle, near Stroud, Gloucestershire
(*Right and below*)
The medieval fortress of Berkeley Castle was built largely in the 14th century, around a Norman keep. It was in a cell in this keep (below) that Edward II was horribly done to death by his gaolers with an iron spit.

with nicknames – Guy Beauchamp of Warwick was 'the Black Dog of Arden', Lancaster 'the Fiddler' – as though heedless of the danger from disaffected barons with large private armies. Within a year of his accession Edward II was obliged to submit to the will of his nobles and exile the hated favourite. Twice Gaveston was obliged to leave the kingdom, and twice he managed to return to his royal patron's side, until eventually a group of his enemies decided the matter by capturing and murdering him, in June 1312.

Though Piers Gaveston was gone, opposition to the incompetent king remained, headed by Thomas of Lancaster, Edward II's first cousin. Lancaster was a dangerously powerful subject; by 1311 he controlled five earldoms and a large private army, and he aimed also to control the kingdom.

In 1314 he showed open defiance to King Edward when he failed to follow him to battle against the Scots. The unwarlike Edward II had hoped to rescue his prestige and his barons' loyalty by earning some military glory, but he failed utterly in the attempt. Against the Scottish hero Robert Bruce Edward's ill-conceived efforts were useless; and at Bannockburn, on Midsummer Day 1314, the English army was utterly routed by a Scots force of one-third its strength. It was one of the most resounding defeats in England's history.

Lancaster, who had stayed out of it, gained immeasurably in political strength. Amid the disorder which followed the defeat at Bannockburn Lancaster became virtual ruler of England; and even after 1318, when a standing council was established to direct the King's actions, Lancaster remained a major force in the land. Edward, deprived of his independent powers, turned to two new favourites for support – Hugh le Despenser and his son, two great Marcher lords from the Welsh borders. With the Despensers' assistance, the King broke away from the nobles' control, rewarding his favourites lavishly in return. Inevitably, the Despensers earned the hatred of their peers, and in 1321 Edward was forced to exile them.

But in the following year the King struck back with surprising success. The other Welsh Marcher lords were forced to yield; Lancaster, deprived of their help, turned traitor and requested the support of none other than Robert Bruce. It was a foolish move, as it turned his countrymen against him. Thomas of Lancaster was finally captured and beheaded in March 1322, and Edward II and the Despensers held sway once more.

A new figure now entered the political

arena – Isabella, Edward's Queen. As a young bride she had suffered her husband's churlish treatment of her and his open preference for Gaveston, and she had dutifully borne Edward four children, but by 1325, with the Despensers triumphant at court, a new side of Queen Isabella emerged, one that was to earn her the nickname of 'the She-Wolf of France'.

In that year she went on a diplomatic mission to her brother, the King of France; and once out of England she began to hold open house for enemies of the Despensers. One of them, a Marcher lord named Roger Mortimer, became her lover, and together

The Battle of Bannockburn, in which the Scots under Robert Bruce utterly defeated the English army.

Isabella and Mortimer began to plot the invasion of England, on behalf of her elder son, Edward, who had joined her in France.

It was a state of affairs which greatly shocked the 'She-Wolf''s brother, the King of France, and so Isabella and Mortimer left his territory and went on to Hainault, where the Count of Hainault had no such scruples. In return for an agreement that his daughter, Philippa, should marry the heir to the English throne, young Edward, he gave his

45

armed support to Queen Isabella's cause, and in September 1326 the Queen, her lover and her son set out on the invasion of England.

Edward II's own shortcomings had made their undertaking an easy one. Few of his subjects rose to his support, and the invaders soon had control of the kingdom. The Despensers and the other few friends of the King were sought out and killed; Edward II himself was captured and deposed in favour of his young son. The former king's treatment was at first reasonably courteous, and during the early part of his captivity he was kept in relative comfort at Kenilworth Castle. But with a new king, Edward III, on the throne, the presence of the previous monarch in the kingdom became an embarrassment. To the brutal Mortimer, the solution was simple, and he gave orders accordingly.

In September 1327, Edward II was put to death in the dungeons of Berkeley Castle, by the hideous means of a red-hot iron thrust up him. Two months later he was buried in Gloucester Abbey, in great splendour, and as if to compound murder with hypocrisy, Queen Isabella attended the ceremony, accompanied by her son Edward III.

Edward III
1327-77

THE FEEBLE, effeminate Edward II was succeeded by a son and heir who was not only handsome, manly and chivalrous, but a famous warrior and a successful king, recalling his grandfather, Edward I. Edward III was also extravagant and warmongering; but for all his faults he did much to restore England's pride after the sorry experiences of his father's reign.

Edward was a boy of 14 when he received the crown of the Plantagenets in 1327. He owed his early accession to the scheming of his mother, Queen Isabella, and her lover Mortimer, and he began his reign under their influence. At the age of 17, however, with the help of Henry of Lancaster, who headed his council of regency, he threw them off completely; Mortimer was tried before Parliament for a long list of crimes and executed, and Isabella was obliged to retire to the seclusion of Castle Rising, in Norfolk. Later, as if to seal his rejection of his mother's actions, Edward built a magnificent tomb

over his father's grave in Gloucester Abbey, and the once-despised Edward II became an object of veneration to pilgrims.

Unlike many mediaeval kings, Edward III was adept at the art of managing his barons. He bound them to him by lavish entertainments and by comradeship in arms; by marriage alliances with his own children and by the brotherhood of chivalry, which was his passion. Energies which might otherwise have been used in plotting were channelled by Edward III into the splendid

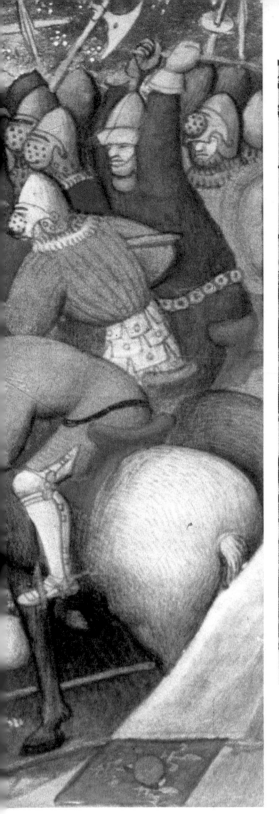

LEFT The Battle of Crécy, 26 August 1346, a resounding English victory over the French.

ABOVE King Edward III, with his son the Black Prince kneeling before him.

BELOW Knights jousting.

sport of jousting, and tournaments, with their pageantry, physical risks and opportunities for glory, became the rage. St George and King Arthur were his heroes; he vowed that he would found an Arthurian Round Table for his knights, and in 1348 he founded the Order of the Garter. According to tradition, the Order was inspired by an incident at court in which a lady's garter slipped off. While the onlookers mocked, the King picked up the offending garter and said 'Honi soit qui mal y pense' – 'evil be to him who evil thinks'. That phrase became the motto of the new Order, and the brotherhood of 26 knights, headed by their King, were pledged to one another as 'co-partners, both in Peace and War'. The symbol of their brotherhood was the garter worn about the left knee.

The co-partners were kept occupied by the demands of war for much of Edward III's reign. To begin with, the Scots suffered his vengeance for his father's military failures and his own enforced signing, as a boy of 15, of the Treaty of Northampton, which recognised Scottish independence. By 1333 Bannockburn had been avenged, and the English were once again in control of the border regions.

In defeat, the Scots turned once more to their old ally, France. Edward was already burning with desire to recover the lost Angevin territories; this threatening alliance

47

IN EDWARD III's ENGLAND

Castle Rising, near King's Lynn, Norfolk
(Below)

When the young King Edward III threw off the influence of his mother, Queen Isabella, she retired to live out her days in the seclusion of this stout Norman castle.

Tomb of the Black Prince, Canterbury Cathedral, Kent
(Right)

Edward III's eldest son, known as the Black Prince, died young and was buried in 1376, behind the high altar at Canterbury. As befits a famous warrior, over his tomb hang his helmet, shield and gauntlets.

gave him additional reason to make war on the French. In 1328 an opportunity presented itself. King Charles IV died without a male heir, and the succession of his cousin, Philip VI of Valois, was disputed. Edward took advantage of the situation to claim the throne for himself, through his mother. For the barons there were rich pickings, as well as knightly glory, to be found across the Channel, and they followed their king eagerly to war. And so began the long-drawn-out-out struggle with France which was to become known as the Hundred Years War.

To begin with there was little satisfaction for the English. A naval victory over a combined French and Genoese fleet at Sluys, in 1340, pleased England's merchants, because it safeguarded trade routes to Flanders, but it did nothing for the booty-hungry barons. Philip VI appeared not to share Edward III's notions of chivalry, and

he declined an invitation to single combat which the English king valiantly offered. In 1345, however, Edward's great commander Henry of Derby captured large areas of Gascony, and the position changed. Edward gathered a huge army and prepared to invade France.

The King's personal popularity and the waiting riches of the French enemy made recruiting no hard task. In July 1346 Edward and his soldiers landed in Normandy and

The Jewel Tower, Palace of Westminster, London SW1

A fragment of the mediaeval Westminster Palace, the Jewel Tower was begun in 1365, as a treasury tower for Edward III's personal belongings.

Edward III's effigy, the Undercroft, Westminster Abbey, London SW1

This is probably the 'effigy in the likeness of a king' made for Edward III's funeral in 1377, at a cost of £22 4s 11d. It shows Edward to have been 5′ 10½″ tall, and, as the face was made from a death mask, gives a good idea of the 65-year-old king's appearance.

made their brutal way towards Flanders. For a sovereign dedicated to the ideals of chivalry, Edward III took a remarkably lenient view of his soldiers' unbridled looting and despoiling on foreign soil. Yet the men-at-arms and bowmen of England proved their military worth on 26 August, at the Battle of Crécy. Fighting in a defensive position, the English won an extraordinary victory, largely through the skill and fire-power of their archers, who 'let fly their

arrows so wholly together and so thick that it seemed snow', creating great mounds of enemy dead before their lines, and eventually forcing the French king to flee from the battlefield in defeat. The surrender of Calais was to follow just a year later; it was on this occasion that six merchants, or burghers, won immortality by offering their lives if Edward would spare the other inhabitants of the city from vengeance – and, on the pleading of his Queen, Philippa, Edward agreed, and spared the burghers too. A major victory over the Scots, won in Edward's absence, set the seal on his triumphs.

Among those who fought gallantly at Crécy was Edward's son and heir Edward, the Black Prince. In the decade that followed, the Black Prince emerged as a warrior to rival his father, and in September 1356 he not only defeated Philip VI of France's successor, John the Good, at Poitiers, but also captured him. With so valuable a hostage in his power, Edward III was able to negotiate a treaty in 1360 which brought the return of huge areas of France, including Aquitaine. It was a glorious but short-lived achievement.

The Black Death, the appalling sickness which ravaged Europe during Edward's reign, broke out again in English-held France during 1361, wiping out large numbers of the inhabitants and helping to weaken England's tenuous hold on the territory. The French commander Bertrand du Guesclin campaigned with skill and success against the occupiers, and despite du Guesclin's capture by the Black Prince, in 1367, nine years later all that remained in Edward's possession was Calais and a narrow area of the south-west.

As his reign drew towards its close, Edward III's personal reputation remained high, but those of his friends and councillors declined. The once capable monarch became feeble, dominated by an ambitious mistress named Alice Perrers; successive Parliaments voiced the people's growing discontent with the poor management of the war and the excessive taxation which it entailed. The so-called 'Good Parliament' of 1376 saw a remarkable attack by the Commons on the King's followers and Alice Perrers, who were openly accused of corruption. The King's fourth son, John of Gaunt, took action to curb this disturbing spirit of dissension. By this time the Black Prince was prematurely dead, of sickness, and John of Gaunt was emerging as the major power in the land. When Edward III died, a worn-out husk of 64, in 1377, he was succeeded by the Black Prince's son, Richard of Bordeaux, as King Richard II. But many feared that John of Gaunt might have other plans for the crown.

Richard II 1377-99

BORN IN Bordeaux, in 1367, Richard was only nine years old when his father died and he became the heir to the throne. The Black Prince had been a magnificent soldier and a man of great promise, but though Richard resembled him physically, he grew up to be a very different character.

At the age of ten, Richard succeeded to the throne, and a regency council was appointed to govern on his behalf. Boy-kings were vulnerable figures, and there was no lack of contenders for King Richard's crown. But the popular suspicions of his uncle John of Gaunt's intentions proved unfounded. Despite all opportunities and temptations, John remained a loyal and valuable servant of his king, and the first major threat to Richard II's security came from quite another quarter.

In 1381 the English peasants revolted. The poll-tax, a 'head-count' tax on every male over 16, sanctioned by Parliament in that year, was the last straw for a people already over-burdened with the costs of the war in France. The peasants rose, and groups from Kent and Essex marched on London.

John of Gaunt, uncle of Richard II, who acted as a regent during his minority.

49

Their target was not the 14-year-old king, whom they claimed to support, but the advisers who made laws in his name; in London they vented their anger in rampaging through the city, looting and burning, and among the buildings destroyed was the Palace of the Savoy, John of Gaunt's royal residence. From the Tower of London, where he had been taken for safety, Richard II was said to have watched the flames as his capital burned.

It was Richard himself who eventually took charge and saved a dangerous situation for the crown. At a first meeting with the peasants' leader, Wat Tyler, the rebels' demands were agreed to, from the abolition of serfdom to a pardon for those who had taken part in the insurrection. But at a second meeting between the King and the rebels, at Smithfield, Wat Tyler was struck down and killed in cold blood by one of the King's party. It was a critical moment – but as the horrified rebels made ready to fight, the young King rode forward. In a ringing voice, he declared that he was their King, and he would be their new captain and leader. It was a master-stroke. The rebels flocked to follow Richard; and though his word proved false, his personal reputation soared. So, to his cost, did his opinion of himself.

As the King grew towards maturity, factions began to develop at court, which Richard himself fostered. Like his predecessor Edward II, whom he increasingly resembled, he became unpopular with some of his most

LEFT The King of Leinster (*right*) confronts the Duke of Gloucester, sent by Richard II in 1394 to secure his homage along with that of three other Irish kings.

RIGHT Scottish troops and their French allies attacking Wark Castle in 1385.

powerful subjects; they complained of his lavish generosity to unworthy favourites, and they resented his inability to make war effectively. Richard's attempt at leading an army into Scotland, in 1385, was a failure, and he abandoned it in a matter of days. In the following year, while his loyal, powerful uncle John of Gaunt was out of the kingdom, Richard's critics acted. Led by another of his uncles, Thomas of Gloucester, and the Earl of Arundel, they forced the king to impeach one of his friends, the Chancellor de la Pole, and to submit to government by a 13-strong commission. It was the first step in a long struggle.

Richard's resistance to his opponents' demands led to open war. In 1387, after failing to bring a group of his favourites to trial as agreed, he was subjected to force. At Radcot Bridge, in Oxfordshire, his supporters' army was defeated by the army of Gloucester and the other barons, who had been joined by John of Gaunt's son, young Henry of Bolingbroke. Their triumph gave the Lords Appellant, as the opposition leaders were called, virtual control of the kingdom, and at what became known as the 'Merciless Parliament' of 1388 they con-

Two characters from Chaucer's *Canterbury Tales*: The Prioress and the Miller.

The famous Wilton Diptych, in the National Gallery, London, shows Richard II (*left*) kneeling before the Virgin and child.

IN RICHARD II's ENGLAND

Westminster Hall, Parliament Square, London SW1 (*Below*)

Richard II rebuilt William Rufus's original hall, giving it its present appearance and dimensions. The fine hammerbeam roof was a particularly important feature added by Richard.

The Tomb Effigy of Richard II, Westminster Abbey, London SW1

Here, cast in copper, Richard II lies beside his Queen, Anne of Bohemia. The effigy was ordered during the king's lifetime, and is presumably a good likeness.

demned to death some of the King's principal friends and supporters.

For a while it seemed as if the young king had learned by adversity. At 22, he declared his intention of ruling in his own right, yet he appeared to remain on cordial terms with the Lords Appellant. He demonstrated, once again, that he had considerable political skills, notably in bringing a settlement to Ireland – always a troubled area – and in concluding a long truce with France in 1396. Richard also showed himself to be interested in the arts; he encouraged building works and painting, and he was a friend of the poet Geoffrey Chaucer. His court was run in magnificent style, and it had a cosmopolitan atmosphere, fostered by the King's foreign marriages, first to Anne of Bohemia and later, as a widower, to Isabella of France. It was an elegant façade which Richard II presented to the world during this period.

In fact, he was secretly preparing a campaign of vengeance, and in 1397, with ruthless suddenness, he acted. His old opponents were arrested and Gloucester, his uncle, was murdered. John of Gaunt's son Henry of Bolingbroke appeared to have redeemed himself by service of the crown; but in 1398 Richard took advantage of a quarrel between Henry and another eminent noble to exile them both. It seemed that the King had triumphed over his adversaries.

By now, Richard II was clearly becoming deranged. He turned into a harsh, extravagant tyrant, bending laws and extorting taxes to suit his own wishes, supported by a private army whose badge, the white hart, was his emblem. Even his political sense appeared to desert him. When the faithful and valiant John of Gaunt died in 1399, Richard made a fatal mistake; instead of becoming reconciled with his uncle's potentially powerful heir, Henry, he made a committed enemy of him by making his inheritance forfeit and extending his period of exile to banishment for life. Then, to compound his folly, he sailed for Ireland, where renewed dissension had erupted, taking some of his strongest supporters with him.

Henry of Bolingbroke wasted no time. He swiftly raised an army and crossed to England to claim his rights. Landing at Ravenspur, in Yorkshire, he gathered eager supporters as he went, and when Richard returned he was soon overpowered and taken prisoner. It was the crown that Henry now sought; and in August, 1399, Richard II was forced to abdicate. Early in 1400, as the new century opened, King Richard was secretly murdered, in Pontefract Castle.

Chronology
THE PLANTAGENETS

HENRY III

1206	*10 Oct* Birth
1216	Coronation
1217	*11 Sep* Treaty of Lambeth Peace with France and withdrawal of invaders
1227	Beginning of Henry's personal rule
1234	Poitevin favourites dismissed
1236	Marriage to Eleanor of Provence
1258–9	Formation of parliamentary opposition
1259	*Oct* Provisions of Westminster defining relations between royal and seigneurial justice
1264	Battle of Lewes; Henry captured
1265	Model Parliament *4 Aug* Battle of Evesham; Simon de Montfort killed
1272	*16 Nov* Death of Henry III

EDWARD I

1239	*17 Jun* Birth
1254	Marriage to Eleanor of Castile
1270	Joins French king Louis IX's Crusade
1274	Returns to claim throne
1282	Unsuccessful uprising in Wales Llewellyn killed
1284	Statute of Wales: transferred to English dominion
1290	Jews expelled from England Death of Eleanor of Castile
1295	'Model' Parliament
1296	Edward invades Scotland and seizes Stone of Scone
1297	Battle of Stirling Bridge; Edward's forces defeated
1301	Prince Edward created first Prince of Wales
1307	*7 Jul* Death of Edward I

EDWARD II

1284	*25 Apr* Birth
1308	Coronation Marriage to Isabella of France
1311	Under tutelage of 21 'Lords ordainers'
1312	*Jun* Murder of Gaveston
1313	Stirling besieged by Robert Bruce
1314	*24 Jun* Battle of Bannockburn; Edward defeated
1319	Two-year truce signed with Robert of Scotland
1321	Edward forced to dismiss Despensers; soon pardons them
1322	*16 Mar* Battle of Boroughbridge; Lancaster defeated
1326	Queen Isabella and Mortimer invade England from France
1327	*20 Jan* Edward forced to abdicate *Sep* Edward killed at Berkeley Castle

EDWARD III

1312	*13 Nov* Birth
1327	Coronation
1327–30	Queen Isabella in power
1328	Marriage to Philippa of Hainault Treaty of Northampton; Robert Bruce acknowledged as King of Scotland
1330	*Nov* Execution of Mortimer; Queen Isabella dismissed
1333	Battle of Halidon Hill; Scots defeated
1337	Beginning of Hundred Years War with France
1340	*24 Jun* Battle of Sluys; English naval victory
1346	*26 Aug* Battle of Crécy *17 Oct* David Bruce, King of Scots, captured
1347	Calais becomes English possesion
1356	*Sep* Battle of Poitiers; French king John the Good captured
1360	*24 Oct* Peace of Calais: treaty with French
1361–2	Black Death
1367	Du Guesclin captured
1375	Truce signed at Bruges
1376	'Good' Parliament Death of Black Prince
1377	*21 Jun* Death of Edward III

RICHARD II

1367	*6 Jan* Birth
1377	Coronation
1381	Peasants' Revolt
1383	Marriage to Anne of Bohemia
1387	Battle of Radcot Bridge; royalist forces routed
1388	'Merciless' Parliament
1394	Expedition to Ireland Truce with France
1396	Marriage to Isabella, daughter of Charles VI of France
1397	Gloucester murdered Bolingbroke exiled
1399	Richard to Ireland. Bolingbroke returns Abdication of Richard Coronation of Henry IV
1400	Richard murdered at Pontefract Castle

Chapter four
THE HOUSE OF LANCASTER

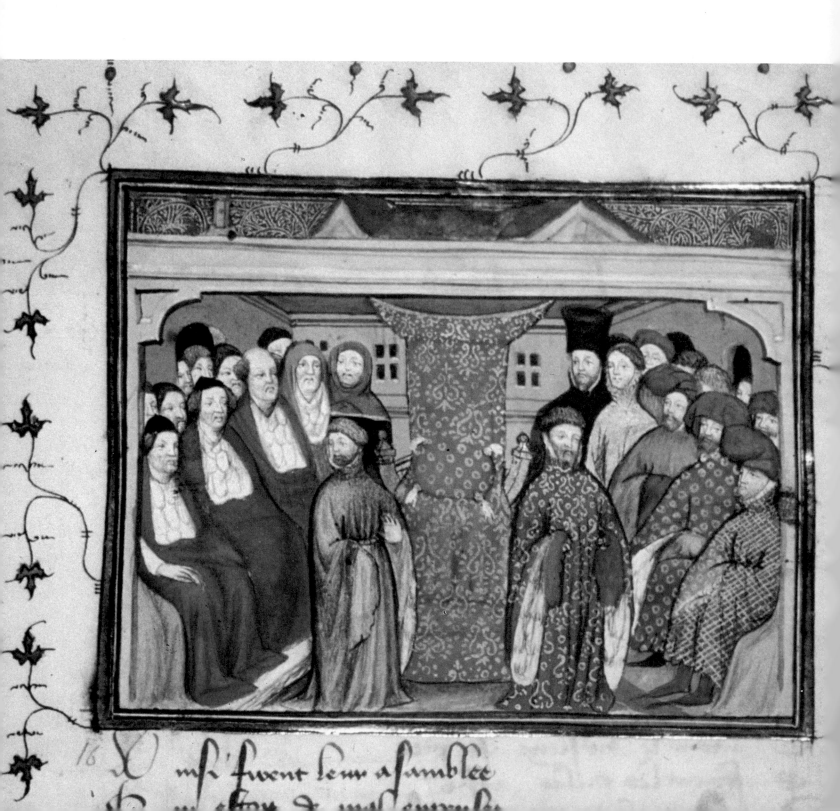

Henry IV 1399-1413

IN THE AUTUMN of 1399 Henry of Bolingbroke became King Henry IV of England on the enforced abdication of his cousin King Richard II. Henry laid formal claim to the throne with a declaration in the English language, which was replacing French in official usage, and Parliament gave its prompt assent.

It seemed in the best interests of the disarrayed kingdom that the victorious Henry should wear the crown, but he was not the immediate heir to Richard II. Henry was, indeed, of doubly royal blood, since his father, John of Gaunt, was Edward III's third surviving son and his mother, Blanche of Lancaster, a direct descendant of Henry III. But one of John of Gaunt's elder brothers had also left a male heir, and this boy, Edmund Mortimer, Earl of March, should technically have succeeded to the throne when the childless Richard vacated it. Out of this break with royal tradition the so-called 'Wars of the Roses' were ultimately to arise, half a century later.

The new King Henry, the first ruler of the House of Lancaster, was a stocky, athletic man, lacking the tall golden looks of the Plantagenet kings, but well-read and courteous in his manner. He had been born at Bolingbroke Castle, in Lancashire, on 30 May 1366. His mother, the gracious Blanche, in whose honour Chaucer wrote the long poem called 'The Book of the Duchess', died when he was in infancy, and Henry of Bolingbroke was the only surviving child of his parents' marriage – though John of Gaunt's third wife, Catherine Swynford, was to provide him with a line of half-sisters and brothers, the Beauforts. At 14 Henry was married to an heiress, Mary de Bohun, and in 1387 their first son was born, the future hero of Agincourt, Henry V. It was in that year that Henry took his first inadvertent step towards the throne, when he joined with the Lords Appellant in opposing King Richard.

The future Henry IV's courage and spirit of adventure were well demonstrated during his early adulthood. He travelled the world, joining with the military Christian order called the Teutonic Knights on a quasi-crusading expedition to Lithuania in 1390, and later he visited the Middle East by way of Prague, returning via Venice, Milan and Paris. The rich experiences of his travels helped to prepare him for the challenges to come.

For a time after his return Henry of Bolingbroke became a king's man, but after quarrelling with another eminent noble, Thomas Mowbray, he was banished from the kingdom by Richard. When he returned, in July 1399, it was at the head of an army. His original aim was solely to reclaim his rightful inheritance and win back the estates which Richard had perfidiously confiscated on John of Gaunt's death. But when others, including the powerful northern leaders, the Percy family, flocked to join his cause, the enterprise acquired a new aim – the crown. By the end of August Henry was master of England, and Richard was a prisoner in the Tower, where once, as a boy, he had awaited the outcome of the Peasants' Revolt.

On 13 October, Henry was crowned King Henry IV. Evil omens were said to have marked the ceremony: one of the new king's golden spurs fell off, a sure sign of rebellion to come. But Henry IV needed no such warnings to remind him of the weakness of his situation. He was threatened on all sides. If friends of Richard did not win the crown

LEFT Henry IV claims the crown before Parliament.
RIGHT The tomb effigies of Henry IV and his second wife Joanna of Navarre in Canterbury cathedral.

back for the deposed King, other great subjects might attempt to do as he, Henry, had done, and claim the throne for the rightful heir, the Earl of March, or themselves; whilst Wales and Scotland might rise at any time.

In the event, it was supporters of the ex-King who struck first, early in 1400. The kingdom's honeymoon with Henry IV was not yet over, however, and the rebels were quickly crushed and put to death. Richard himself had now no hope. He was secretly murdered, certainly with Henry's agreement, at Pontefract Castle.

In the autumn of that year, the Welsh patriot Owen Glendower rose to fame. Glendower was a fine soldier and a rousing leader of men, and he inspired his countrymen to successful defiance of the English for the next eight years. Scotland rebelled also, and when the Earl of Northumberland's heir, Henry Percy, won a great victory over the Scots in 1402, it further increased King Henry's difficulties. Young Percy, who was known as 'Hotspur', was as dashing and hot-tempered as his nickname implied, and the

power of the Percies in the north was immense. Hotspur now turned against the king, supported by his family; and the fact that he was connected by marriage to Owen Glendower made the situation critical.

Before Hotspur and Glendower could join forces, King Henry acted, with characteristic energy. On 21 July 1403, in a crucial battle near Shrewsbury, Hotspur was killed, and so one threat was removed. But the insurrections continued. The Earl of March, senior claimant to the throne, found strong support for his cause, from Percy's powerful father, the Earl of Northumberland, and Owen Glendower among others. To this dangerous alliance was added the backing of the Church, in the person of the Archbishop of York; and when the revolt was put down, Henry took the decision to execute all the ringleaders, including the Archbishop.

There was great public outrage at the execution of the Archbishop – and when the King was afterwards struck down by an unpleasant, unidentified disease, which his contemporaries believed to be leprosy, the superstitious saw it as a punishment sent by

God. But as if to disprove such rumours Henry was also granted relief from his most urgent dangers. The death in battle of the Earl of Northumberland in 1408, the capture of King James I of Scotland and the quelling of the worst of the Welsh defiance by 1409 left the sick King more secure on his throne, to face his other problems of debt and discontented ministers.

Campaigning on so many fronts was a costly business, and Henry IV was constantly subjected to criticism and demands from the Commons, who objected to his financial management and sought concessions before they would grant him taxes and customs revenues. As his disease grew worse, he became less able to fulfil an active role in government, and rival factions emerged within his ruling council. King Henry placed his faith in Archbishop Arundel, his Chancellor, but his son Henry, the Prince of Wales, displayed an impatience for power, and by 1409 he had come to dominate the council. There were rumours that the Prince intended to depose his own father; as if to assert his failing strength, in 1411 Henry IV

IN HENRY IV's ENGLAND

Alnwick Castle, Northumberland
(*Below*)
This was the main stronghold of the Percy family, who helped put Henry of Lancaster on the throne but later rebelled against him. It was substantially restored in the 19th century.

Pickering Castle, near Malton. North Yorkshire
Henry IV, before his accession, stayed at Pickering while journeying to London to claim the throne in 1399. Today it is an impressive ruin.

dismissed his son's faction.

Any widening of the breach between father and son was prevented by Henry IV's early death at the age of 47. On 21 March 1413, whilst at his prayers in Westminster Abbey, he collapsed and was carried into the Abbot's withdrawing-room, known as the Jerusalem Chamber, where he died that night. An old prophecy, that Henry IV would die 'in Jerusalem', had been fulfilled.

Henry V
1413-22

HENRY V was a boy of 12 when his father seized the crown of England and founded the royal House of Lancaster. At Henry IV's coronation his heir was created Prince of Wales, and it was in the Principality that the future hero of Agincourt gained his first experience of warfare, in defence of his father's throne.

A separate royal establishment was set up for Prince Henry at Chester in 1400. The 15-year-old prince took part in a battle for the first time at Shrewsbury, in 1403, helping to defeat Hotspur, but most of his early fighting was against the patriot Owen Glendower, whose Welsh rebels troubled the English successfully for eight years.

As he grew up, Prince Henry also played a part in English political affairs, and he became a dominant force on his father's governing council. There were disagreements between the King and his energetic heir; the Prince was rumoured to be impatient for Henry IV to abdicate, or die, and in 1411, when he was 23, the prince was summarily dismissed from the council. Two years later, however, Henry IV died, and his son had the power he desired, as King Henry V.

Shakespeare's history plays followed tradition in showing Henry V becoming a changed man on his accession to the throne. Earlier writers described him as 'a new man' once he became King. The roistering and potentially troublesome prince gave way to a thoughtful and determined king, who began his reign by making gestures of peace towards former – and possible future – enemies of his House. He had the remains of Richard II reburied with great splendour at Westminster, and he restored to favour the

heirs of several nobles regarded as opponents by his father, including the Earl of March, son of the deposed King Richard's rightful heir. It was Henry V's intention to unite the English and rally them to the cause of a glorious war with France. His policy succeeded: apart from a religious uprising early in 1414 and one abortive coup among the aristocracy, he was untroubled by rebellion at home.

The threat from the religious reformers, known mockingly as Lollards, who followed the teachings of the 14th-century radical John Wycliffe and roamed the countryside in groups, was put down with great severity.

Thomas Hoccleve (c 1370–c 1450) presents his book *Regement of Princes* to the Prince of Wales, later Henry V.

Henry V was deeply pious (he had spent the night of his accession in meditation in Westminster Abbey) but he was merciless in his response to the Lollards, and the persecution begun under his father, with burnings of heretics, was ferociously carried on. Even one of Henry's own former friends, Sir John Oldcastle, the original for Shakespeare's Falstaff, was sentenced to death, though Henry made efforts to save him.

59

The Battle of Agincourt, St Crispin's Day 1415, Henry V's famous victory over the French.

IN HENRY V's BRITAIN

Portchester Castle, near Portsmouth, Hampshire
(*Below*)
It was here that Henry V assembled his troops before embarking for France and the battle of Agincourt, in 1415.

Monmouth Castle, Gwent, Wales
Here Henry V was born, in 1387. Now a ruin, it is nevertheless worth visiting in summer for the atmosphere of its ancient keep and great hall.

Catherine de Valois' Effigy, the Undercroft, Westminster Abbey, London SW1
The effigy of Queen Catherine, Henry V's French wife, shows her to have been 5′ 4″ tall. In widowhood she married the Welshman Owen Tudor, and was thus the grandmother of Henry Tudor, who became Henry VII.

Henry V's Chantry Chapel, Westminster Abbey, London SW1
The Chantry Chapel where Henry V's body rests is decorated with illustrations of events in his life – including, of course, the triumph at Agincourt, in 1415.

The weak situation of the French king, Charles VI, who suffered bouts of mental illness, gave Henry V the opportunity to revive the old claim of the English monarchs to the throne of France. After complex negotiations with the powerful rival factions in France, the Burgundians and the Armagnacs, and having reassured himself of the legality of his claim, Henry made preparations for an invasion of France.

Whatever the morality of the enterprise, Henry's generalship was outstanding. On 11 August 1415 his army crossed the Channel, and by the end of September they had taken the town of Harfleur. This early success seemed unlikely to be repeated when the exhausted, disease-ridden and, by then, hungry English force met the far larger French army near Agincourt, on 23 October. But through Henry's skill and the power of the legendary English longbowmen, the result was a swift and astonishing rout of the French. The flower of France's chivalry fell that day, while England's casualties were remarkably low, and the victory at Agincourt on St Crispin's Day passed into history as a national triumph which made a hero of Henry V. One of the earliest Agincourt songs has been preserved: it begins 'Our King went forth to Normandy, With grace and might of chivalry'.

In fact, Agincourt had been no more than the first step towards Henry's ambition of the reconquest of France. Over the next five years the King of England needed all his skills as a diplomat, as well as a soldier, to carry out his purpose. He won over the Holy Roman Emperor to his cause, and he made the most of the continuing rivalries in France, between the Burgundians and the Armagnacs.

With the support of Duke John of Burgundy, Henry landed in France again in the summer of 1417, and after a series of arduous sieges he made himself master of all Normandy by the spring of 1419. In July of that year his ambitions seemed to receive a check, when the warring Burgundian and Armagnac parties united, in the face of his conquest, to defend Paris. But trouble flared between them again, and when the Duke of Burgundy was murdered, with a wound to the head, their hatred was confirmed. The Burgundians now turned to Henry for alliance, and so arose the saying that Henry V entered Paris through the hole in the Duke of Burgundy's skull.

By May 1420 the English king was in the ascendant and able to impose his demands on the French king – though not on his heir, the Dauphin, who was carrying on the fight from his territories south of the Loire. By the Treaty of Troyes, it was agreed that Charles

VI should continue to rule in his lifetime, but on his death Henry V of England should succeed to the French crown. To seal the arrangement, Henry married Charles's daughter, the Princess Catherine, at Troyes Cathedral.

The couple returned to England to a rapturous welcome, and in February 1421 the new Queen was crowned. They went on a royal progress through England, and before long Queen Catherine was pregnant with the child who was to become Henry VI, inheritor of the thrones of England and France. But Henry V's success was not yet complete.

In June of that year he returned to the wars in France, fighting the Dauphin, who had the backing of the Armagnacs. There were victories for the English king; in May 1422 the Dauphinist stronghold of Meaux, on the Marne, fell. But that was to be his last achievement. He was already ill, and by July he was too weak to sit on his horse, but had to be carried in a litter. Early on 31 August 1422, he died in the Bois de Vincennes. He was 35 years old and had reigned for nine years; in that short time he had established himself as one of England's most famous kings.

Henry VI
1422-71

HENRY VI, son of the legendary victor of Agincourt, was a mild, virtuous and often pitiable figure. Born on 6 December 1421, he was only nine months old when his father died, and he was crowned King of England when a child.

Within weeks of his accession to the English throne Henry also became King of France, on the death of his mother's father, the mentally unstable King Charles VI. The child on whom this vast inheritance had fallen was carefully schooled for his role; while his uncle Bedford governed France on his behalf, young Henry VI was brought up by the Earl of Warwick, one of his father's loyal supporters. But both men ultimately failed in their efforts. French resistance to English rule mounted dangerously, fostered by Joan of Arc, and King Henry grew up to be

LEFT Henry VI and Margaret of Anjou with their courtiers.

A 15th-century depiction of the Court of King's Bench; the prisoners wear ankle chains.

quite inadequate for the heavy tasks which lay ahead of him.

As an adult, Henry VI was far more interested in spiritual matters than in war and politics. He had many of the qualities of a monk: he hated bloodshed, wore a hair shirt, and was deeply shocked by sexual irregularities. 'Forsooth and forsooth' was the strongest language he permitted himself. Two great memorials to his piety and charity are King's College, Cambridge, with its glorious chapel, and Eton College, both of which he founded at the beginning of the 1440s. A good man, Henry was nevertheless a poor king.

His naïvety and unquestioning loyalty to those whom he regarded as his friends made it hard for him to control the factions which flourished at his court. He put his trust in the party of the Beauforts – his kinsmen by John of Gaunt's third marriage – and the Earl of Suffolk, who favoured a peaceful settlement with France. Though the French warrior-saint Joan of Arc had been burnt to death by the English in 1431, the same year that young Henry was taken to Paris and crowned King of France, six years later the French King Charles VII entered Paris in triumph. In England, opinion was divided over French policy: Henry and his advisers hoped to make peace and thereby save some of England's possessions across the Channel, but it was an unpopular view. Among the leaders of the opposition party was an ominous figure – Richard, Duke of York, next in line to the throne.

The peacemakers seemed to prevail when, in 1445, Suffolk negotiated a marriage between Henry and Margaret of Anjou, niece of King Charles VII. Suffolk's power and influence soared. But the marriage proved no safeguard. Still greater losses followed, and by 1451 Normandy and Guienne were gone. As the author of such a national disaster, Suffolk could not survive; despite Henry's loyal efforts to save him, he was impeached by Parliament and subsequently killed, in 1450. It was a measure of the nation's discontent when, a few months after Suffolk's death, the popular rising known after its Kentish leader as 'Jack Cade's Rebellion' erupted, but the saintly Henry would not heed warnings.

He continued to govern with unwise and unpopular advisers, notably his great-uncle, Edmund Beaufort, Duke of Somerset, and he did nothing to conciliate Somerset's enemy and his own heir presumptive, the Duke of York. In 1453, however, York suddenly found himself in the ascendant, through two dramatic events: the unfortunate king went mad, and two months later a son and heir was born to him. The child was christened

63

IN HENRY VI's ENGLAND

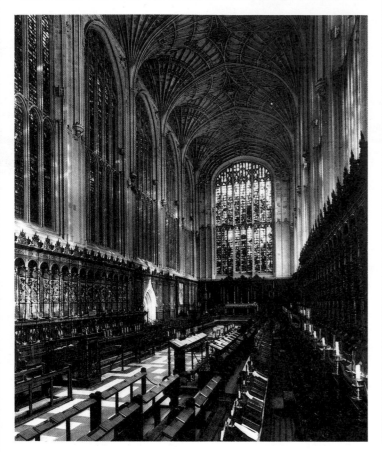

King's College, Cambridge, Cambridgeshire
(Top left)
King Henry VI founded the College, with its glorious chapel, in the early 1440s. In music, as well as architecture, King's Cambridge provides a fine memorial to a pious king.

The Duke of Bedford's Cup, British Museum, London WC1
(Top right)
The royal gold cup of kings, made in 1380–1 by order of the duc de Berry for Charles V of France. It was given to Henry VI by the Duke of Bedford.

Bamburgh Castle, near Belford, Northumberland
(Above)
To this remote royal castle Henry VI came as a fugitive, in 1463, after his deposition by Warwick the Kingmaker. Much of the castle was later rebuilt, but the 12th-century keep still stands.

Eton College, Windsor, Berkshire Henry VI's famous charitable foundation for poor scholars was begun in 1441. Though the original 70 pupils have now become closer to 1,400, and their status has changed likewise, the name of their royal founder is still revered by Etonians.

Prince Edward. York became Protector, in March 1454, and he took advantage of his new-found power to send Somerset to the Tower. But the pendulum swung again, and when the king recovered his wits York was dismissed, Somerset restored.

What followed was the first battle in the long civil war which the Romantic novelist Sir Walter Scott christened 'The Wars of the Roses'. On 22 May 1455 York and his supporters fought a battle against Somerset and Henry VI at St Albans, after Henry refused to hand over Somerset to his enemies. In the ensuing fighting Somerset was killed, and for a time it seemed that peace would now prevail, as the pacific King Henry so devoutly desired. But Henry's queen, the hot-tempered Margaret, had no intention of letting her infant son's rights be endangered and in 1459, when trouble flared again, it was she who took the initiative, dominating the King, raising an army, and attacking the Yorkists near Ludlow, scattering their defeated leaders. Yet again there was a change of fortunes. The Yorkists returned to rout the Lancastrian king's army at Northampton, in 1460, capturing the unhappy king, and this time the Duke of York took decisive action. He formally requested the throne of England from Parliament.

His wish was not granted, but he was promised that he would inherit the throne on Henry's death. Now Queen Margaret's militant maternal instincts were truly roused, in defence of her son's rights. She gathered a fresh army, and brought her son's disinheritor to battle at Wakefield, at the end of December 1460. It was York's last battle: he was killed in the fighting. But it was not the end of the war. His heir, Edward, now took up the Yorkist claim, supported by one of his father's strongest allies, the Earl of Warwick, who was to earn himself the name of 'the Kingmaker'.

Edward was the first king whom Warwick helped to make. As Edward IV, he entered London in triumph, and was accepted as king in Westminster Hall on 4 March 1461. A handsome young man, not yet 20, he possessed great military skill; and when, at the end of March, he met the forces of Henry and Margaret at Towton, near Yorkshire, in a battle for the throne, the result was an overwhelming victory for King Edward and the House of York. The defeated King and Queen fled across the border into Scotland for safety, and Edward IV returned victorious to London for his coronation.

For the next nine years, the throne was Edward's. While the indomitable Margaret continued to seek support from Scotland and France for the Lancastrian cause, Henry

Chronology
THE HOUSE OF LANCASTER

HENRY IV

1366	*30 May* Birth
1380	Marriage to Mary de Bohun
1390	Joined Teutonic Knights' Crusade to Lithuania
1399	Returned to England from exile
1399	*13 Oct* Coronation
1400–1	Rising of Owen Glendower joined by northern Earls
1402	Battle of Homildon Hill; Hotspur defeats the Scots
1403	*21 Jul* Battle of Shrewsbury; Hotspur killed
1405	Archbishop of York executed
1406	Capture of the future James I of Scotland
1408	Battle of Bramham Moor; Earl of Northumberland killed
1413	*21 Mar* Death of Henry IV

HENRY V

1387	*9 Aug* Birth
1400	Own establishment set up in Chester
1411	Dismissed from his father's council
1413	Coronation
1415	Invasion of France *Sep* Seizure of Harfleur *25 Oct* Battle of Agincourt
1417	Second invasion of France
1420	Treaty of Troyes; peace with France. Henry V accepted as heir to French throne Marriage to Princess Catherine of France
1421	*Feb* Queen Catherine crowned
1422	*31 Aug* Death of Henry V at siege of Meaux

HENRY VI

1421	Birth
1429	Joan of Arc relieves Orléans Coronation as King of England
1431	Joan of Arc burned at the stake
1440s	Eton and Kings College founded
1445	Marriage to Margaret of Anjou
1449–51	Loss of English possessions in northern France
1450	Jack Cade's rebellion
1453	End of Hundred Years War
1455	*22 May* Battle of St Albans; Somerset killed
1460	*10 Jul* Battle of Northampton; Lancastrians defeated by Yorkists; Yorkists capture King *30 Dec* Battle of Wakefield; Richard Duke of York killed
1461	*4 Mar* Edward IV accepted as king Henry VI ousted Battle of Towton; Edward victorious
1463	Henry's wife and son to France
1465	Henry captured, put in Tower
1470	Exiled Earl of Warwick takes London; Edward flees kingdom; Henry reinstated
1471	*14 Apr* Battle of Barnet; Warwick killed; Edward king again *3 May* Battle of Tewkesbury; defeat of Lancastrians, death of Edward Prince of Wales *21 May* Murder of Henry VI in the Tower

drifted about the borders of his lost kingdom, until in 1463 his wife and son crossed to France, leaving him in the northern stronghold of Bamburgh. In the summer of 1465 he was taken prisoner by Yorkist supporters and brought to degrading captivity in the Tower.

Warwick the Kingmaker had not finished with Henry VI, however. When a breach arose between the new King Edward IV and Warwick, in 1470, Edward temporarily fled the kingdom, and the Kingmaker, having joined forces with Queen Margaret, had Henry brought out of the Tower – where he was 'not so cleanly kept as should seem such a prince' – and reinstated as King of England. He was no more than a pathetic pawn in Warwick's game, and the 'readeption' of King Henry VI ended in the spring of 1471,

with the return of Edward IV. At the Battle of Barnet, on 14 April, Warwick was killed, and Queen Margaret's army was defeated soon afterwards, in the bloody Battle of Tewkesbury. Edward IV was King once more, and Henry VI was sent back to the Tower, never to emerge. His only son, young Prince Edward, was killed on the field of Tewkesbury, and soon after the battle Henry was murdered in the Tower of London, on the night of 21 May.

Today, on the anniversary of King Henry VI's death, two sheaves of flowers are delivered to the Tower – white lilies from Eton College, roses from King's College, Cambridge. They are a tribute to a pious king from his two great foundations.

Chapter five
THE HOUSE OF YORK

Edward IV enthroned.

Edward IV
1461-83

IN APPEARANCE, King Edward IV took after the Plantagenet forebears from whom he claimed his throne. At the time of his coronation on 28 June 1461, he was 19 years old, tall, fair-haired and handsome, and he enjoyed immense popularity among his subjects. But those who hoped that the accession of Edward of York would mean an end to civil war in England were soon disappointed.

Edward IV had many talents. He had already proved, on his path to the throne, that he was an able soldier, and once he had matured he was to display considerable political skills. At first, however. he was too deeply under the influence of his ambitious cousin Warwick, the 'Kingmaker', who had helped him to win the crown, to assert his own authority. Richard Neville, Earl of Warwick, was of semi-royal status, as a descendant of Edward III, and through several profitable marriage alliances in the Neville family he had become one of the richest landowners in England. As the power behind the throne of young Edward IV it was he who virtually ran the kingdom and organised the suppression of remaining Lancastrian opposition, while the King pursued his favourite occupations of drinking and womanizing.

Edward IV's ungovernable passion for women – preferably sophisticated older women – was the cause of many of his troubles. It certainly led to his breach with Warwick, which came about in 1464. In the autumn of that year Warwick was negotiat-

66

could be suitably punished, the Kingmaker fled to France. There, encouraged by Louis XI, he made an ironic new alliance – he joined forces with Queen Margaret of Anjou, wife of the captive Lancastrian king, Henry VI. When Warwick returned to England to fight Edward again, in September 1470, it was on behalf of Henry VI, whom he had once helped to depose.

On this occasion, Warwick sealed the pathetic Henry's fate. For a time he was brought out of the Tower and made to act as king again, under Warwick's direction. But Edward, who had fled abroad, returned in the spring of 1471 with the support of the Duke of Burgundy and his own youngest brother, the trusty Richard of Gloucester. On 14 April, Easter Day, Edward won a great victory at the Battle of Barnet, in which Warwick was killed. When Queen Margaret landed with her son Edward, Henry VI's heir, there was a further bloody battle, at Tewkesbury; and again the skilful King Edward IV was victorious. Lancastrian opposition was crushed at Tewkesbury; when the battle was over, Henry VI's heir lay dead and the tragic old king was murdered in the Tower. Any future Lancastrian threat to the House of York now depended on a distant descendant of John of Gaunt, a 14-year-old boy named Henry Tudor, and for his safety he was spirited away to France.

ing an important peace treaty with France, which involved a diplomatic marriage alliance between Edward and a princess of France. To the Kingmaker's outrage, matters had to be broken off when Edward revealed that he had been secretly married, several months earlier; to complete Warwick's discomfiture, the lady was a widow named Elizabeth Woodville, whose family were ardent Lancastrians. As the Woodville clan began to fill King Edward's court, eager for advancement, Warwick's influence declined, and it soon became clear that Edward intended to think for himself in future. While Warwick continued to conduct his own negotiations with the King of France, Louis XI, Edward treated with a rival power, Burgundy; and when his sister, Margaret, married the Duke of Burgundy, after which the new brothers-in-law proposed a joint

The execution of Edmund Beaufort after the battle of Tewkesbury in 1471.

invasion of France, Warwick's displacement was complete.

The Kingmaker responded by seeking to make a new king. For this he had the ideal candidate in Edward's foolish, ambitious heir presumptive, his brother the Duke of Clarence. With Clarence as his pawn, Warwick rose against King Edward, backed by his friend and Edward's enemy, Louis XI of France. At first the rebellion succeeded; by July 1469 Edward was a prisoner in Warwick's hands.

Fortunately for the King, his popular support in the realm was so great that, instead of deposing him, Warwick was obliged to release him, to restore order in England. Before Warwick and Clarence

Caxton presents his translation of the *Tales of Troy*, the first book he printed, to Margaret of York, sister of Edward IV and wife of the Duke of Burgundy.

67

IN EDWARD IV's ENGLAND

Tewkesbury Abbey, Gloucestershire
(Below)
This 11th-century Benedictine Abbey is close to the 'Bloody Meadow' where the Yorkists under Edward IV won a decisive victory over the Lancastrians, led by Queen Margaret,

the Duke of Somerset and Prince Edward.

St George's Chapel, Windsor Castle, Berkshire
To replace the original chapel founded by Henry III and enlarged by Edward III, Edward IV founded the present St George's Chapel. Work began in the late 1470s, and it was not complete when KingEdward IV died. His body lies there now, on the north side of the Choir.

For the rest of Edward IV's reign the crown remained secure, and the birth of the heir to the throne, also christened Edward, in 1470, seemed to ensure the Yorkist succession. King Edward emerged as a wise ruler and administrator; he set about reforming the Crown's finances, he built up trade, and he made successful efforts to keep down taxation. As well as putting down lawlessness on the English highways, he sought to curb the unruly Welsh, and he established a household for his son at Ludlow, where the infant Prince of Wales presided over the Principality in his name.

The French King Louis XI had proved himself Edward's enemy; now Edward retaliated, by intervening in French affairs. In the summer of 1475 he set sail for France at the head of a 10,000–strong invasion force. Though he was let down by several allies, including the Duke of Burgundy, Edward came out of the situation with credit: instead of fighting, he signed a truce with King Louis and agreed to withdraw in return for a large annual payment. Certain high-minded Englishmen, including the King's youngest brother, Richard, Duke of Gloucester, thought the settlement inglorious, but it benefited Edward's finances and thus his security.

Throughout the reign of Edward IV, Richard of Gloucester served his brother loyally. The second brother, the Duke of Clarence, was a constant source of trouble, however. When his dealings with Warwick the Kingmaker were at an end he involved himself in other dangerously ambitious projects, such as seeking to marry the great Duke of Burgundy's daughter; he seemed heedless of warnings, and finally action was taken to stop his plots for good. In February 1478 he was put to death; according to contemporary tradition, he was drowned in a butt of Malmsey wine. Certainly the killing had the King's consent.

Edward was himself fond of good wine and food, among other pleasures. He was genuinely cultured, possessing a considerable library of his own, and he encouraged the setting up of the first printing-press in England by William Caxton. But Edward IV's greatest passion was women, and his last, and most famous, love was the tradesman's wife Jane Shore.

Edward IV had many faults and vices, including greed, promiscuity and idleness, but he was in general a successful king. When he died of fever on 9 April 1483, he was succeeded by his 12-year-old son Prince Edward; and to act as Protector, he appointed his capable brother Richard, Duke of Gloucester.

Edward V 1483

THE ELDER SURVIVING son of Edward IV and Elizabeth Woodville, Edward V succeeded his father in April 1483, was deposed by the end of June and disappeared without trace some time in July, to become the centre of a celebrated unsolved mystery.

Edward V was born in Westminster Abbey, where his mother had taken sanctuary during Warwick the Kingmaker's attempted coup to reinstate Henry VI as monarch. His father was then abroad, gathering forces for a final defeat of Warwick and the Lancastrian threat; this he achieved at the battles of Barnet and Tewkesbury, and by June 1471 Edward IV was securely re-established as king, and his heir was created Prince of Wales. Much of the prince's boyhood was spent at Ludlow, where he learned the business of government at first hand, as his father's nominal representative in Wales. The Queen's brother Anthony Woodville, Earl Rivers, was appointed as governor to the Prince, and Sir Richard Grey, his mother's son by her first marriage, was one of young Edward's closest advisers.

The influence of Rivers and Grey over the King, as Edward became on 9 April 1483, was clearly unwelcome in certain quarters. Edward IV's youngest brother, Richard of Gloucester, who had been appointed Protector, took action: he met the king's party on the journey from Ludlow to London, arrested Rivers and Grey – who were later executed – and escorted young Edward to his state lodgings in the Tower of London. The Queen, Elizabeth Woodville, retired to sanctuary in Westminster Abbey once more, with her younger son, nine-year-old Richard, Duke of York, and her five daughters. On 16 June, however, she was obliged to surrender her son Richard to his uncle Gloucester's care, and the boy joined his brother in the Tower.

Before Edward V's coronation could take place, a startling allegation was made. On 22 June, Dr Ralph Shaw, a supporter of Gloucester, preached a sermon in which he publicly declared that Edward IV's marriage to Elizabeth Woodville had not been lawful, as the King had previously entered into a contract with another lady. The Woodville

The Great Sword of State, which was first carried before Edward V, and the three Swords of Justice.

69

A stained glass window in Canterbury cathedral, portraying the family of Edward IV. *Left to right*: Richard Duke of York, Edward Prince of Wales, Edward IV, Elizabeth Woodville, Princesses Elizabeth, Cecilia, Anne, Catherine and Mary.

IN EDWARD V's ENGLAND

Ludlow Castle, Salop
(*Below*)

Edward IV sent his heir, Prince Edward, to govern Wales (in name, at least) from Ludlow. At his accession in 1483 the little King Edward V left Ludlow for London, to be met on the way by his uncle, the future Richard III, who escorted him to the Tower.

The Tower of London, London E1

Edward V and his brother Richard, Duke of York, are perhaps the best known and most pathetic of all the spectres from the Tower's history. They were lodged in the Bloody Tower, known then as the Garden Tower.

children, most importantly young Edward and his brother, were thus bastards, and debarred from the throne.

Three days after this revelation, Parliament met, and the matter was discussed. The outcome was that the late king's sons were held to be illegitimate, and Richard of Gloucester was thus the rightful heir to the throne. He was formally requested to become king, and after appearing to hesitate, he accepted. On 26 June, the reign of Edward V was over.

The two boys remained in the Tower, where they were sometimes seen playing and shooting together. But late in July they disappeared, and were never recorded alive again. Suspicions were voiced at the time, both in England and in France, that they had been murdered; and in the reign of Henry VII a man named Sir James Tyrell claimed that

he had been paid by Richard III to smother the children while they were asleep, and that he then buried their bodies beneath a staircase.

Two centuries later, in the reign of King Charles II, some workmen digging beneath an old staircase in the Tower came upon a coffer containing children's bones. They were taken to be the bones of the two Princes, and reverently re-interred in an urn – designed by Sir Christopher Wren – in Westminster Abbey. In 1933 the remains were forensically examined and pronounced to be parts of the bodies of two boys aged about twelve and ten years – the ages of Edward V and his brother Richard of York in 1483. The case remains unproven, but it would seem likely that the uncle who usurped their throne did indeed order the deaths of the Princes in the Tower.

Richard III
1483-5

WHEN RICHARD III came to the throne in 1483 he was 30 years old, with a long record of service to the crown. The youngest surviving son of Richard, Duke of York and Cecily Neville, he was born at Fotheringhay Castle on 2 October 1452, and spent his childhood under the shadow of the Wars of the Roses. He was eight when his father was killed at the Battle of Wakefield, and his mother fled with him to the safety of Burgundy; but a year later the victory of his

Richard III.

RICARDVS · III · ANG · REX ·

eldest brother, Edward, at Towton brought about a dramatic change in the family fortunes. As King of England, Edward created young Richard a Knight of the Garter and Duke of Gloucester, and Richard repaid him with his steadfast loyalty.

Like his elder brother Clarence, Richard of Gloucester married a daughter of Warwick the Kingmaker, Anne Neville, who became his wife in 1471. But unlike Clarence, who succumbed briefly to Warwick's promises of kingship, Richard remained loyal to Edward, for whom he fought valiantly at the crucial battles of Barnet and Tewkesbury. When Clarence was finally put to death, Richard showed great grief for him. There were many good reports of Gloucester during these years. His relationship with the Queen, Elizabeth Woodville, was, however, not cordial, and he spent much of his time away

from court, acting as his brother's Lieutenant in the North, or as Warden of the West March. Shortly before King Edward died he recognised Richard's valuable work by making the Warden's post hereditary and granting him the royal estates in the county of Cumberland. It was a fine inheritance for Richard's son, named Edward, who had been born in 1473.

When King Edward IV died, in April 1483, he entrusted the care of his own son, and of the realm, to Richard's Protectorship. It was a decision which the boy's mother and her Woodville relations found unacceptable. A resolution was hurried through, before Richard arrived from the north, replacing his authority with that of a council of regency, and young Edward began his journey from Ludlow to London. On the way, however, he was met by Richard; and as the Protector

took charge of Edward, having arrested his governor, Earl Rivers, the Woodville Queen fled into sanctuary at Westminster with her other son and daughters.

On 4 May Richard entered London, and from then on events moved swiftly. He requested support from his loyal followers in the north, officially to protect him from the Queen and her adherents; and on 16 June the younger Prince, Richard of York, was removed from his mother in Westminster Abbey, and sent to join his brother. The Princes' uncle was planning their disinheritance.

Lord Hastings, who opposed the action, was arrested during a council meeting, and beheaded at once; on 22 June, Dr Ralph Shaw preached the sermon in which he made the startling claim that the little King was ineligible to rule, as his father had

IN RICHARD III's ENGLAND

Sudeley Castle, near Winchcombe, Gloucestershire
(Above)
The Great Hall at Sudeley was almost certainly built while Richard held the castle. It is now a ruin.

The ceiling of the reconstructed great hall, Crosby Place, which was Richard III's London residence.

already contracted a marriage before he made Elizabeth Woodville his wife. With both of Edward IV's sons thus declared illegitimate and debarred from succeeding, the rightful heir to the throne was Richard of Gloucester, and Parliament duly made a formal request to Richard that he should become their King. After some demurring, he accepted, and on 6 July the English people witnessed the coronation, not of Edward V, but of Richard III.

What became of the two little boys in the Tower may never be known for certain. After they ceased to be seen, rumours quickly began to circulate that they had been killed on their uncle's orders, and in January 1484 the French Parlement was told formally that Richard had murdered his nephews; but Richard III never produced the boys to stop the stories. Amidst the centuries-old speculation and circumstantial evidence, a few facts remain: the scraps of bone found beneath a staircase in the Tower two centuries later, and subjected to forensic tests in 1933, were found to be those of two boys of the ages of the Princes in 1483. Richard's successor, Henry VII, who has sometimes been charged with the crime, showed a marked (and unusual for the time) reluctance to kill even his proven enemies, as his lenient treatment of the dangerous pretenders Lambert Simnel and Perkin Warbeck demonstrated. And despite Richard's energetic service of his brother Edward IV during his lifetime, and his motto 'Loyauté me lie' – 'loyalty binds me' – there was little loyalty in the exposure of that brother's reputed earlier marriage, the swift disinheritance of his nephews and his acceptance of their throne.

Whatever the means by which he won it, Richard III did not enjoy his throne for long. His reign was not tranquil; though an early attempt at rebellion, led by his former supporter the Duke of Buckingham, was swiftly put down, the threat of invasion from Henry Tudor remained ever-present. In the spring of 1484, a personal tragedy struck when Richard's only son, Prince Edward, died. Not only did Richard and his wife Anne seem half-mad with grief, but the King's position was now doubly vulnerable, since only his life now lay between another claimant and the throne. Just a year later, Anne herself died; and the rumours which seemed to cling to Richard III now whispered that he had killed her, so that he could marry his niece, Elizabeth of York, whom the Lancastrian Henry Tudor had publicly pledged to marry as soon as he had won the throne.

Despite Richard's intensely loyal following in the north, he was by no means universally loved by his subjects. The unpopularity of his advisers Catesby, Ratcliffe and Lovell, and his own emblem of the white boar, were celebrated in the biting rhyme,

'The Cat, the Rat and Lovell our Dog
Rule all England under a Hog'.

There were disaffected Yorkists, as well as ardent Lancastrians, among the supporters who welcomed Henry Tudor to England in August 1485. The Tudor claimant landed in South Wales and made his way towards Leicester, gathering men as he went. Finally his army and Richard's took up their positions at Ambien Hill, near the Leicestershire village of Market Bosworth, and on 22 August 1485 the last battle of the Wars of the Roses began.

Richard had a far larger army than the invader, and he was experienced in battle, unlike Henry Tudor; but the desertion of two powerful former Yorkists, the Stanleys, to Henry's side helped to tip the balance. Richard was killed, fighting valiantly 'in the thickest press of his enemies', and according to tradition the royal circlet was found hanging on a thornbush, and placed reverently on the head of the new King, Henry VII. Richard's body was slung across the back of a nag to be carried, in unkingly fashion, to Leicester.

The people of York risked Tudor displeasure by recording their sorrow at the death of King Richard, 'piteously slain and murdered, to the great heaviness of this city'. But the struggle between York and Lancaster was over at last, and the age of the Tudors had begun.

Chronology
THE HOUSE OF YORK

EDWARD IV

1442	*28 Apr* Birth
1461	*28 Jun* Coronation
1464	Marriage to Elizabeth Woodville
1469	*Jul* Battle of Edgecote; Edward briefly Warwick's prisoner
1470	Henry VI briefly restored
1471	*14 Apr* Battle of Barnet; Warwick killed; Edward reinstated *21 Apr* Henry VI murdered *4 May* Battle of Tewkesbury; Margaret defeated
1475	Leads army to France; Treaty of Picquigny with Louis XI
1476	Caxton sets up first English printing press
1478	*Feb* Duke of Clarence killed
1483	Death of Edward IV

EDWARD V

1470	*Nov* Birth
1483	Accession to the throne; Richard of Gloucester appointed Protector *16 Jun* Joined by brother, Prince Richard, in Tower *22 Jun* Edward IV's marriage declared unlawful *26 Jun* Richard of Gloucester replaces his nephew as king *Jul* Last recorded sighting of Princes in Tower

RICHARD III

1452	*2 Oct* Birth
1471	Marriage to Anne Neville *14 Apr* Battle of Barnet; Warwick killed
1473	Son Edward born
1483	*6 Jul* Coronation *2 Nov* Buckingham beheaded
1484	Death of Prince Edward
1485	Death of Anne Neville *Aug* Arrival of Henry Tudor in England *22 Aug* Battle of Bosworth; death of Richard III

Chapter six
THE TUDORS

Henry VII
1485-1509

IN THE aftermath of the Battle of Bosworth, the new King of England circulated an open letter among his subjects. Announcing his victory and the overthrow of 'Richard, Duke of Gloucester, lately called King Richard', he bade them go home and keep the king's peace, 'and pick no quarrels for old nor new matters'. Henry VII had won the crown of the Plantagenets on a doubtful claim, out of civil war and disorder, to become the fifth English king in less than 25 years. If he was to keep that crown and establish the House of Tudor securely on the throne, he would have to end old quarrels and bring a lasting peace to England.

The upheavals of the Wars of the Roses had dominated Henry Tudor's early life. The son of a half-Welsh nobleman named Edmund Tudor, Earl of Richmond, and the Lady Margaret Beaufort, a Plantagenet heiress, he was born at Pembroke Castle in Wales on 28 January 1457. When he was 14 years old, the deaths of Henry VI and the Prince of Wales, resulting from the Battle of Tewkesbury, had left Henry Tudor as the senior male representative of the royal House of Lancaster; and though his claim to the throne was slight, resting on his mother's descent from John of Gaunt's second son, whose legitimacy was in question, young Henry was hurried away for his own safety to France by his loyal uncle, Jasper Tudor. There he remained in political exile until his successful bid for the English throne ousted the Yorkist Richard III, and brought the Wars of the Roses to an end.

At the time of his coronation, which took place with ostentatious pomp on 30 October 1485, Henry VII was 28 years old. His years of hardship and exile had helped to mould him into a shrewd, far-sighted ruler, with a strong sense of the value of money and an

76

instinct for political survival. In one of the first acts of his reign, he dated his rule from the day before Bosworth; thus those who had fought against him were guilty of treason against their rightful king. Twenty-eight of Richard III's leading supporters were deprived of titles, lands and power by Henry's first Parliament, and throughout his reign the Tudor king was constantly vigilant in keeping down over-mighty subjects who might threaten the royal security. Acts were passed which forbade the keeping of private armies and limited the wearing of liveries and badges by great men's retainers; whereas for the sovereign's own personal protection, Henry VII instituted the Yeomen of the Guard, the scarlet-uniformed royal bodyguard which survives to the present day.

As a major step towards healing old quarrels, Henry took as his wife the principal Plantagenet claimant to the throne – Edward IV's eldest daughter, Elizabeth of York, sister of the vanished Princes in the Tower. The flaxen-haired, 20-year-old Elizabeth became Henry's Queen on 18 January 1486; to the joy of those who desired peace, she gave birth to a son nine months later, and the warring claims of the red and white roses of Lancaster and York were reconciled at last, in the infant 'rosebush of England', the first Tudor prince. In 1485, Caxton's printing-press had published Malory's classic tales of King Arthur, *Le Morte d'Arthur*, and the newborn heir to the throne was named Arthur, as a token of past and future greatness. When a second son, christened Henry, was born in 1491, the future of the House of Tudor seemed assured.

There were several attempts by pretenders, both real and fraudulent, to claim the throne during the early years of Henry VII's reign. In 1487, an Oxfordshire tradesman's son named Lambert Simnel was actually crowned 'King Edward VI' in Dublin Cathedral. He had been coached by a group of Yorkist conspirators who hoped to pass him off as Edward IV's nephew the Earl of Warwick, and the plot nearly succeeded. At the Battle of Stoke, on 16 June 1487, Henry VII narrowly defeated the conspirators, and to show the world his opinion of the so-called 'Edward VI', he had young Lambert put to work in the royal kitchens.

Another challenge came from a plausible rogue named Perkin Warbeck, who received widespread support from foreign courts. The kings of France and Scotland, and even the powerful Holy Roman Emperor, were willing to accept him as Richard, Duke of York, the younger of the Princes in the Tower. For six years Warbeck troubled Henry VII's and England's security, until he was finally captured whilst abetting a rebellion in Cornwall in 1497. Again Henry showed mercy, putting 'Prince Richard of England' under comfortable house-arrest at court, but Perkin continued to stir up trouble until Henry was obliged to execute him. Henry Tudor's reluctance to make martyrs of his enemies showed a rare degree of wisdom and tolerance for the age.

Though, as the years passed, England became settled and prosperous under Henry VII's wise rule, he never acquired great personal popularity. His public image was of a somewhat cold, stately monarch, over-fond of amassing wealth. His extortion of money from his subjects was much resented, and the rich complained of the forced loans,

The splendid effigies of Henry VII and Elizabeth of York, by Torrigiano, on Henry's tomb in Westminster Abbey.

IN HENRY VII's BRITAIN

Richmond Palace Gatehouse, Surrey
(*Below*)
When the old royal palace of Sheen, in Surrey, burned down Henry VII rebuilt it in magnificent Gothic style, and gave it the new name of Richmond Palace, after the title which he had borne before his accession. The original gatehouse can still be seen from the outside.

Pembroke Castle, Pembrokeshire, Wales
(*Below right*)
The birthplace of Henry VII, on 28 January 1457, now a dramatic ruin.

Henry VII Chapel, Westminster Abbey, London SW1
(*Right*)
Begun in 1503 as a resting-place for the bones of his Lancastrian forebear Henry VI, which were never laid there, the Chapel remains a glorious memorial to Henry VII. It is famous for its fine vaulting and for its numerous royal tombs, which include those of Henry VII himself and his wife Elizabeth of York, as well as his famous descendants such as Mary Queen of Scots and Elizabeth I.

or 'benevolences', which one of Henry's chief advisers, Cardinal Morton, extracted by the ingenious method known as 'Morton's fork'. Those living well could clearly pay large sums, said Morton; those living simply must have saved plenty, and so could also pay plenty.

Henry himself was frugal by nature, but he was no miser. The account-books over which he liked to pore reveal that he enjoyed music, dancing and sports, and show details of payments to charity and to entertainers. Henry's private tastes were simple, but he believed in spending large sums on food, clothing and jewels, to maintain the lifestyle befitting a great king, and on public occa-sions no expense was spared to make an impressive show. His building works, too, were magnificent. He built the fine modern palace called Richmond, after his former title, to replace the old palace of Sheen, which burnt down; but probably his greatest monument was the Henry VII Chapel in Westminster Abbey, intended to house the revered remains of King Henry VI, his Lancastrian predecessor on the throne. Henry VII and many of his descendants lie there now.

Henry Tudor was not much given to innovations in government; he preferred to make the most efficient use of existing administrative machinery. But the King's Council took on a new look under the first of the Tudors, as the old aristocracy lost its hold and 'new men' of humbler origins rose through the royal favour. Henry VII's justice was administered fairly, through the powerful new Court of Star Chamber; he encouraged exploration and trade; above all he brought peace to England, both at home and abroad. He married his daughter Margaret to the King of Scots, James VI, and his heir Prince Arthur to Catherine of Aragon, the King of Spain's daughter, thus securing two valuable alliances for England. Though Arthur died in 1502, at the age of 15, the Spanish princess stayed on in England to become the bride of the new heir, Henry, instead.

The kingdom which Henry Tudor seized in 1485 was rich, peaceful and prospering when he died, aged 52, at Richmond Palace, on 21 April 1509. It was a measure of his success that his son Henry succeeded him unchallenged by any Yorkist claimant to what was now the Tudor throne.

Henry VIII 1509-47

KING HENRY VIII came to the throne in the spring of 1509 with every gift that heaven and the 16th-century world could shower upon him. He was 17 years old, 6 feet tall, intellectual, athletic and fun-loving, with a face so handsome 'it would become a pretty woman', and muscular legs which he liked to show off. The pattern of a Renaissance prince, he could compose part-songs or worst an opponent in the tiltyard with equal skill, and he appeared to enjoy theological debate as much as hunting, singing and dancing. Henry had inherited a stable kingdom and a full treasury, thanks to the efforts of his careful father; and unlike Henry VII, who had accrued those benefits, the gorgeous young

Catherine of Aragon, Henry VIII's Catholic first wife.

Anne Boleyn, his second wife.

Henry VIII was the darling of his subjects.

When he was born, on 28 June 1491, he was not expected to inherit the throne; according to one account, he was to become Archbishop of Canterbury when his brother Arthur was king. Like Arthur, Henry received a first-class education – for a time the poet John Skelton was his tutor – and at the age of eight he impressed the great Dutch scholar Erasmus with his cleverness. After Arthur's death in 1502 he was trained for kingship by his father, who supervised him as strictly as if he were a girl. But for all his care the frugal, peace-loving and merciful Henry VII failed to pass on his principles to his son; as king, Henry VIII soon showed himself to be extravagant, eager for war, and all too ready to destroy those who crossed him.

In marrying, however, he obeyed what he claimed was his father's dying wish, and on 11 June 1509 he took as his wife his brother Arthur's widow, the pretty and dutiful Catherine of Aragon. Politically it was a wise move, re-allying England with mighty Spain, but the union seemed also to be a love-match. To Henry VIII, love and marriage were closely associated, and for much of their 20-year-long marriage he and Catherine of Aragon were happy together – despite their

constant failure to produce a surviving son. Yet Henry remained optimistic. 'By the grace of God, the sons will follow', he declared after the birth of their only surviving child, Mary, in 1516.

The business of government, which had so concerned Henry VII, was not to Henry VIII's liking. He preferred to leave the detailed work to able, ambitious servants, 'new men' of humble origins, such as Cardinal Wolsey and Cromwell. Thomas Wolsey, son of a Suffolk butcher, rose to giddy heights, becoming Cardinal and Lord Chancellor by 1515, and living in splendour, with ornate palaces at York Place (or Whitehall) and Hampton Court – both of which Henry later acquired himself. King Henry's glory-seeking zest for war had led him into action in France early in the reign, but Wolsey embarked on ambitious plans for peace throughout Europe, with England holding the balance between the great powers, Spain and France. It was Wolsey who organized the dazzling diplomatic affair known as the 'Field of Cloth of Gold', in 1520, when Henry, Catherine and most of the English aristocracy crossed to France to join in a fortnight of festivities with Henry's sometime enemy and rival, King Francis I.

Wolsey's attention was increasingly

The title page of Cranmer's Great Bible, showing Henry VIII handing it to the clergy via whom the word of God in English reaches his grateful subjects.

occupied during the 1520s with what became known as 'The King's Great Matter' – the divorce which Henry came to desire from Catherine, so that he could marry his vivacious, black-eyed new love, Anne Boleyn. As Queen Catherine ceased child-bearing, with only the Princess Mary to inherit the Tudor throne, Henry convinced

himself that he had sinned in marrying his brother's widow, and that his lack of male heirs was God's punishment. But the papal annulment he sought was not forthcoming. Negotiations with Rome dragged on; Catherine insisted, in court, that her marriage to Arthur had not been consummated, and that she was thus Henry's lawful wife; finally, in 1529, Wolsey fell, having failed his master, and was replaced by Thomas Cromwell. With Cromwell's assistance, Henry VIII decided on a momentous step – he would deny the Pope's authority in this and all

other English affairs, replacing the Pope's supremacy with his own. Typically, in defying Rome, Henry did not give up the title of 'Defender of the Faith', which a previous Pope had granted him in 1521. In his own eyes, he remained a devout Catholic to the end of his life.

The Act of Supremacy of 1534 established Henry VIII as Supreme Head of the English Church, and in 1539 a version of the Bible translated into English was placed in every parish church for the first time. The Reformation Parliament, which sat between 1529 and 1536, approved the break with Rome, as well as the King's divorce and re-marriage. Growing nationalism and resentment at Church corruption had paved the way for this culmination of the centuries-old struggle between Kings of England and the Papacy. Sir Thomas More refused to acknowledge the Act of Supremacy and was executed in July 1535; a year later a group of rebels in Yorkshire, calling themselves the Pilgrimage of Grace, demanded the restoration of the Pope's supremacy and the powers of the Church, but were brutally suppressed; resistance otherwise was limited, and the Dissolution of the Monasteries went ahead, under Cromwell's expert direction. As the vast wealth of the Church was transferred to the Crown, the confiscated buildings and lands were sold off to the new nobles and gentry who were coming to prominence under the Tudors. Henry VIII thus emerged far richer, as well as more powerful, from the Reformation which his love for Anne Boleyn had set in motion.

That love, unlike the Reformation, did not last. Anne's eagerly-awaited child, born on 7 September 1533, was, disappointingly, another girl – the future Elizabeth I. Anne grew neurotic and shrewish, she failed to provide a son, and Henry grew tired of her. Eventually he convinced himself that she had committed adultery with five lovers, and on 19 May 1536, she was executed. With indecent haste, Henry married again, and this time his queen, a Wiltshire knight's daughter named Jane Seymour, bore him a healthy son, on 12 October 1537. The Queen died in childbed, but the infant, Prince Edward, lived, 'the whole realm's most precious jewel'.

In 1536 Henry VIII had united Wales with England. Through Prince Edward he sought to unite the crowns of England and Scotland also, by betrothing his only son and heir to Mary, the infant Queen of Scots. The plan found no favour in Scotland, however; the Scots had no wish for English control. It was now up to Henry himself to marry.

Excommunicated by the Pope, threatened

A painting by Holbein of Henry VIII in his prime.

IN HENRY VIII's ENGLAND

Hampton Court Palace, Hampton Wick, Surrey
(*Right and below*)

On the downfall of Wolsey, who built this palace for himself. Henry VIII acquired it, and it became one of his favourite residences. He expanded and decorated the palace, adding the Great Hall and the tennis court. In the entrance courtyard, the initials of H and A, for the King and Anne Boleyn, can be seen, but the dominating feature is the magnificent astronomical clock, with its three dials, giving the time of day, the position of the moon, and the stars' relation to the earth, as the Tudor age saw them.

King Henry's Writing-Box, Victoria and Albert Museum, London SW7

Henry VIII disliked writing letters, but he was moved to write a series of passionate love-letters (now in the Vatican Archives) during his courtship of Anne Boleyn. This exquisite writing-box bears the royal arms and the Tudor rose.

St Peter-ad-Vincula, the Tower of London, London EC2

Here lie the bodies of Henry VIII's two executed wives, Anne Boleyn and Catherine Howard. Both were brought into the chapel from the scaffold site nearby, on Tower Green, which is marked with a plaque.

82

Fountains Abbey, near Ripon, Yorkshire

One of the loveliest ruins in England, this once-thriving Abbey suffered at the Dissolution of the Monasteries, and was broken up in 1539. Later, Fountains Hall was built nearby, from stones taken from the demolished Abbey.

Deal Castle, Kent

A fine example of the rugged ring of castles built on Henry VIII's orders for England's coastal defence. In the late 1530s, following Henry's breach with Rome and excommunication, there was a real danger of invasion by the Catholic powers, France and Spain.

Henry VIII's Armour, White Tower, Tower of London, London E1

Henry VIII encouraged the founding of Britain's famous armouries at Greenwich. His own suits of armour preserved in the Tower are of great interest; the variations in their sizes amply illustrate the effects of time and indulgence on the King's figure.

Rievaulx Abbey, near Helmsley, Yorkshire (*Below*)

Rievaulx Abbey was dissolved in 1536. It is in a particularly beautiful setting.

with invasion by the newly-allied French and Spanish rulers, the Tudor King sought a foreign diplomatic alliance, and in 1540 a daughter of the Protestant Duke of Cleves arrived in England as his bride. Henry had been assured that she was beautiful, and a Holbein portrait had seemed to confirm the reports; but his first sight of Anne of Cleves disillusioned him. Unable to consummate the marriage with this 'Flanders mare', he obtained a swift and amicable divorce from her, and in July 1540 Henry VIII married his fifth wife, the young and pretty Catherine Howard, niece of the Duke of Norfolk. His raptures with Catherine, his 'rose without a thorn', were short-lived. Catherine, it transpired, had had lovers, both before and after her marriage; the King had even been cuckolded by one of his young courtiers, Thomas Culpeper. In his rage and misery the gross, ageing King swore that he would cut off Catherine's head with his own sword, but in the event it was the professional executioner who beheaded the girl, on 13 February 1542.

Henry VIII self-pityingly cursed his fortune in 'meeting with such ill-conditioned wives', yet in 1543 he embarked on one more marriage. Catherine Parr was 33 and had been twice widowed; a clever and kindly woman, she brought a sense of family unity to the King and his three children by different marriages, and she provided intelligent companionship for the ageing Henry in the difficult closing years of his life. Renewed war with France and a growing religious struggle at home troubled him, and as the rift between right-wing, orthodox Catholics and the more radical reformers grew, so did the danger to his successor, the nine-year-old Prince Edward.

Before he died, Henry did what he could to ensure peaceful government in England during Edward's minority. He cut down the Duke of Norfolk and his heir, the Earl of Surrey, whose great blood and power might have threatened the Tudor supremacy, and he appointed not one Protector, but a council of 16 to rule on the boy-king's behalf. The succession question was resolved by the expedient of naming first Mary, then Elizabeth, as heirs after their brother; the problem of their technical illegitimacy, since his marriages to both their mothers had been annulled, was left unresolved.

On 28 January 1547, Henry VIII died. He left behind him a legacy of stout coastal castles and ruined abbeys; a 'puissant navy' and a reformed Church; and a marital record unequalled in the history of the British monarchy.

Chronology

HENRY VII

1457	*28 Jan* Birth
1485	*30 Oct* Coronation
1486	*18 Jan* Marriage to Elizabeth of York
1487	Lambert Simnel crowned in Dublin Court of Star Chamber licensed by Parliament
1497	Execution of Perkin Warbeck End of Wars of the Roses
1501	Marriage of Prince Arthur to Catherine of Aragon
1502	Death of Prince Arthur
1503	Marriage of Princess Margaret to James IV of Scotland
1509	*21 Apr* Death of Henry VII

HENRY VIII

1491	*28 Jun* Birth
1509	*11 Jun* Marriage to Catherine of Aragon
1513	*9 Sep* Battle of Flodden; James IV of Scots killed
1516	*18 Feb* Birth of Princess Mary
1520	Field of Cloth of Gold
1529	Death of Wolsey
1533	Marriage to Anne Boleyn *Apr* Catherine of Aragon's marriage declared invalid *7 Sep* Birth of Princess Elizabeth
1534	Act of Supremacy; Henry Supreme Head of the English Church
1536	*Jan* Death of Catherine of Aragon *May* Execution of Anne Boleyn
1536–9	Dissolution of the Monasteries
1536	*May* Marriage to Jane Seymour Pilgrimage of Grace
1537	*12 Oct* Birth of Prince Edward Death of Jane Seymour
1540	Marriage to and divorce from Anne of Cleves *Jul* Marriage to Catherine Howard
1542	*Feb* Catherine Howard beheaded Battle of Solway Moss; English victory over Scots
1543	Marriage to Catherine Parr
1547	*28 Jan* Death of Henry VIII

Edward VI 1547-53

EDWARD VI, 'the boy of wondrous hope', was a slight, fair-haired child of nine when he was crowned King of England on 19 February 1547. Archbishop Cranmer performed the coronation, and during the lavish ceremonials – which were shortened to only seven hours, because of the King's youth – Edward VI became the first English monarch to be crowned as Supreme Head of the English Church.

As the only surviving son to result from Henry VIII's six marriages, Edward had been brought up and educated for kingship from the time of his birth. King Henry himself had laid down exact rules as to the precautions to be observed in the royal nursery, to guard his heir against every ill from infection to treason, and as Prince Edward grew older he had the benefit of some of the finest scholars in England as his tutors, among them the Cambridge humanist John Cheke. 'Learning of tongues, of the Scriptures, of philosophy and the liberal sciences' were among the precocious prince's studies, and by the time he succeeded to the throne he was a solemn, highly intelligent boy who took his royal

An anti-papal allegory of the death-bed of Henry VIII, painted in about 1548. Henry VIII, on the left, gestures to his successor, Edward VI.

responsibilities intensely seriously.

Yet beneath the kingly exterior, Edward VI was still a child and therefore vulnerable. Henry VIII had sought to protect him against the ambitions of powerful men by appointing 16 joint councillors to govern during his minority. Within hours of Henry's death, however, his will had been overridden: at their very first meeting the Council elected the boy-king's senior uncle, Edward Seymour, as Protector of all the Realms and Dominions of the King's Majesty. Created Duke of Somerset, and living in semi-royal state, Seymour became increasingly autocratic. 'A dry, sour, opinionated man' was one ambassador's description of Protector Somerset, and Edward VI apparently felt little affection for him.

'My uncle of Somerset deals very hardly with me', he once observed, 'but my lord Admiral both sends me money and gives me money'. The Admiral was his youngest Seymour uncle, Thomas, who set out to win the King's affections by a dexterous mixture of bribes and jollity. A born plotter, Thomas Seymour cast his nets wide; having married Henry VIII's widow, Queen Catherine Parr, against the Protector's wishes, he went on to conduct a risky flirtation with the young Princess Elizabeth, whilst ingratiating himself with the King in the apparent hope of ousting Protector Somerset. The Admiral's schemes brought him, inevitably, to the block, in March 1549, and at court the great Bishop Latimer preached a thundering sermon against him, declaring, 'He was an ambitious man: I would there were no more in England!' It was a vain hope.

Lady Jane Grey

Edward made a business-like note of his uncle's death in his diary. The King's Journal, which he kept for much of his short life, revealed a great deal about his character and tastes, as well as the daily events of his reign. Accounts of audiences with ambassadors, and reports of his communications with foreign rulers, alternated with results of archery contests, in the boy-king's careful handwriting. The executions of uncles were recorded with no apparent emotion. His entry for 22 January 1552, when he was 14, read simply, 'The Duke of Somerset had his head cut off upon Tower Hill between eight and nine o'clock in the morning'.

The downfall of Somerset had been skilfully engineered by another 'ambitious man' – John Dudley, Earl of Warwick. Unlike Dudley, Somerset had been a man of some principle. Under his Protectorship, England advanced rapidly down the Protestant road, and in 1549 the First Prayer Book was issued in English; yet he believed in a measure of religious tolerance. He tried to prevent the growing move towards the enclosure of common land by powerful landowners, and among the ordinary people he was known as 'The Good Duke'. John Dudley, who replaced Somerset, and was made Duke of Nor-

Edward VI. In the background is Hunsdon House, near Ware in Hertfordshire.

84

IN EDWARD VI's ENGLAND

Edward VI's grammar school, Guildford

Edward VI's love of learning is commemorated in foundations such as this Royal Grammar School, refounded in 1553.

Eltham Palace, Kent
(Below)

Much of Edward II's original palace has disappeared since falling into disuse under the later Tudors. However, the 15th-century Great Hall has been skilfully restored; its fine hammerbeam roof now looks much as it would have done when Edward VI visited the palace during his boyhood.

thumberland, had no such name. His goal was power, both during and after the boy-king's lifetime.

In Edward VI, England had a monarch of great promise. Deeply concerned with the spread of learning, Edward lent his name to a number of fine grammar-schools, and his concern for religion was reflected in the publication of the first English prayer-books. Eminent scholars came away from interviews with King Edward deeply impressed: 'If he lives, he will be the wonder and terror of the world', was the comment of one bishop.

Edward was not destined to live, however. The sickness to which Tudor boys in their teens, from Prince Arthur to Henry VIII's illegitimate son the Duke of Richmond, were always prone, struck him down at the age of 15; tuberculosis was almost certainly the cause of his death, though there were whispers that the Duke of Northumberland had poisoned him. Certainly Northumberland profited from King Edward's death. He had laid his plans carefully. First, his son Guildford Dudley was married to the Lady Jane Grey; she was the grand-daughter of Henry VIII's younger sister, who had married the Duke of Suffolk. In his will King Henry had deliberately by-passed Mary, Queen of Scots, the descendant of his elder sister, and named Lady Jane as successor to the throne after his own daughters. Once Mary and Elizabeth were removed from the succession – as Northumberland now proceeded to do – the crown was Lady Jane's. Edward wrote out laboriously what he called 'My Device for the Succession', but the devising was probably Northumberland's. When the boy-king died, in terrible pain, on 6 July 1553, it was Northumberland, father-in-law of the new young Queen, who was left in control of the kingdom. The summer thunderstorm that rent the skies on the night of Edward VI's passing was seen by many as a portent.

His successor, the 'very small and short' 15-year-old Queen Jane, was the victim of her elders' ambitions. A girl of outstanding intellectual ability, who was never happier than when reading Plato, she had had an unhappy childhood, with constant 'pinches, nips and bobs' from her 'sharp, severe parents', the Marquess and Marchioness of Dorset. The Dorsets had already lent themselves and their daughter to the schemes of one plotter, Thomas Seymour, in 1547; they now fell in eagerly with Northumberland's attempted coup.

Queen Jane was received at the Tower in state on July 10. She remained there as Queen for nine days, and as a prisoner for the rest of her short life.

Mary I
1553-8

THE QUEEN who was to pass into history as 'Bloody Mary' was a well-meaning, short-sighted woman of deep religious convictions, fond of fine clothes, children and merrymaking, yet haunted by guilt and sorrow. Her life had been disrupted when she was in her late teens by Henry VIII's divorce from her adored mother, Catherine of Aragon, and the break with Rome. After great ill-treatment by Henry and his new Queen, Anne Boleyn, Mary was coerced in 1536 into signing an agreement acknowledging that her parents' marriage had been invalid and she herself was a bastard. Having submitted, Mary was restored to favour and named in the succession to the throne in Henry VIII's will; but for the betrayal of her mother and her own conscience Mary Tudor never forgave herself.

During her half-brother Edward's reign, while England became a Protestant nation, Mary resolutely upheld the Catholic faith. At times she was under strong pressure from the King and his councillors, who feared she might become a focus for Catholic dissension, but she had the support of her mother's country, mighty Spain; in 1551 the Emperor Charles V of Spain threatened war if Mary was forbidden to practise her religion. Edward VI could be in no doubt that his older half-sister would restore Catholicism to England if she should inherit the throne on his death; it was one of the major reasons why he fell in with Northumberland's plan to alter the succession in favour of the staunchly Protestant Lady Jane Grey. When Edward died, in the summer of 1553, it was Queen Jane and not Queen Mary who was ceremonially received as England's monarch at the Tower of London, on 10 July.

For once in her life, Mary acted with dashing heroism. Warned of what was afoot, she eluded Northumberland's urgent attempts to capture her and took refuge at Framlingham Castle, in Suffolk. There she prepared to fight for her throne, while the English flocked to her support. Even the Spanish ambassador thought her chances slight, but he, like Northumberland, had underestimated the power of the Tudor name. Religious questions aside, the English wanted Henry VIII's own daughter, the rightful Tudor heiress, for their ruler, and within nine days the reign of Lady Jane Grey

was over, as the country rallied to Mary. Without bloodshed or Spanish intervention she had won her rights, and on 19 July 1553, she was proclaimed Queen in London, while the crowds went wild with joy.

In her newfound happiness, Mary was eager to be merciful. The traitor Northumberland was, inevitably, executed, but she was determined to spare her cousin Lady Jane Grey, despite the contrary advice of the Spanish ambassador Simon Renard, on whom she came to lean heavily. 'Mary, Mary, quite contrary' wanted only to restore the true faith to England, and repair the damage of the Reformation. She would not

Queen Mary and Philip of Spain, whom she married in July 1554.

even be harsh with her Protestant half-sister Elizabeth, the hated Anne Boleyn's daughter, but welcomed her to court, and took her to Mass, which the first Parliament of the reign restored throughout the realm.

Mary was 38 when her first Parliament met. A dumpy, spinsterish figure, dressed in over-elaborate clothes, she seemed older than her years; but it was generally assumed that she would marry. Parliament and her subjects earnestly hoped that she would choose an English husband, but the am-

IN MARY I's ENGLAND

Framlingham Castle, Suffolk
(*Below*)

At Framlingham, home of the Dukes of Norfolk, Mary made her headquarters during Northumberland's attempt to oust her from the succession in 1553.

Her growing band of supporters camped out on the slopes below the castle walls; tradition has it locally that the Queen's lodging was the one looking north above the now-ruined bridge over the ditch.

Winchester Cathedral, Hampshire

Here Mary married Philip of Spain, on 25 July 1554. The bridegroom had commented, 'I am going not to a marriage-feast, but to a fight', and so it almost proved; though Wyatt's rebellion against his coming had been put down, the Prince remained intensely unpopular.

Martys' Memorial, Oxford, Oxfordshire
(*Below*)

The memorial marks the spot where three of the most famous Marian martyrs, Latimer, Cranmer and Ridley, were burnt to death as Protestant heretics, on 16 October 1555. Latimer went to his death with the famous words, 'Be of good comfort, Master Ridley, and play the man. We shall this day light such a candle, by God's grace, in England, as I trust shall never be put out'.

bassador Renard was instructed by his master, the Emperor Charles V, to propose a far more dazzling bridegroom – his own son, Prince Philip, the heir to the Spanish throne. A handsome young widower of 26, Philip was the greatest Catholic match in the world, and after some modest delaying, Mary rapturously accepted him.

The Spanish marriage marked the beginning of Mary Tudor's real unpopularity. Parliament petitioned her against it; her subjects viewed it with hostile dislike, fearful that they would now become subjects of Spain, caught up in Spanish wars and politics. When resistance turned to rebellion, early in 1554, and Sir Thomas Wyatt marched on London with some 5,000 insurgents under the rallying-cry, 'We are all Englishmen!', Mary could no longer afford to be merciful. After some fierce street-fighting, Wyatt was taken prisoner at Temple Bar; in the aftermath of the rising not only Wyatt, but Lady Jane Grey and Guildford Dudley

were beheaded, and the Lady Elizabeth, whom the Protestant rebels had hoped to make Queen, was sent to the Tower of London. Only Mary's strict sense of justice, and insufficient proof of her complicity, saved Elizabeth, too, from execution.

Mary Tudor married Philip of Spain on 25 July 1554, at Winchester Cathedral. Tragically, the ageing, virtuous Queen fell deeply in love with her magnificent young bridegroom. Philip tried to be affable, but to him the marriage was a political sacrifice. With the abdication of his father, in the winter of 1556, he became King of Spain, King of Naples, master of the Spanish Netherlands and Spain's American territories; duty and pleasure alike caused him to spend less and less time in his wife's inhospitable kingdom. Even Mary's desperate hopes of bearing a child were to be disappointed: two false pregnancies ended in fruitless embarrassment – hysteria, or possibly a tumour, having created her medical symptoms. The

prayers for women in childbed in Queen Mary's prayerbook are said to be stained with her tears.

Early in 1555, six months after Mary's Spanish marriage, the burnings of heretics began in earnest. Execution by burning was an established punishment for heresy in Tudor England; but under Mary it was carried out on an unprecedented scale, and some 300 men and women, rich and poor, eminent and ignorant alike, were burnt in the four years of her reign. As an attempt to save souls, the Marian persecution was a disastrous failure. Men such as Edward VI's Bishop Latimer, who died in the Oxford market-place with the valiant words, 'By God's grace, we shall this day light such a candle as shall never be put out!', impressed the world with their faith, and advanced the cause of the Reformation which Mary Tudor so ardently sought to extinguish. Though the deaths were not of Philip's making, and his father Charles V had tried to urge moderation

88

A Tudor depiction of the port of Calais, England's last possession on French soil.

Elizabeth I 1558-1603

on Mary, it seemed to many that Spanish, Catholic rule and persecution were closely allied; the Protestant Elizabeth, whose proud boast was to be that she was 'mere English', became the focus of the people's hopes.

As had been feared, England became involved in Spain's hostilities abroad, and in 1558 the last English possession on French soil, Calais, was lost. It was a bitter blow to the Tudor Queen; she was said to have declared that 'Calais' would be found engraved on her heart after her death. That death came as a release to Mary Tudor, on 17 November 1558; she was 42. She was buried in Westminster Abbey, but her heart and bowels were entombed separately, in the Chapel Royal in St James's Palace. Whether the word 'Calais' was written on them was not recorded.

ELIZABETH was at Hatfield House when she became Queen of England, on 17 November 1558. According to tradition, she was seated beneath an oak tree when the news reached her, and the reputed oak is still preserved there. At Hatfield the young Queen held her first council meetings and made her first official appointments; her lifelong favourite Robert Dudley became her Master of the Horse, and wise, loyal William Cecil her First Secretary. Together, Queen Elizabeth I and Cecil were to guide England through the dangers and triumphs of the next four decades.

Elizabeth Tudor had had an arduous training for monarchy. She was only three years old when her mother, Anne Boleyn, was executed and she herself declared a bastard, and by the age of ten she had had four stepmothers. Fortunately for Henry VIII's children, his last wife Catherine Parr was a kind and sensible woman, who not only showed them affection but took an interest in their education. Elizabeth was, even by the high standards of the time, an outstanding scholar; among the documents which survive from her childhood are letters in exquisite handwriting, written in French and Italian, to Catherine Parr, and the translation of a theological work done by the ten-year-old princess for her stepmother as a Christmas present.

On the death of King Henry VIII in 1547 it was to Queen Catherine's household in Chelsea that the orphaned Elizabeth went to live, with her own servants and governess, Kat Ashley. But a domestic crisis ensued; Catherine's new husband, the scheming

The defeat of the Spanish Armada in 1588.

Lord High Admiral, Thomas Seymour, began a dangerous flirtation with the young princess, bursting into her bedroom to romp with her, and kissing her in the garden, until Catherine reluctantly sent her away. When Thomas Seymour's plots brought him to the block, in 1549, the charges against him included the accusation that he had conspired to marry the Princess Elizabeth, second-in-line to the throne. He was executed, amid rumours that the princess was pregnant by him. Indignantly denying these 'shameful slanders', the 15-year-old Elizabeth set herself to live down the scandal, living quietly in the country, studying hard and earning herself a reputation for scholarship and high-mindedness.

After her sister Mary's accession she was frequently in grave danger. Following Wyatt's Protestant rebellion, in 1554, she was imprisoned in the Tower of London, under threat of execution. But through Mary's strict sense of justice, and her own sharp wits, Elizabeth survived with both her life and her religion intact, to succeed her sister, amid great popular rejoicing, when she was 25 years old.

Though never a beauty like her cousin Mary, Queen of Scots, Elizabeth was attractive enough in youth, with her pale skin and auburn hair, and there was no shortage of suitors for her hand. Even her former brother-in-law and future enemy, Philip of Spain, proposed marriage in the first year of her reign. Elizabeth loved the rituals of courtship; to the end of her days she revelled in the flattery and flirtation of handsome men, and as a young, eligible woman she welcomed proposals from the King of Sweden, a brace of Habsburg Archdukes, and, later, from the young King of France and two of his brothers. But from the outset she adopted the tactic of shilly-shallying, giving 'answers answerless', and keeping herself always available.

It was a policy which became increasingly unpopular with her ministers and subjects, and great pressure was brought to bear on the Queen to marry and settle the succession. When, in 1562, Elizabeth caught smallpox and seemed close to death, there was grave anxiety as to who should be her heir; the opportunity for Mary, Queen of Scots to enforce her claim to the throne, aided by the Catholic powers, was all too obvious. When Elizabeth recovered, she stated that in another such emergency, Lord Robert Dudley should be made Protector of the

IN ELIZABETH I's ENGLAND

The Lord Leicester Hospital, Warwick, Warwickshire
(Below)
This is one of the finest existing examples of Tudor building. Queen Elizabeth personally donated a linen-press to the occupants (it served as an almshouse) and may well have come here while visiting her favourite Robert Dudley.

Queen Elizabeth's Virginals, Victoria and Albert Museum, London SW7
(Bottom of page)
Queen Elizabeth inherited her father, Henry VIII's love of music, and she played the virginals with exceptional skill. This instrument in the V & A bears the arms of her mother's family, the Boleyns.

Kenilworth Castle, near Coventry, Warwickshire. Contrary to Sir Walter Scott's fictional account, Robert Dudley's wife Amy Robsart was not found mysteriously dead at Kenilworth, but at Cumnor Place, in Oxfordshire. But Kenilworth did later belong to Robert Dudley and Elizabeth visited him here on progress.

Hatfield House, Hertfordshire
In the grounds of the Jacobean palace is the Old Palace, where Elizabeth spent much of her youth.

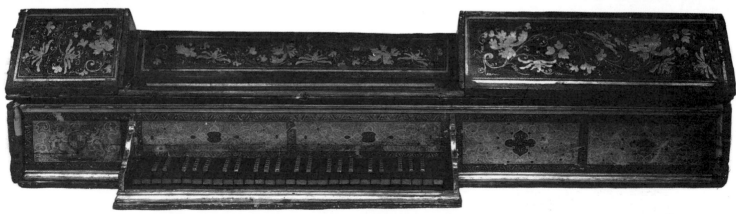

92

realm. Dudley was a dark, handsome son of the traitor-Duke of Northumberland; a married man, distrusted by many, he was nevertheless Elizabeth's best-loved favourite. Even when his wife Amy Robsart suddenly and conveniently died, falling downstairs at her home at Cumnor Place, in Oxfordshire, the Queen continued to place absolute trust in her 'sweet Robin', though she would never yield to his importunate desire to marry her.

Politically, Elizabeth Tudor was dangerously isolated at her accession, and her Protestantism made her a natural target for French and Spanish aggression. The danger from Catholics, both at home and abroad, was increased when in 1570, the Pope declared her deposed and absolved Catholics from their allegiance to her; yet the growing forces of Puritanism in Parliament proved almost as burdensome at times. Elizabeth sought to steer a middle course in religion, and she stated early in the reign that she did not intend to 'open windows in men's souls'. As long as outward conformity was maintained, her subjects' consciences were their own. The Queen's attitude was demonstrated at her coronation, when her title was given as 'Supreme Governor', not, as her father and brother had been, 'Supreme Head', of the Church of England.

Compromise was always Elizabeth's favoured policy; the compromise she conceived as a solution to Mary, Queen of Scots' threat was that Mary should marry her own trusted favourite, Robert Dudley. To fit him for a royal marriage Elizabeth created him Earl of Leicester in 1565 – but to her chagrin, Mary married another English subject instead, the handsome 'long lad', Lord Darnley. When that marriage came to grief, with Darnley's murder, in which Mary was suspected of complicity, the Scots queen was eventually forced by her own subjects to seek refuge in England. There she remained, a thorn in Elizabeth's side, for nearly 20 years. Through a series of Catholic plots, in which Mary involved herself, Elizabeth steadfastly refused to execute her lovely cousin; but after the Babington Plot, Mary Stuart was finally beheaded, at Fotheringhay, in 1587. A year later, the greatest threat of all was launched – the Spanish Armada.

The 'Enterprise of England', as it was known, was the climax of long hostilities with Spain. Elizabeth had sent troops under her beloved Leicester to fight the Spanish in the Netherlands, in support of the Dutch Protestants, and the Elizabethan seadogs had raided Spanish vessels and possessions on the high seas, in Spanish America and in Cadiz harbour itself. Mary, Queen of Scots had willed her much-prized right to Elizabeth's throne not to her own infant son James, but to Philip of Spain; and in 1588 it seemed as if Philip might make good that claim.

In the hour of invasion Elizabeth showed her magnificent Tudor mettle. She went down to Tilbury Camp, and addressed her troops, rousing them with her words: 'Let tyrants fear! I have always so behaved myself that, under God, I have placed my chiefest strength and goodwill in the loyal hearts and goodwill of my subjects ... I know I have but the body of a weak and feeble woman, but I have the heart and stomach of a king – and a king of England, too!' Through the ingenuity of Drake, Hawkins and Frobisher, and the courage of the English fighting-men, the mighty Armada fleet was scattered and thrown off course before ever linking up with the Spanish land-army as planned, and the result was a splendid victory for England.

Elizabeth had brought a glorious spirit of unity to her subjects. Her reign saw a flowering of talent of all kinds, from the seamanship of Drake and Hawkins to the unrivalled poetry and drama of Shakespeare, Sidney and Marlowe. Elizabeth herself, the Virgin Queen, was the focus for the nation's new-found sense of pride; even in old age, bewigged and heavily painted, she was 'Gloriana', the divine, ageless object of adoring flatteries from brilliant young courtiers such as Sir Walter Raleigh, who sought to make her the queen of an American colony which he named Virginia in her honour. Another of her last favourites, the Earl of Essex, was less well chosen – he disastrously mishandled the Earl of Tyrone's rebellion in Ireland, and ended by stirring up rebellion himself, which brought him to the block in 1601.

By then the Elizabethan age was nearing its end. In November 1601 Elizabeth delivered what came to be called her 'Golden Speech' to the Commons, in which she told them '... And though God has raised me high, yet this I account the glory of my crown, that I have reigned with your loves'. To the last she refused to name her successor, but there was increasing certainty that it would be the King of Scots, Mary Stewart's son James VI, and Robert Cecil – son of the great William – had been in secret correspondence with King James, preparing for the transfer of power. When Elizabeth Tudor, perhaps the greatest of all Britain's monarchs, died, on 24 March 1603, it was the Scots king who succeeded her, and so at last the crowns of England and Scotland were united.

Chronology

EDWARD VI
1537 *12 Oct* Birth
1547 *19 Feb* Coronation
1549 *Mar* Thomas Seymour executed; First Prayer Book in English issued
1552 Execution of Protector Somerset
1553 *6 Jul* Death of Edward VI

MARY I
1516 *18 Feb* Birth
1553 *10 Jul* Lady Jane Grey received at Tower as Queen; *19 Jul* Mary proclaimed Queen in London
1554 Wyatt rebellion; Lady Jane Grey executed; *25 Jul* Marriage to Philip of Spain
1555 Martyrdom of Latimer, Ridley and Cranmer
1557 War against France
1558 Loss of Calais; *17 Nov* Death of Mary I

ELIZABETH I
1533 *7 Sep* Birth
1554 Imprisoned in Tower
1559 Coronation; Act of Uniformity
1564 Birth of Shakespeare
1568 Mary Queen of Scots imprisoned in England
1570 Elizabeth excommunicated
1577–80 Drake's circumnavigation of world
1587 Drake's raid on Cadiz harbour
1588 Defeat of Spanish Armada
1596 Capture of Cadiz
1598 Campaigns in Ireland
1603 *24 Mar* Death of Elizabeth I

Chapter seven
THE ROYAL HOUSE OF SCOTLAND

Caerlaverock Castle. The Maxwell family, to whom Edward I entrusted it, switched their allegiance to Robert Bruce after his death.

Robert I Bruce 1306-29

THE THRONES of England and Scotland first came close to being united after the death of the King of Scots, Alexander III, in 1286. At the Treaty of Birgham, King Edward I of England promised that, whatever happened, Scotland would always remain independent, and thereby persuaded the Scots guardians – the six elected wardens of the kingdom – to agree to a marriage between his heir Edward, Prince of Wales, and Alexander's granddaughter and only surviving descendant, Margaret, the daughter of the King of Norway. The plan was thwarted, however, when little Margaret died in the Orkneys on her way to Scotland.

On Margaret's death there were no less than 14 'competitors' for her throne. Fearing an open conflict, the Bishop of St Andrews invited Edward I to keep the peace in Scotland. Edward came north in 1291, basing his right to intervene on the feudal suzerainty which previous Kings of England had claimed over the Scots. Once the Scots barons had recognised his authority by paying grudging homage to him, he agreed to judge between the competitors, most of whom claimed descent from King Duncan I.

Duncan had been the first king to rule the whole of Scotland. He only ruled for six years – in 1040 he was murdered by his cousin

94

Robert Bruce, from the Seton Armorial.

Macbeth, and it was another 17 years before his son, Malcolm, wrested the throne from the usurper. But thereafter, while the Normans conquered England, Duncan's descendants ruled in Scotland. In 1124, his grandson, David I, who had been brought up in England, on his accession granted Scottish estates to his foreign friends, including a Breton called Fitz Alan and three Normans called de Comyn, de Balliol and de Bruce, and in the years that followed members of their families married royal children. When King Edward came northwards in 1291, the two foremost 'competitors', who were both descended from King David's granddaughters, were John Balliol and the old leader of the Bruces, the Lord of Annandale.

Fortunately for the ambitious Edward, the weakest 'competitor', John Balliol, was also the one with the best claims, since he was descended from the elder granddaughter. Balliol was chosen, and Edward then imposed such intolerable terms that he renounced his allegiance to England and made an alliance with the King of France. With an army that was already assembled, Edward returned from England and routed the Scots at Dunbar. By the end of 1296, Balliol was in the Tower of London, 2,000 Scots had been compelled to recognise Edward as their king, the ancient crowning stone which the Scots had brought from Ireland had been removed from Scone to England, and Scot-

land was under the oppressive government of an English viceroy.

One of the knights in King Edward's army at Dunbar was the 22-year-old grandson of the Lord of Annandale, Robert Bruce. When the Scots rebelled against their viceroy, under Sir William Wallace, Bruce changed sides and fought with Wallace. But Bruce had more to lose than Wallace or his Scots – his estates in England were as rich as his estates in Scotland, and he even owned a house in London. When Wallace's cause began to fail, Bruce returned his allegiance to the King of England, and by the time Wallace was defeated the King had forgiven him enough to appoint Robert Bruce with John Comyn and the Bishop of St Andrews as regents of Scotland.

In spite of their office, however, Bruce and the Bishop continued to correspond secretly with the rebels, and by 1306, when Bruce's father and grandfather were dead and Balliol was in exile, Robert Bruce had become the leading claimant to the Scots throne. In that year he arranged a secret meeting with John Comyn in the Greyfriars Church at Dumfries. What followed is a mystery. Perhaps Bruce was already planning rebellion, and intended to kill his fellow regent for betraying him; or perhaps he invited the 'Red Comyn' to join him and then lost his temper when he refused. All that is certain is that Bruce emerged from the church a 'murderer', and since he had committed his 'crime' on consecrated ground, he was also guilty of sacrilege. His excommunication was inevitable, and if King Edward were to capture him, so was his execution. Robert Bruce could not change sides again.

On Palm Sunday, 1306, Robert Bruce was enthroned at Scone. The Scots rallied to his

The 1320 Declaration of Arbroath, in which the people and clergy of Scotland successfully protested to the Pope about the proposed excommunication of Robert Bruce.

ROBERT BRUCE's SCOTLAND

The tomb of Robert Bruce, Dunfermline Abbey, Fife
(Below)
Robert Bruce's body was buried here, though his heart was buried later at Melrose Abbey.

Battlefield of Bannockburn, Stirling, Central Region
At Bannockburn, on 23–24 June 1314, Robert Bruce routed the English under Edward II. The field of battle has changed greatly over the centuries, but just off the Glasgow Road at Bannockburn the National Trust for Scotland have provided an informative exhibition at the Monument, describing and illustrating the course of the battle.

Melrose Abbey, Roxburgh
In accordance with Bruce's dying wish, his heart was cut from his body and taken on a Crusade, by Sir James Douglas. Afterwards, it was buried here – possibly below the East window.

banner, but in June they were defeated at Methven by an English army, and for nearly a year, excommunicated and outlawed, Bruce lived in hiding. By the time Edward I died in July 1307, however, Bruce was on the offensive. While the spineless Edward II left Scotland to his English garrisons, Bruce and his friend and principal commander, Sir James Douglas, captured town after town; and in every assault the King and the Black Douglas were in the forefront of the fighting. By 1314 King Robert was in control of his entire kingdom except for Stirling.

At last King Edward II marched north with an army, and on 24 June, as he advanced to relieve the siege of Stirling, he met the Scots at Bannockburn. Bruce's army was outnumbered three to one, but King Edward II was an incompetent commander. Hampered by a deep marsh, and without the protection of their archers, who had been driven from the high ground before they had time to deploy, the advancing English knights fell easy prey to the agile Scots spearmen. It was the most terrible slaughter ever inflicted on the baronage of England. By midday the English survivors and their king were in headlong flight.

Scotland was free. Although the war continued, England was never victorious. In 1320, when Edward II invited the new Pope to confirm Bruce's excommunication, the people and clergy of Scotland answered with the famous Declaration of Arbroath, protesting most eloquently that they fought only for their liberty and that Bruce was their lawful king. The excommunication was revoked, and in 1328, at the Treaty of Northampton, Edward III recognised Scotland as an independent kingdom and Robert as its ruler.

A year later, on 7 June 1329, Robert Bruce died at Cardross. His body was buried in Dunfermline; but in accordance with his dying wish, his heart was cut from it and carried on a crusade by Sir James Douglas. When it returned, it was given separate burial at Melrose Abbey.

The name of Bruce passed into the legends of Scotland: ballads were sung, and children were taught how, while he was hiding, their half-Norman liberator had learned perseverance from watching a spider spin. But the name was not to last long in the royal lineage. On the death of his worthless son, David II, in 1371, the throne passed to his grandson, Robert II, the son of the marriage between his daughter Margery and Walter Fitz Alan. The Fitz Alans had been created hereditary High Stewards of Scotland by King David I, and it was from this office that the new royal family took its name – the House of Stewart.

James I
1406-37

JAMES I, the third son of Robert III, was born at Dunfermline in July 1394. His father, who succeeded his own father, Robert II, in 1390, had never fully recovered from being kicked by a horse a few years earlier; by his own admission he was too weak to rule. At the beginning of his reign he naïvely resigned the government of his kingdom to his ambitious brother, whom he created Duke of Albany. Although his elder surviving son, David, managed to usurp the regency in 1399, Albany recovered it two years later, and a few months after that David vanished mysteriously. In 1406, fearing that Albany was planning to deliver his only remaining son to the English, Robert sent the 12-year-old James to France for safety.

James never completed the journey. Intercepted by an English ship off Flamborough Head, he was taken to London and handed over to Henry IV. When the news reached Scotland the crippled king died from the shock. For the next 18 years, while the regent, Albany, made no more than token efforts to secure his release, the new King of Scots grew to manhood as an honoured prisoner in England.

When Albany died, in 1420, the Scots began to negotiate in earnest for James's release, but the real chance to gain his freedom did not come until after the death of England's King Henry V in 1422. At the end of his reign Henry had been fighting the French Dauphin, who had been receiving so much military support from Scotland that the tide of war was turning in his favour. The regents who ruled England on behalf of the infant Henry VI were now eager for a truce with the Scots. When the Scots agreed to pay a ransom and withdraw their troops from France, the English promised to release their king, and, to James's delight, consented to his marriage to their own king's cousin, the Lady Joan Beaufort. In 1424, after the marriage and the payment of part of the ransom, King James I returned to his kingdom with his beloved queen.

James had been well educated in England. He had wide interests in the arts and philosophy, was a skilful musician, and had become an accomplished poet. But he was also vigorous and athletic; though small, he was heavily built, and above all he was ruthless and fearless. For the first time in almost a hundred years, a strong man ruled Scotland. He was determined to restore the authority of the crown, and it was his aim to bring order to the kingdom and curb the defiant autonomy which the barons and Highland chiefs had enjoyed under Albany.

Within a week of his coronation, which took place at Scone on 14 May 1424, James began the programme of administrative, legislative and fiscal reforms which was to earn him the name of 'the Lawgiver'. He provided for the representation of the shires in his parliament, he attempted to found a second chamber, on the pattern that he had seen in England, and there was hardly an area of his subjects' lives which he did not touch with his legislation. Precautions were prescribed against the dangers of fire and leprosy; archery was encouraged, whilst football was forbidden; and when poaching had been prohibited, close seasons were instituted for game and salmon.

At the same time, James set about taming his barons. The arrests began even before he was crowned. In 1425 he executed Albany's heir, together with his father-in-law and two of his sons. Two years later, he summoned the Highland chiefs to his Parliament, arrested 40 of them and executed others, and when rebellions followed (two in the Highlands and one in the Lowlands) he suppressed them mercilessly.

In the course of strengthening and centralising his government, James also became rich. By the end of his reign he had doubled the revenue from customs alone and trebled the income from crown lands, which had been augmented by the reversion or forfeiture of as many as half a dozen earldoms. No more afraid of the English than he was of his barons, he renewed the alliance with

James I of Scotland, who returned from captivity in England in 1424 to become king.

97

IN JAMES I's SCOTLAND

Linlithgow Palace, Linlithgow Loch, West Lothian
One of the loveliest of Scotland's royal palaces, and steeped in royal history, Linlithgow was begun by James I, in its present form, in 1425.

France, supporting it with expensive contingents of soldiers, and cementing it by marrying his eldest daughter, Margaret, to the Dauphin.

James lived and dressed splendidly, and he turned Linlithgow into a magnificent palace. But the inevitable price of his success was the hostility of the barons. Where rebellion had failed, they turned instead to treachery. At the instigation of his uncle, the Earl of Atholl, in 1437 his cousin and chamberlain Sir Robert Stewart and Sir Robert Graham went to his court at Perth, and on 20 February murdered their King in front of his Queen.

The 32-year-old King was buried in the Charterhouse which he had founded in Perth. But his death brought no profit to his murderers. Pursued and arrested on the orders of his vengeful widow, they died in agony, under tortures which, even by the standards of a brutal age, were horrifying.

James II 1437-60

JAMES II, known as 'James of the fiery face' because of a red mark on his cheek, was the only surviving son of James I. He was born at Holyrood on 16 October 1430, and since he was only six years old when he succeeded his murdered father, his kingdom was ruled by a regent, the powerful Earl of Douglas, descendant of the companion of King Robert I.

Under Douglas the barons began to recover some of the licence that they had lost in the previous reign. But when Douglas died in 1439, leaving two sons, of whom the elder

was only 14, the regency passed to his rival, Sir William Crichton. Knowing that it would not be long before the barons were inciting the young Douglases to recover the regency, Crichton took drastic steps to prevent them: having invited the young earl and his brother to dine with the King at Edinburgh Castle, he brought forward a black bull's head, the symbol of death, and then murdered them.

As impetuous and masterful as his father, James took over the government when he was 19, shortly after his marriage to Mary of Guelders, the niece of the Duke of Burgundy. With the able support of Crichton and his cousin, Bishop Kennedy of St Andrews, he continued his father's programme of administrative reforms. But it was not long before he brought himself into open conflict with the Douglases. While the new earl, the second cousin of the murdered brothers, was on a pilgrimage to Rome, James invaded his estates. On his return, Douglas and his brothers formed an alliance with the Earl of Crawford and the Lord of the Isles and opened treasonable negotiations with the Yorkists in England. When an attempt at reconciliation failed, James resorted to the lesson that he had learned from his regent. He invited Douglas to dine under safe conduct at Stirling Castle, and after dinner took him alone into an inner chamber, where he demanded that he abandon his alliance, then stabbed him to death when he refused.

After the murder, Crawford and the Lord of the Isles soon came to terms. But the murdered earl's four brothers continued in open rebellion until, in 1455, the power of the Black Douglases was finally crushed, when James defeated them at the Battle of Arkinholm and confiscated all their estates.

Although three of the Douglas brothers died at Arkinholm, the eldest, who was now the ninth earl, escaped to England, where the kingdom was divided in civil war between the Houses of York and Lancaster. In 1460, after Henry IV had been captured and his wife and son had fled to Scotland, James intervened in the war. Partly as a gesture of support for Henry, partly to punish the Yorkists for giving refuge to the fugitive Douglas, and partly to recover the remains of a town which rightly belonged to Scotland anyway, James laid siege to the Yorkist-held Castle at Roxburgh.

On 3 August he was watching his precious artillery bombarding the walls when a cannon burst beside him and killed him. A few days later, after the castle had been taken, the king's broken body was carried away and given reverent burial at Holyrood.

James II of Scotland.

IACOBVS 2 D·GRATIA
REX·SCOTORVM

IN JAMES II's SCOTLAND

Edinburgh Castle, Lothian
It was here that the two sons of the Earl of Douglas were murdered to prevent them claiming the regency before James's majority.

James III 1460-88

JAMES III, eldest son of James II, was born on 10 July 1451; shortly after his father's death he was crowned at Kelso Abbey, in the summer of 1460, at the age of nine. Once again, and not for the last time, the government of Scotland was entrusted to regents, during the minority of a Stewart king.

On the whole, however, James III was well served by his regents. The first, Bishop Kennedy of St Andrews, concluded a welcome truce with England, in which the Scots recognised the supremacy of the Yorkists; and the second, Lord Boyd, negotiated a prestigious marriage between James and Margaret, the daughter of King Christian of Denmark, which brought with it the annexation of the Orkneys and Shetlands. When, like his father, James took control of his kingdom after his marriage, at the age of 18, he could not have hoped to do so in more favourable circumstances: his domains were enlarged and at peace, and some of the more dangerously independent barons were so well disposed towards him that four years later they were ready to fight on his behalf against the Lord of the Isles.

But James was more interested in music and architecture than in government. Cultured and clever, but moody and superstitious, he spent most of his time with his low-born intellectual and artistic favourites. It was not long before the barons were blaming all the ills of Scotland on the king and his companions, and when at last they turned against him they found their leader in Archibald Douglas, Earl of Angus, the head of the Red Douglases, 'who rose upon the ruins of the Black'.

In 1479, fearing with justification that his more able brothers, the Duke of Albany and the Earl of Mar, were plotting with his disaffected barons, James imprisoned them. Soon afterwards, Mar died suspiciously in his bath, but Albany escaped, clambering precariously down the walls of Edinburgh Castle, and fled via France to England. There, through the agency of the fugitive ninth Earl of Douglas, he entered into an agreement with King Edward IV, promising to restore Douglas to his earldom and recognize Edward as his overlord in return for the Scots throne.

In 1482 Albany and Douglas marched north with an English army under the command of Richard, Earl of Gloucester. As James advanced his little army to meet them, he was overtaken at Lauder by Angus and the disaffected barons, who hanged his favourites from the bridge and carried him captive back to Edinburgh. Leaving the

James III at prayer.

IN JAMES III's SCOTLAND

Kelso Abbey, Roxburgh
In this once-magnificent 12th century abbey, the nine-year-old James III was crowned, in the summer of 1460. Today it is a splendid ruin.

English to take Berwick, Albany rode on to join them and, with the support of Angus, was reconciled with his brother and installed as Lieutenant-General of Scotland. But as soon as the liberated king discovered the extent of his treason with Edward IV, Albany was forced to fly again. Although he and Douglas returned to Scotland with a small English army in 1484, they were defeated by Borderers at Lochmaben; Albany fled for ever to France, and the last Earl of Douglas spent the rest of his life as a prisoner in the monastery of Lindores.

Four years later, supported by Lord Home and Colin Campbell, first Earl of Argyll, the Earl of Angus took the field in earnest. Having won over the governor of Stirling, who held the king's 15-year-old heir, James, Duke of Rothesay, in his custody, they proclaimed the boy their leader. King James marched on Stirling, but the governor refused to open the gates, and on 11 June 1488, he met the rebel army at Sauchieburn.

James was no horseman. Thrown and injured when his horse bolted from the battlefield, he lay helpless and calling for a priest – and died on the dagger of an unknown passer-by, who pretended to be one. He was buried beside his wife at Cambuskenneth. Within days his son was crowned at Scone, and a letter was sent to the courts of Europe, discreetly announcing that the late King had been killed in battle.

James IV 1488-1513

FROM THE day he was crowned in 1488 until the day he died, James IV wore an iron belt as a penance for the shameful, though innocent, part that he had played in the downfall of his father. Born on 17 March 1473, he was at least old enough, by the time he was crowned, to be involved in the affairs of state, and although at first the real power lay with the Earl of Angus, it was not long before the king had taken control. Inadvertently, Angus had done Scotland a great service: he had set out only to rid her of a feeble king, but in so doing he had hastened the accession of the most able and popular of all the Stewart monarchs.

At the end of the 15th century the Renaissance came to Scotland, and the man

Margaret Tudor, James IV's widow, with the Duke of Albany, who acted as regent after his death.

then on her throne was a true Renaissance prince. Cultured, charming, confident, chivalrous and courageous, he was enthusiastic in his pleasures, and yet tireless and conscientious in his duties. A pious man, he nevertheless had many mistresses and countless bastards; the great theological scholar Erasmus, who was employed for a time as tutor to one of these bastards, wrote that the King 'had a wonderful force of intellect, an incredible knowledge of all things'. Under James's patronage, art, architecture, music and literature flourished. In 1495 King's College was founded at Aberdeen, adding a third university to those of St Andrews, which had been founded during the imprisonment of James I, and Glasgow, which had been founded in 1451. Ten years later, in 1495, James IV passed a statute providing that all the sons of barons and freeholders should be sent to grammar

schools until they had perfected Latin, and that they should then go on to a university.

James IV's reign was not without its share of rebellions, but they were few and easily suppressed. Once the King had established royal strongholds in the Highlands and annexed the title of Lord of the Isles to the Crown, the kingdom was comparatively peaceful. Although relations with England were strained for a while when James offered half-hearted support to the pretender Perkin Warbeck, many of his councillors believed that it was time they were at peace with their neighbour, and when James failed to find himself a royal bride in Spain, he acceded to their wishes. In August 1503, at the age of 28, he married Henry VII's 13-year-old daughter Margaret, in a ceremony that was marked by magnificent tournaments such as the English guests had never seen, and celebrated by the poet William Dunbar in his work, 'The Thistle and the Rose'. A year later, a treaty of perpetual peace was signed between Scotland and England.

At the time it did not seem that the treaty with England would preclude Scotland's traditional friendship with France. But in 1511 the Pope, the King of Spain and the Doge of Venice formed the Holy League, with the express intention of partitioning France, and soon afterwards they were joined by the Holy Roman Emperor and the new King of England, the warlike Henry VIII. Convinced that an independent France was essential to the balance of power in Europe, James ignored the advice of his cautious councillors, renewed the 'Auld Alliance', and sent an ultimatum to his brother-in-law in England. When Henry VIII dismissed the ultimatum with contempt and embarked his soldiers for France, James invaded England with the largest army that Scotland had ever raised.

Before leaving for France, Henry VIII had delegated the defence of England to the 70-year-old Earl of Surrey. Collecting soldiers as he went, Surrey raced north. On 9 September 1513, he met the Scots below Branxton Hill in Northumberland, on the 'Fatal Field of Flodden'.

When the fighting began the advantage lay with the attacking Scots, but as time passed the lack of cohesion between Highlanders, Lowlanders, Borderers and French allies began to tell, and in the end Surrey's younger subordinates siezed the initiative. In the centre of the battle King James's column was surrounded. Rejecting the last chance of escape, he fought on till he fell, and the barons in the ranks beside him followed his example.

Next day, when the King's naked body was identified among thousands of others, it was sent to London, and later buried at Sheen in Surrey. His glorious reign had ended in humiliating disaster. For the nobility of Scotland, Flodden had been the same tragic slaughter that Bannockburn had once been for the nobles of England. In the words of the lament, later written for Flodden, 'The flowers of the forest are a'wede awa.'

James V 1513-42

TWO WEEKS after the Battle of Flodden, James v, the only legitimate son of the fallen King James IV, was crowned King of Scots at Stirling. Not only was the new King a baby less than 18 months old, but the kingdom was in mortal danger: its army had been destroyed, its nobility had been decimated, its only ally, France, was beleaguered, and on top of all that, in accordance with the late king's will, the regent was the Queen Mother, the foolish sister of the King of England.

Fortunately, however, the English were too preoccupied in France to follow up their victory, and in the next year, on the death of

the old Earl of Angus, who had gone home in tears on the eve of Flodden after the King refused his advice, Queen Margaret married his grandson and successor, thereby forfeiting her regency. At the request of the Scots, the Duke of Albany – son of James III's fugitive brother – came over from France to rule in her place. The Auld Alliance was renewed, and when Albany discovered that Angus and his wife were planning to kidnap the King and hand him over to Henry VIII, they fled to England.

In 1525, after Albany had gone back to France, Angus returned to Scotland. By the time James was formally declared fit to govern in the following year, at the age of 14, Angus had defeated his opponents in a battle in the streets of Edinburgh, and placed such a heavy guard on the young King that he was virtually a prisoner. Two years later, however, James escaped from Edinburgh dressed as a

James v of Scotland and his wife Marie de Guise.

IACOBVS.QVINTVS.SCOTTORVM.REX   MARIA.LOTHORINGIA.ILLIVS.IN.SECVNDIS.NVP
ANNO.ÆTATIS.SVE.   TIIS VXOR ANNO ATATIS SVE. Z 4

IN JAMES V's SCOTLAND

Falkland Palace, Fife
This Renaissance Palace was a favourite residence of King James V; his tennis court, dating from 1539, has been preserved. Here he came to die, in December 1542, with the famous last words, 'It came with a lass and it will gang with a lass'. *left* The King's Bedchamber. *below* The Chapel Royal.

groom and went to Stirling, where he raised the support to be able to drive Angus over the border and take control of his kingdom.

James had inherited some of his father's good qualities, and some of his weaknesses. He was charming and forceful, and he had many bastards. But the experience of his childhood had left him suspicious and uncompromising; although he earned the affection of the common people with his genuine concern for their welfare, his merciless suppression of every sign of rebellion did not endear him to his barons. 'He was called of some a good poor man's king', wrote John Knox, 'of others he was termed a murderer of the nobility'.

In 1537 James went to France and married the French king's daughter Madeleine, who succumbed tragically to the Scottish climate and died within six months, and in the following year he married a French widow, Marie, daughter of the Duke of Guise. Marie bore two sons, but in 1541 the boys died within two days of each other.

With his French marriages and his loyalty to the Pope, who sent him a cap and a sword, James was firmly aligned with France and Catholicism. To the now excommunicated Henry VIII, Scotland seemed more of a threat than ever. Relations between uncle and nephew grew more and more hostile, until, in 1542, after James had been offered the throne of Ireland, Henry revived an English claim for homage and sent an army against Scotland.

Since his support from his barons was only minimal, James was forced to rely on his clergy for soldiers. His army was pitifully inadequate, and, on 24 November 1542, it was routed at Solway Moss. When he heard the news the King, already seriously ill, broke down in utter despair. He wandered aimlessly from palace to palace, and, after spending a few days with his pregnant wife at Linlithgow, ended at Falkland, where he took to his bed.

It was there that he received more bitter news: on 8 December the anxious Queen had given birth prematurely to their child – a daughter. It had been a woman who brought the crown to the House of Stewart, and now there was only a woman left to inherit it. 'It came with a lass and it will gang with a lass', said James, and a few days later, on 14 December, he turned his face to the wall and died.

Mary Queen of Scots 1542-67

WHEN JAMES V died in December 1542, his fragile, six-day-old daughter Mary succeeded him as Queen of Scots. Within seven months her regent, the Earl of Arran, had concluded a treaty betrothing her to Henry VIII's heir, Prince Edward. But her mother, Marie of Guise, had other plans; by the end of the year she had persuaded the Scots to repudiate the unwelcome treaty. When Henry VIII retaliated with two devastating raids, the 'rough wooing' only strengthened Scotland's defiance, and five years later, Mary was betrothed instead to the heir to the French throne, the Dauphin Francis.

For the next ten years Mary was brought

up in France by her mother's kinsmen, the Guises. In 1558, the year in which her cousin, Elizabeth, was crowned in England, she married Francis, and a year later the Dauphin succeeded his father. Mary was now not only Queen of Scots and Queen Consort of France; in the eyes of Catholic Europe, which regarded Elizabeth as illegitimate, she was the rightful Queen of England as well.

The union between Scotland and France was closer than ever. Not only were they ruled in name by a husband and wife, they were ruled in fact by a brother and sister: Marie of Guise had become regent in Scotland, and her brother, the Duke of Guise, governed France on behalf of the simple-minded Francis. But the Scots soon began to resent the overbearing French influence – their kingdom was full of French soldiers, and there was even a Frenchman sharing the chancellorship – and at the same time, supported by England, led by men like John Knox and further fired by Catholic-French persecution, the Reformation swept through Scotland. In 1560, fate and the reforming spirit combined to alter the course of Mary's life. In June her mother died; in July, by the Treaty of Edinburgh, her subjects recognised Elizabeth as Queen of England, expelling French soldiers from Scotland; in August they abolished Papal authority and forbade the celebration of the Mass; and in December her young husband died. Next year, proud, beautiful, only 18 and already widowed, the Catholic Mary Queen of Scots returned to her newly Protestant people.

She was received with considerable suspicion, but she was willing to be conciliatory. The young Queen assented to the maintenance of the new religion, asking only that she should be allowed to hear Mass in her private chapel, and the only act which she refused to ratify was the Treaty of Edinburgh; she was not prepared to recognise Elizabeth as Queen of England unless Elizabeth recognised her as her heir.

When the Scots councillors began to look round for a second husband for the Stewart Queen, Elizabeth proposed her own favourite, Lord Robert Dudley, but she also permitted a visit to Edinburgh by Mary's cousin, Lord Darnley. Mary fell in love with him, and, after a rumoured marriage in the apartments of a favourite secretary called David Rizzio, they were publicly married at Holyrood on 29 July 1565. For the 'Virgin Queen' of England theirs was a dangerous match: Darnley was the grandson of Mary's

A portrait of Mary Queen of Scots in Hardwick Hall, Derbyshire.

grandmother, Margaret Tudor, by her second marriage to the Earl of Angus. After Mary, he could claim to be next in line to the English throne.

It was not long, however, before Mary tired of the depraved, effeminate boy. By the time she bore him a son, James, in June 1566, his supporters had dragged his opponent and, as he thought, rival, Rizzio from her presence and murdered him, and although the birth of the Prince brought a brief reconciliation between husband and wife, it did not last. On 10 February 1567, the house of Kirk o' Field, where Darnley was staying, was blown up by a massive explosion of gunpowder. Next day, he was found in the garden, strangled.

There were many who suspected that the

RIGHT   The execution of Mary Queen of Scots.

BELOW   The murder of Darnley. The figures of Darnley and his servant appear top right. *Left*, the infant James cries 'Judge and avenge my cause, o lord!'

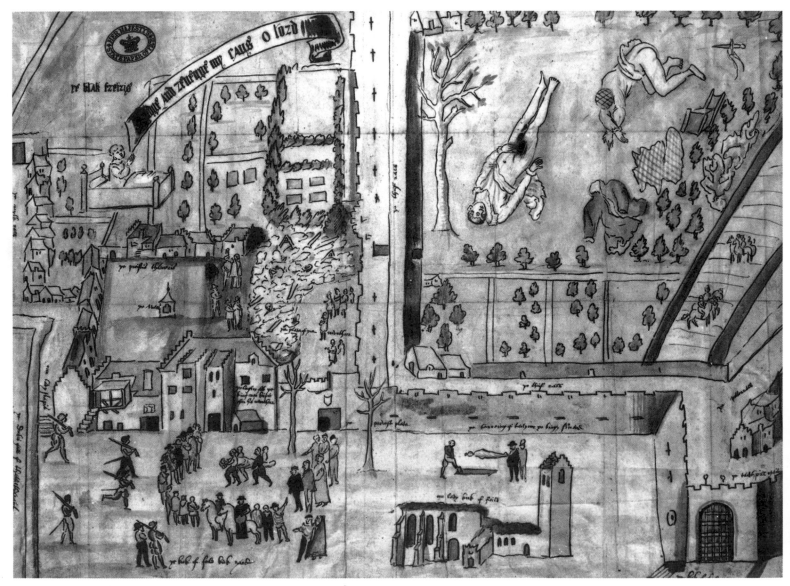

108

Holyrood House, Edinburgh, Lothian
(*Below*)
Despite extensive alterations to the palace in the 17th century, the north-west tower remains much as it was in Queen Mary's reign, when her Italian secretary, David Rizzio, was murdered there before her eyes in 1566. The spiral staircase up which his murderers climbed can still be seen, and there is a memorial on the spot where the killing took place.

IN MARY QUEEN OF SCOTS' BRITAIN

Tutbury Castle, near Burton-on-Trent, Staffordshire
Mary's prison in 1568 and again in 1585. The castle was partially refurbished before she was sent there, but nevertheless the Queen found it a cold and bleak prison.

Mary, Queen of Scots' Tomb, Westminster Abbey, London SW1
In 1612 King James VI and I had his mother's remains brought from Peterborough Abbey for reburial at Westminster, where he built a splendid tomb to house them.

Craigmillar Castle, near Edinburgh, Lothian
This splendid ruin was a favourite residence of Queen Mary. The view from its 14th century tower is well worth seeing.

The Queen's Prayerbook and Rosary, Arundel Castle, Sussex
(*Below*)
This golden rosary and prayerbook were carried by Mary, Queen of Scots at her execution at Fotheringhay, on 8 February 1587. She bequeathed them to the Countess of Arundel, whose descendant, the Duke of Norfolk, is their present owner.

Queen had been involved in the murder, and there were even more who were certain that the real culprit had been the ambitious Earl of Bothwell. When Mary married the divorced Bothwell three months later, in a Protestant ceremony, there was a public outcry. A confederacy of Lords raised an army, and on 15 June 1567 they met the Queen and Bothwell at Carberry Hill, outside Edinburgh. Deserted by most of her followers, and consenting to the terms that were offered by the French ambassador, the Queen agreed to surrender, on condition that her beloved Bothwell was allowed to retire in safety. That evening she was taken under guard to Edinburgh, accompanied by shouts of 'Burn the whore!' from the hostile crowds. From there she was taken to imprisonment on the island stronghold of Lochleven, where, on 24 July, she abdicated in favour of her infant son.

Mary still had supporters, but although they managed to arrange for her escape from Lochleven in the following year, they were not strong enough to recover her throne. After they had been defeated at Langside, near Glasgow, Queen Mary fled across the border into England. For the next 19 years, while Elizabeth consistently refused to grant her a personal interview, Mary lived in increasingly strict confinement in England. Still anxious for the recovery of her throne, and still ambitious to gain Elizabeth's, she became the centre of a series of Catholic plots, including a proposed invasion of England by the Duke of Guise. Eventually, in 1586, when English agents revealed that Mary Stewart was at least aware that an assassin called Anthony Babington had been engaged to murder Elizabeth, she was tried and found guilty of 'compassing and imagining ... matters tending to the death and destruction of the Queen of England'.

For a while, fearing the reaction in Scotland, Elizabeth delayed, but once she was assured that James VI was more interested in his own succession to the throne of England than he was in his mother's life, she

109

signed the death-warrant. On 8 February 1587, with courage and dignity, and proclaiming her innocence, Mary died on the block in the great hall of Fotheringhay Castle. Five months later her body was buried at Peterborough, but in 1612 it was removed to Henry VII's Chapel in Westminster Abbey, and laid in the tomb which her son, the first King of England and Scotland, had built in her honour.

James VI
1578-1625

JAMES VI, the only child of Mary, Queen of Scots and Lord Darnley, was born at Edinburgh Castle on 19 June 1566. Just over a year later, after the murder of his father and the imprisonment of his mother, he was proclaimed King of Scots.

During his childhood four successive regents struggled to eliminate the remnants of his mother's supporters. Known as 'the Queen's Lords', some of them seized Edinburgh Castle and held it until 1573, when they were forced out by heavy cannon that had been specially imported from England. For his own safety, the King was kept at Stirling Castle. Over-worked by his exacting tutors, he excelled as a scholar and developed precocious literary ambitions, but his intellectual gifts were not matched by any great strength of character: he was terrified of violence and he longed for affection. By the time he became nominal ruler, at the age of 12, he was deeply infatuated with his French cousin, Esmé Stewart, Seigneur d'Aubigny, whom he created Duke of Lennox and Lord High Chamberlain.

Lennox had ousted the last Regent, and was attempting to make James a Catholic, and use him as the figurehead of a Catholic rising in Scotland and England. In 1582, despairing of any other means of preventing him, a group of staunchly Protestant barons, led by the Earl of Gowrie, kidnapped the young King and forced him to exile his favourite.

Ten months later, the 17-year-old James escaped. After ordering Gowrie's execution,

James VI at the age of eight.

he turned his attention to the defiantly independent Protestant Church. By now the Church in Scotland was organised on the Presbyterian system, with graded courts ranging from general assembly to kirk session; but James preferred the English system, with a hierarchy of Bishops and the monarch, ruling by the 'Divine Right of Kings', at its head. In 1584, he persuaded his Parliament to pass the 'Black Acts', asserting his authority over his church and confirming his right to appoint Bishops. Although these acts were later partially repealed, and James was forced to allow a full Presbyterian system of government for his church, he still retained the right to create titular bishops with seats in Parliament.

In his dealings with his Church, as in everything else, James's actions were dominated by his overwhelming ambition to succeed the childless Queen of England. He intrigued with Spain and with his cousins, the Guises, he was lenient with Catholic rebels, and in 1584 he even wrote to the Pope implying that he was ready to turn Catholic himself in return for support. But at the same time he was careful not to antagonize Elizabeth. He knew that in the long run there was more to be gained from her good will than from the support of her enemies. On the execution of his mother he made no more than a token protest, he signed a treaty with England, and, in 1589, he married Anne of Denmark, a Protestant princess.

Although Elizabeth always refused to name her heir, James's perseverance and patience were rewarded in the end. Early on the morning of 24 March, 1603, the Queen of England died, and the senior surviving descendant of Henry VII was declared her successor. At 10 o'clock that morning, at Whitehall Gate in London, King James VI of Scotland was proclaimed King James I of England.

Chronology

ROBERT BRUCE
1274 Birth
1290 Treaty of Birgham; England recognises Scottish independence / Death of Margaret, heir to the throne
1292 Edward I awards Scottish crown to John Balliol
1296 Battle of Dunbar; Edward I defeats Scots and dethrones John Balliol / English vice-regency / Stone of Scone stolen
1306 Coronation of Robert Bruce
1314 Battle of Bannockburn; Edward II defeated
1328 Treaty of Northampton; Bruce recognised as ruler of Scotland
1329 *7 Jun* Death of Robert Bruce
1329–71 Reign of David II
1371–90 Reign of Robert II, first Stewart King
1390 Accession of Robert III
1390–9 / 1401–20 Regency of Earl of Albany
1406 Death of Robert III

JAMES I
1394 *Jul* Birth
1406 Captured by English
1412 Foundation of St Andrews University
1424 Truce with England; release of James and marriage to Lady Jane Beaufort / *14 May* Coronation at Scone
1427 Suppression of Highland chiefs
1436 Marriage of daughter Margaret to French Dauphin
1437 *20 Feb* Assassination of James I at Perth

JAMES II
1430 *16 Oct* Birth
1437 Coronation

1449 Marriage to Mary of Guelders; takes government
1451 Foundation of Glasgow University
1455 Battle of Arkinholm; James II defeats Douglases
1460 Siege of Roxburgh Castle by Scots; *3 Aug* accidental death of James II

JAMES III
1452 *10 Jul* Birth
1460 Coronation
1468–9 Orkneys and Shetlands acquired by Scotland
1469 Marriage to Margaret of Denmark; takes over government
1482 James III captured by rebel Scottish earls at Launder / Berwick-on Tweed lost to England
1484 Battle of Lochmaben; defeat of Earl of Angus and Duke of Albany
1488 *11 Jun* Battle of Sauchieburn; death of James III in battle

JAMES IV
1473 *17 Mar* Birth
1495 Foundation of Aberdeen University
1503 *Aug* Marriage to Margaret Tudor, daughter of Henry VII
1511 Formation of Holy League
1513 Battle of Flodden; defeat of Scots by English / *9 Sep* James IV killed

JAMES V
1512 *10 Apr* Birth
1513 Accession to throne
1526 Beginning of personal rule
1537 Marriage to Madeleine of France / Death of Madeleine
1540 Marriage to Marie de Guise
1542 *24 Nov* Battle of Solway Moss; rout of Scottish army / *8 Dec* Birth of daughter Mary / *14 Dec* Death of James V

MARY QUEEN OF SCOTS
1542 *8 Dec* Birth / Accession to throne
1547 Battle of Pinkie; defeat of Scots by English invasion force
1548–58 Mary in France
1558 Marriage to Francis II
1559 Return of John Knox
1560 Reformation Parliament / *Jun* Death of Marie de Guise / *Jul* Treaty of Edinburgh; Elizabeth recognised as Queen of England, French soldiers expelled from Scotland / *Dec* Death of Francis II
1561 Mary returns to Scotland
1565 Marriage to Lord Darnley
1566 *Mar* Murder of Rizzio / *Jun* Birth of son James
1567 *10 Feb* Murder of Darnley / *15 May* Marriage to Bothwell / *15 Jun* Battle of Carberry Hill; defeat of Mary and Bothwell / *Jul* Mary surrenders to Scottish lords and abdicates in favour of James VI (*24 Jul*)
1568 Mary flees to England; imprisoned
1582 Foundation of Edinburgh University
1586 Babington Plot
1587 *8 Feb* Execution of Mary

JAMES VI
1566 *19 Jun* Birth
1567 Accession to throne
1582–3 Kidnapped by Protestant barons
1584 Black Acts establishing crown's right to appoint bishops
1589 Marriage to Anne of Denmark
1603 Union of Crowns of England and Scotland

Chapter eight
THE STUARTS

James I
1603-25

KING JAMES VI and I arrived in England in the summer of 1603 with a high reputation for wisdom and good government. On his 400-mile journey south, 'The people of all sorts rode and ran, nay rather flew to meet him', and as he approached London the Great North Road was churned to mud by the coach-wheels of the crowds who flocked to welcome him. Yet within months the popularity of the vain, pedantic king, whom Henry IV of France called 'the wisest fool in Christendom', had begun to decline; and only two years after his coronation he became the target of an assassination attempt – the celebrated 'Gunpowder Plot'.

The padded doublet which King James habitually wore, for fear of assassins' knives, would have been of little use against the massed barrels of gunpowder which a group of hotheaded Catholic gentlemen laid beneath the Houses of Parliament in November 1605. Their intention was to blow up the King and his ministers, 'all at a clap', when he came to open Parliament, but by chance the plan was discovered, and Guy Fawkes, the group's explosives expert, caught and terribly tortured. Not only was the Gunpowder Plot a total failure, it left England's Catholics worse off than before. Although King James could be fanatical, on subjects such as the evils of witchcraft and tobacco-smoking, he favoured religious tolerance where possible, and his own wife, Anne of Denmark, was known to hold strong Catholic sympathies. But Robert Cecil, who had become his Chief Minister, lived in fear of plots and foreign agents, and he constantly urged stricter measures against Catholics; in the aftermath of the Gunpowder Plot, King James was obliged to assent.

In the eyes of his Puritan subjects,

however, the King still showed suspicious 'softness' towards 'Popish practices'. Early in the reign, in a conference at Hampton Court, he refused Puritan demands to remove the powerful bishops from the Anglican Church, with the telling phrase, 'No bishop, no king!' Although he ordered a new translation of the Bible into English (the resulting Authorised Version of 1611, the 'King James's Bible', still bears his name), James Stuart's religious policies, both at home and abroad, reflected his conservative, peace-loving nature. It was left to his elder son and daughter, Prince Henry and Princess Elizabeth, to emerge as zealous champions of Protestantism.

The English people's early expectations of King James were not fulfilled. For all his scholarship, he lacked common sense. He saw himself as 'an old experienced king, needing no lessons'; under the 'Divine Right of Kings', in which he ardently believed,

A pamphlet showing the conspirators in the Gunpowder Plot and their punishment of hanging, drawing and quartering.

Parliament was there to do his bidding, for kings were 'breathing images of God upon earth'. As God's image, James VI & I cut a poor figure. Bandy-legged and dribbling, with a relish for obscene jokes, he loved to hang on the necks of handsome young men, showering them with caresses and extravagant gifts. The first of these favourites in England, the Scotsman Robert Carr, became involved in a poisoning scandal; the last, the gorgeously handsome George Villiers, Duke of Buckingham, wielded a political influence for which he was quite unsuited, and which further antagonised Parliament. James,

James I of England by Van Somer, with the new Banqueting House, Whitehall, in the background.

112

IN THE ENGLAND OF JAMES VI & I

The Queen's House, Greenwich, London SE10
(*Below*)

Begun by Inigo Jones in 1616 for Queen Anne, the Queen's House was unfinished at her death. It was completed for Charles I's wife Henrietta Maria.

Raleigh's Rooms, the Tower of London, London E1

Soon after James I came to the throne, he imprisoned the former Queen's favourite, Sir Walter Raleigh, on suspicion of plotting, and Raleigh remained in the Tower for the next 13 years. His life was made relatively comfortable; his wife joined him, and their second son was born there and christened in the Chapel of St Peter-ad-Vincula; he received many celebrated visitors, including the Queen, Anne of Denmark, and Prince Henry, the heir to the throne; and he wrote constantly, producing his many-volume

'History of the World', as well as a wealth of poetry and pamphlets. For exercise he was allowed the liberty of the wall-walk.

Hatfield House, near St Albans, Hertfordshire

After giving Hatfield to Robert Cecil in 1607, James often visited the magnificent new palace which Cecil built there. His effigy stands in the Grand Drawing-room and the King James Bedroom bears his name.

GLOBE · SOUTHWARKE ·

A watercolour of the Globe Theatre, where many of Shakespeare's plays were performed.

George Villiers, Duke of Buckingham.

Jones also built the elegant new Banqueting House on Whitehall, introducing the classical style of architecture into England, and he designed the Queen's House at Greenwich for Anne. When James's only daughter, the beautiful Princess Elizabeth, married the young Elector Palatine, one of the leading German Protestant princes, on St Valentine's Day, 1613, the wedding-celebrations were of breathtaking splendour and expense. Even the sudden death of the heir to the throne, the brave, popular Prince Henry, of typhoid, in November 1612, caused little more than a lull in the festivities.

Elizabeth's marriage to the Elector Palatine was pursued by tragedy. In 1619 the young Elector and Electress acquired the disputed throne of Bohemia, by invitation, but after one year of monarchy they were expelled by the Catholic Holy Roman Emperor, at the start of the Thirty Years War which devastated Germany. Deprived of lands, money, even their home at Heidelberg, they became known throughout Europe as the 'Winter King and Queen'. Contrary to the wishes of many of his subjects, who urged armed support for the popular Elizabeth and the Protestant cause in Europe, James was anxious not to involve England in the war. He saw his role as that of a peacemaker, and undertook endless negotiations on his daughter's behalf, with little result.

His master-plan was that his surviving son Prince Charles, now his heir, should marry a Catholic princess and thus bring pressure to bear on the Catholic powers to end the war. To this purpose, Charles and the Duke of Buckingham set off on a madcap mission, disguised as ordinary citizens, travelling through Spain in quest of the Spanish Infanta for Charles's bride. They left in 1623; James, then 57 and nearing the end of his life, missed his 'sweet boys' badly, and wrote dotingly after his 'Baby Charles' (Prince Charles was 23 years old) and 'Sweet wife' Buckingham. Their mission a failure, they returned to their 'dear Dad and Gossip' and, at Buckingham's instigation, James declared war on Spain. On 27 March 1625, he died.

Though James VI and I brought together peacefully the crowns of England and Scotland, he was denied one of his most cherished wishes – to preside over a united Great Britain. The Scottish Parliament passed an Act of Union in 1607 but the English did not, and James remained King of Great Britain in name only. War with Spain, an impoverished Treasury and a growing rift with Parliament were among the failures of his reign, and he left a grim legacy for his successor, Charles I.

capriciously took a deep dislike to a former royal favourite, the great Sir Walter Raleigh, and imprisoned him in the Tower of London for 13 years, before executing him for conspiracy. 'Who but my father would keep such a bird in a cage?' Prince Henry was said to have demanded angrily.

James had none of the traditional Scots carefulness with money, but spent recklessly what he saw as England's wealth. Entertainments at his court were lavish; the pleasure-loving Queen Anne commissioned elaborate musical entertainments called 'Masques', with fantastic scenery and costumes, often designed by the architect Inigo Jones, and words by writers such as Ben Jonson. Inigo

Charles I
1625-49

IF HIS elder son Prince Henry had lived, James I would have been succeeded by a talented, popular young man of rare personality and intellect, and the tragedy of civil war might have been avoided. As it was, the second Stuart to be crowned in Westminster Abbey was Charles I, who came to the throne in 1625 ill equipped to rule, and died on the scaffold 24 years later, the victim of rebellion and regicide.

'Baby Charles', as James dotingly called him, had grown up in the shadow of his elder brother and sister, who captured the people's hearts with their good looks and charm. Unlike Henry and Elizabeth, Charles was a nervous, undersized child with feeble legs and a stammer which he never lost. The Stuart tendency to unusual tallness – confirmed in their genes by the marriage of Mary, Queen of Scots and the 'long lad' Darnley – appeared to be reversed in Charles I, and he grew no higher than 5ft 4ins, though portrait-painters were at pains to make him look taller. It may have been a sense of personal inadequacy which led him, in early adulthood, to fall deeply under the spell of his father's favourite, the Duke of Buckingham.

Charles I's rigid sense of morality almost certainly ruled out any physical relationship between him and the magnificent Duke, but he followed Buckingham's advice devotedly during the early years of his reign, and paid little attention to his wife, Henrietta Maria of France, whom he married two months after becoming king. Under Buckingham's influence he involved England in wasteful wars against France, as well as Spain.

When Parliament, deeply distrustful of the royal favourite, refused to subsidise Charles's war-making ventures, the King's response was to raise funds through other means, such as spending his wife's dowry and exacting the Customs duties known as tonnage and poundage without Parliamentary authority. The Parliament of 1628 forced through a petition, the 'Petition of Right', condemning the king's actions (which included imprisoning subjects who refused to pay forced loans); but when the impeachment of his beloved Buckingham was threatened, Charles felt obliged to adjourn Parliament without delay.

The murder of Buckingham in August

116

The execution of Charles I, by the Spanish artist Gonzales Coques.

IN CHARLES I's ENGLAND

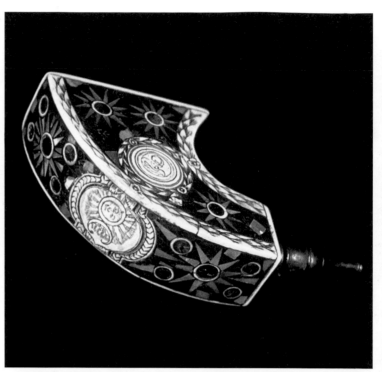

Carisbrooke Castle, near Newport, Isle of Wight
(Above)
Charles I was held here in 1647–8, but continued to bargain with Cromwell and the Scots for his restoration to the throne. These relics of him can still be seen there.

Cromwell's priming flask, Cromwell Museum, Huntingdon
(Top right)
Oliver Cromwell used this flask in battle to charge his personal set of pistols.

The Queen's Chapel, St James's Palace, London W1
(Bottom right)
Designed by Inigo Jones for Charles I's intended bride, the Infanta Maria of Spain, the Chapel was afterwards completed for Queen Henrietta Maria, in 1625. From Easter to July the public may attend morning service here on Sundays.

The Banqueting House, Whitehall, London SW1
(Opposite)
On the site of earlier royal Banqueting Houses, Inigo Jones began the present building in 1619, for James I. An early example of the new Palladian style of architecture, it was described at the time as 'too

handsome for the rest of the palace'; fortunately it survived the fire in 1698 which destroyed the rest of Whitehall Palace. Charles I, a connoisseur and art-lover, commissioned Rubens to decorate the interior with glorious painted ceilings in 1635; this one shows the Apotheosis of James I. Ironically, King Charles had to walk beneath these paintings on the way to his execution on 30 January 1649; the scaffold had been erected outside the northern end of the Banqueting House, and he stepped out of the window over the door onto it.

Westminster Hall, Parliament Square, London SW1
The scene of the trial of Charles I, in 1648, it is one of the only parts of the original Palace of Westminster which he would recognise today – the rest of the old buildings were destroyed by fire in 1834.

City of Oxford, Oxfordshire
With London in Parliament hands, King Charles I made his headquarters in royalist Oxford during the Civil War. He lived in Christ Church and Queen Henrietta Maria at Merton College; tradition has it that a secret passageway, now lost, linked the two.

1628 by a knife-wielding fanatic named John Felton came too late to turn Charles I from the path of political confrontation. Into the gap left by the Duke's death Henrietta Maria now stepped; and as the little king and queen discovered their attachment for one another, a remarkable royal love-story developed. Unfortunately, Henrietta Maria was as politically inflexible as her husband, and she encouraged his hard-line attitudes. To the Puritans, already resentful of the king's support for the High Church prelates known as 'Arminians' (followers of a Dutch theologian called Arminius), the Queen's Catholicism was a further outrage.

There were dramatic scenes in the House of Commons in the spring of 1629. While resolutions were passed condemning 'innovations' in religion, and the levying of all illegal taxes, the Speaker, whom the King had ordered to adjourn the House, was held in his chair, weeping, while outside the usher called Black Rod hammered on the locked doors for admission. Eventually, Charles threatened to bring troops in. After that, he called no more Parliaments for 11 years.

In this period of outward calm, King Charles enjoyed the pleasures of court and family life. A true connoisseur and patron of the arts, he collected paintings and sculptures, gave royal support to artists such as Van Dyck and Samuel Cooper, and commissioned Rubens to embellish the Banqueting House with its glorious painted ceilings, on such mythical and allegorical themes as 'The Apotheosis of James I'. His married happiness was completed by a series of royal births; though several infants died young, a healthy heir, Charles, was born in 1630, James in 1633, and Mary in 1631, with a last baby, Henrietta, in 1642. For all his faults, Charles I was a model of royal domesticity, unlike his unbridled father and his womanising son, Charles II.

By 1640, the storm had begun to break. In 1636, a Parliamentarian named John Hampden had gone to court rather than pay the unpopular Navy Tax called 'Ship Money'. In religion, too, Charles had made enemies. With his unpopular Arminian Archbishop of Canterbury, William Laud, he had sought to

Oliver Cromwell, portrayed as the Saviour of England. Born on 25 April 1599, this Huntingdon MP emerged as a formidable general in the Civil War. After the execution of Charles I and the abolition of the monarchy, England became a 'Commonwealth'; but in December 1653 Cromwell was appointed Lord Protector for life. On his death, on 3 September 1658, he was succeeded by his son Richard – an unworthy successor. To general rejoicing, the monarchy was restored in May 1660.

impose a new Prayer Book on the Church of Scotland, to enforce religious uniformity on his two kingdoms. Defiant, the Presbyterian Scots swore a National Covenant of loyalty to their own Kirk and, when the King tried to impose his will by arms, he was humiliatingly defeated at the hands of the Scots in the 'First Bishops' War'. To finance a second war, Charles at last summoned Parliament – to find himself faced with open hostility from both Houses. Urged on by the brutal Lord Strafford, one of his most trusted friends, who believed in rule by force, Charles swiftly dissolved this 'Short Parliament'. But by November 1640 defeat in the 'Second Bishops' War' and desperate financial straits had forced him to call another, and the 'Long Parliament', which would not be dissolved in his reign, began.

With feelings in the capital running high, and the life of his Roman Catholic queen arguably in danger, Charles made a concession for which he never forgave himself: he signed a bill of attainder, consenting to the execution of his friend Strafford for treason. On other points he would not yield, notably the Parliamentary demands to determine major reforms in the Church of England and to control the militia, the only permanent armed force in the kingdom apart from the King's personal guard. In January 1642, Charles risked everything on a coup. He entered the House of Commons, accompanied by soldiers, intending to arrest the five Members whom he saw as his principal opponents. The five, warned in advance, had fled; Charles could only say, 'I see all my birds have flown', and depart, humiliated. Civil war was now inevitable. Charles fled London, and on 22 August 1642 he raised his battle-standard at Nottingham.

The conflict between King and Parliament divided not only the realm, but regions, social classes and even families. Broadly, the traditional conservative groups such as the old nobility and the rural north and West Country were Royalist, while the industrial towns, the minor bourgeoisie and those who sought religious reform were for Parliament, as was the key city of London; Charles's headquarters for most of the war was Oxford. Some of those who fought for the King did so out of old loyalty, rather than a belief in the justice of his cause. His standard-bearer, Sir Edmund Verney, spoke for many when he said 'I have eaten his bread and served him near thirty years, and will not do so base a thing as to forsake him.' Charles's courage was inspiring, however, and in the first two years of the war a Royalist victory seemed likely.

With the dashing leadership of the King's half-German nephew Prince Rupert, son of his sister Elizabeth, the Winter Queen, the Cavaliers had the early advantage of strong (if at times unruly) cavalry. But by 1644 the balance was shifting. Parliament made a Solemn League and Covenant with the Scots, obtaining their help in return for an undertaking to impose Presbyterian worship in England. And a new and formidable leader began to emerge – a former Huntingdon MP named Oliver Cromwell. At the battle of Marston Moor, in Yorkshire, in July 1644, Cromwell's cavalry decisively beat the King's. Under the command of Cromwell and Sir Thomas Fairfax a large and well-disciplined new force, the 'New Model Army', was built up, and in August 1646, after major defeats at Naseby and Langton, King Charles I made his way to the Scots, and surrendered.

He was handed over to the Roundheads in 1647, and attempts were made to reach an honourable settlement between the King and his opponents, but Charles Stuart still scorned compromise. After comfortable house-arrest at Hampton Court, he was sent to the Isle of Wight, and from there tried to bargain with his former subjects in England and Scotland. In 1648 the Scots, with whom he had come to terms, invaded England on his behalf, and were joined by English Presbyterians and Royalists, in a short-lived second civil war.

There was no more hope of a settlement; Cromwell came to the decision that the monarchy must end, in the execution of the small, stubborn King Charles I. 'We shall cut off his head with the crown on it', was his summing-up.

Westminster Hall, begun by a very different monarch, William Rufus, in the 11th century, was the setting for the trial of Charles I. He was condemned to death; and by cruel design his execution took place at the Banqueting House at Whitehall, built and decorated by the Stuarts as the setting for their lavish amusements.

On the morning of 30 January 1649, crowds lined Whitehall in awed silence to see King Charles beheaded. It was a Cromwellian supporter, the poet Andrew Marvell, who wrote the famous lines,

'He nothing common did or mean
Upon that memorable scene'.

Unreliable, obstinate and oppressive in life, in death Charles I was magnificent. The dignity with which he met his trial and execution had a profound effect on his subjects, and may have hastened the end of the short-lived Protectorate and Commonwealth governments which followed.

Chronology

JAMES VI AND I

1566	*19 Jun* Birth
1589	Marriage to Anne of Denmark
1603	*24 May* Proclaimed James I of England
1605	*5 Nov* Gunpowder Plot
1607	Founding of Jamestown in Virginia
1611	King James's Bible (Authorised Version)
1612	*12 Nov* Death of Prince Henry
1613	*14 Feb* Marriage of Princess Elizabeth to Elector Palatine
1620	Voyage of the *Mayflower*
1623	Death of Shakespeare Publication of First Folio of his plays
1624	War with Spain
1625	*27 Mar* Death of James I

CHARLES I

1600	*19 Nov* Birth
1625	Coronation Marriage to Henrietta Maria of France
1628	Petition of Right *Aug* Murder of Buckingham
1629	Parliament dissolved
1630	Birth of Prince Charles
1634	Imposition of 'Ship Money' tax
1640	First Bishops' War; Short Parliament Second Bishops' War; Long Parliament
1641	*Jan* Attempted arrest of the Five Members Grand Remonstrance *12 May* Execution of Strafford
1642	*22 Aug* King raises standard at Nottingham; Civil War begins *23 Oct* Battle of Edgehill; indecisive
1644	*2 Jul* Battle of Marston Moor; Parliamentary victory
1645	*14 Jun* Battle of Naseby; Parliamentary victory *Apr* King surrenders to Scots
1647	King handed over to Roundheads
1648	Second Civil War
1649	*30 Jan* Charles beheaded
1649–1660	Interregnum

Charles II 1660-85

Among the crowds who thronged Whitehall to see the execution of Charles I was a schoolboy named Samuel Pepys. Eleven years later, Pepys was present at the triumphant return to the country of Charles II, and he recorded the events in his celebrated diary: the King landed at Dover, he wrote, to be received 'with all imaginable love and respect. Infinite the crowd of people!' On 29 May 1660, his 30th birthday, Charles II re-entered London, amidst scenes of wild rejoicing. The bleak experiment of Cromwell's Protectorate had failed, and in the words of a popular Cavalier song, the King enjoyed his own again.

In temperament and appearance there was little resemblance between the new King and his father. A cheerful, sensual cynic, highly attractive to women, Charles II was very tall, with dark hair and skin – Henrietta Maria had called him her 'black baby' – and his enemies, seeking him after the Battle of Worcester, had circulated a description of 'a tall black man, upwards of two yards high'. Much of Charles's youth had been spent under the shadow of civil war; at the age of 12, with his younger brother James, he had witnessed the Battle of Edgehill, at 14 he was given nominal command of his father's forces in western England and by the age of 17 he was a royal refugee on the Continent.

With the help of the Scots, who crowned him as their King in 1651, after his father's death, Charles led an army into England in 1651, but suffered a severe defeat at the Battle of Worcester, where he fought bravely. After a series of adventures, hiding out in country houses, disguising himself as a servant and even sheltering in a leafy oak tree while his enemies searched for him below, Charles escaped to exile once more, to plan, fight and wait for the restoration of his kingdoms. At last, two years after the death of Oliver Cromwell, the former Parliamentary General Monck carried out a bloodless military coup in Charles's favour. After issuing the Declaration of Breda in April 1660, by which he promised to pardon his old enemies and to submit to the will of Parliament, Charles Stuart was restored to his inheritance, with popular assent.

Charles's II's label of the 'Merry Monarch' reflects the mood of gaiety and optimism which the Restoration unleashed. The arts flourished, and so did science; 1662 saw the founding of the Royal Society, with John Evelyn and Robert Boyle among its first members and King Charles as its official founder. Theatres, closed since the beginning of the Civil War, re-opened, delighting the audiences with lively new comedies such as Wycherley's *The Country Wife* and Dryden's *Marriage à la Mode*, while authors as diverse as Milton, Bunyan and Rochester were composing some of the finest poetry and prose in the English language. The king tried his own hand at writing verses, and he showed himself to be a keen patron of the theatre – and of actresses, then a novelty on the London stage. In a licentious age, Charles was famous for his sexual appetite, and he was known as 'Old Rowley', after his favourite stallion. The King's mistresses ranged from the haughty beauty Barbara Castlemaine, Duchess of Cleveland, to Nell Gwynn, a lively actress with an earthy sense of humour, and Frances Stewart, whose likeness is still preserved as Britannia on some coins of the realm. By a sad irony, while Charles's liaisons produced at least eight royal bastards, some of whom he created Dukes, his marriage to the Portuguese princess Catherine of Braganza was childless. As it became known that the King's brother

An engraving of Nell Gwynn, Charles II's famous mistress, after a painting by Lely.

Charles II.

IN CHARLES II's ENGLAND

The Crown Jewels, Tower of London, London E1
Because most of the original Crown Jewels were sold or destroyed during Cromwell's Protectorate, many of the present Regalia were specially made for the coronation of Charles II. He was thus the first British monarch to wear the Crown of St Edward (the Coronation Crown) and St George's Spurs, and to carry the Orb and Sceptre.

St Paul's Cathedral, London EC4
(Above)
Christopher Wren's masterpiece, built on the site of the old Gothic St Paul's which was destroyed in the Great Fire of 1666. Charles II took a keen interest in Wren's plans, but did not live to see the works completed.

Royal Hospital, Chelsea, London SW3
In Charles II's reign the first British standing army was formed. To provide for sick or impoverished former soldiers, King Charles founded a hospital, or home, and commissioned Wren to build it, in 1682. It is still in use today, as a home for former servicemen.

Charles II's Effigy, the Undercroft, Westminster Abbey, London SW1
Among the royal funeral effigies preserved here is that of Charles II. The figure is 6′ 2″ in height, and the face may have been cast from life; one contemporary wrote, 'Tis to the life, and truly to admiration', on seeing it in 1695. His Garter robes are the earliest surviving in England.

The King's Dining-Room, Windsor Castle, Berkshire
(Right)
Charles II's extensive alterations to Edward III's apartments have largely disappeared, but the Queen's Presence Chamber and the King's Dining Room still reflect his taste. Here Charles II dined in public, and anyone dressed suitably could come and watch him eat. The portrait above the fireplace is of Catherine of Braganza.

Audley End, near Saffron Walden, Essex
Charles II paid £50,000 for this mansion in 1667, and often stayed here, as it was convenient for Newmarket racecourse.

The Royal Observatory, Greenwich, London SE10
On 22 June 1675, Charles II declared by royal warrant 'In order to be finding out of the longitude of places and for perfecting navigation and astronomy, we have resolved to build a small observatory within our park at Greenwich'. Flamsteed House, built by Wren as the Astronomer Royal's dwelling, contains one of the rare original Wren interiors.

Boscobel House, near Wolverhampton, Salop
On the run after his defeat at Worcester, Charles II hid out at Boscobel; it was here that he sheltered in a leafy oak tree, while the Roundheads searched for him beneath. Boscobel House contains relics of the young king, and a reputed descendant of the original tree can be seen in the grounds.

and heir presumptive, James, Duke of York, was an ardent Roman Catholic, Charles II's lack of legitimate children was to cause increasing constitutional problems.

King Charles never lost his popularity, despite the reversals of his reign. The years following the Restoration saw a series of disasters: England's unsuccessful war against her commercial and colonial rivals, the Dutch, was still in progress when the two great calamities of fire and plague struck at home. The tragic outbreak of the Great Plague raged through the kingdom in 1665, to be followed a year later by the Great Fire of London. Starting in a bakery in Pudding Lane, on 2 September 1666, the fire blazed for five days, destroying much of the huddled, teeming city, including the old St Paul's Cathedral. Charles II took a close interest in the rebuilding of his capital, and approved the plans for Sir Christopher Wren's magnificent new St Paul's. (He employed the great Wren again in 1682, as the architect for a project close to his heart – the Chelsea Hospital for old soldiers.)

Rumours were spread that Papist agents had caused the Great Fire – a sign of the absurd heights which anti-Catholic feeling reached in Charles II's reign. Charles successfully concealed his own strong leanings towards the Catholic Church, but in 1670 he entered into a close alliance with the powerful Catholic King of France, Louis XIV, from whom he received much-needed financial support, and he also tried to introduce religious toleration for all his subjects, including Catholics. These measures incurred the hostility of the House of Commons, with the result that Charles was obliged not only to pass a Test Act, excluding Catholics from holding public office, but also to threaten war against France, and to agree to a marriage between the Dutch Protestant Prince William of Orange and the Princess Mary, elder daughter of his brother and heir James, Duke of York.

Much of the religious dissension of the later years of the reign centred round James's Catholicism. The efforts of a hysterical agitator named Titus Oates helped to bring matters to a crisis in 1679. Oates declared that a 'Popish Plot' was being hatched to overthrow the King and the Church of England, with great bloodshed, and put James on the throne at the head of a Catholic government. Parliament accepted the story, and the upshot was the introduction of an Exclusion Bill intended to debar James from the succession, and make Charles II's favourite illegitimate son, the Duke of Monmouth, heir to the throne in his place. Anthony Ashley Cooper, the Earl of Shaftesbury – a former member of Charles's inner council of five, known as the 'Cabal' from the

The Banqueting House and Whitehall Palace from Horse Guards' parade, by Jan Wyck.

initial letters of their names – organised an opposition party, of those who supported Monmouth, while the court faction staunchly supported James's rights. The names 'Whig' and 'Tory' – derived from slang names for religious rebels – became bandied about, initially as terms of abuse directed at Exclusionists and anti-Exclusionists respectively, and so the origins of the two-party system began to be seen in Parliament.

Charles responded calmly and sensibly to crises. His personal preference was almost certainly for his son Monmouth, but he would not entertain the idea of depriving his brother of his hereditary rights. Wisely, he sent James into exile for a time, to allow the storm to blow over, which it gradually did. The pro-crown, pro-establishment 'Tory' faction gained the ascendancy, and for the last four years of his reign, Charles ruled without Parliament altogether.

On 1 February 1685, Charles II was taken ill. Charming to the last, he apologised on his deathbed for being 'such an unconscionable time a-dying', and asked , 'Let not poor Nelly starve'. He was finally received into the Catholic Church, and on 6 February, aged only 54, he died, and was succeeded by his rightful heir, James, Duke of York.

Scenes of the Great Plague in 1665.

James II 1685-88

JAMES II, like his elder brother, had spent his boyhood years amid the dramas and tragedies of the Civil War. Born on 14 October 1633, he was 12 years old when the Royalist head-quarters, the city of Oxford, sur-rendered, and the monarchy was overthrown. He was taken as a prisoner to St James's Palace in London, but in 1648 a daring escape was organised for him, and he managed to flee in disguise to Holland, to the court of his sister Mary and her husband, William II of Orange. In exile, he showed himself to be a brave and capable soldier; and when the Restoration came, in the spring of 1660, James, Duke of York was welcomed home to England almost as warmly as his brother the King.

It was a state of affairs which could not last. While in exile, James had not only contracted a secret marriage, to Lord Clarendon's daughter Anne Hyde, he had also become attracted to Roman Catholi-cism, and by 1668 it was known that the heir presumptive to the thrones of England and Scotland was a Catholic convert. He continued to attend Anglican services, and his loyalty to his brother was unaltered; as Lord High Admiral James played an import-ant part in the wars against the Dutch, who actually sailed up the River Thames into the Medway in 1667 and raided the English fleet. But James's Catholicism became the cause of increasing unrest, and in 1673, when Parliament passed the Test Act forbidding Roman Catholics to hold rank in public life, he was obliged to give up his office of Lord High Admiral. As though to affirm his devotion to his new religion, in the same year James, now a widower, was remarried – to the ardently Catholic princess, Mary of Modena.

The anti-Catholic hysteria engendered by Titus Oates and his allegations of a 'Popish Plot' led to the Exclusion Crisis of 1679, when attempts were made to pass a bill excluding James from the succession. Wisely, King Charles responded by sending his brother into exile abroad for a time, until the fuss had died down. By 1680 James had returned to public office as Lord High Commissioner for Scotland (where he brut-ally persecuted Presbyterians) and soon he was back in London and restored to the Admiralty. The king resisted all attempts to have his brother disinherited; and by the time Charles II died, on 6 February 1685, James Stuart had recovered sufficient popularity to allow him to succeed to the thrones of England and Scotland in peace.

He was then 51 years old, a man of high principles but little common sense, who more resembled his stubborn father Charles I than his easy-going cynic of a brother. Like Charles II he was a sensualist, but even in this the brothers differed; it was Charles's joke that James's mistresses (who were usually very plain) must have been chosen by his confessor, for penance. Religion was, indeed, never very far from James's thoughts.

The example of his father's downfall and execution, which had overshadowed his early life, had left James II with an attitude of wary hostility, rather than conciliation, towards the people whom he now ruled; the English, he believed, 'could not be held to their duty by fair treatment'. He regarded it as his duty to re-establish Catholicism in England, and although in May 1685 he assured Parliament that he would protect the Anglican Church, 'whose members have shown themselves so eminently loyal in the worst times', he speedily set about redressing the balance of religious power in the king-dom, by appointing Catholics to positions of influence.

Parliament remained loyal to the new king during the early months of his reign, and those who assumed that James's ac-

A miniature of James II as Duke of York, 1661, by Samuel Cooper.

126

cession would rouse the country to rebellion were proved wrong. A rebel force which landed in Scotland, under the Marquis of Argyll, met with failure, as did an attempt on the throne by the illegitimate Duke of Monmouth. After Monmouth's defeat at the Battle of Sedgemoor on 6 July 1685, his followers were hunted down and tried by the notorious Judge Jeffreys, whose ruthless sentences gave these trials the name of the 'Bloody Assize'. Monmouth himself was beheaded.

In the wake of the rebellions, dissension arose between King and Parliament. James sought to staff the army with Roman Catholics on whom he could rely; Parliament, fearing the prospect of a king with a powerful army at his bidding, disagreed. As a result, Parliament was prorogued in November, 1685, and not recalled for the rest of James II's brief reign, while the king,

unrestricted, carried out his policy of granting important offices to Catholics. He appointed them as officers in the army, to the Privy Council, even to key positions in Oxford colleges, and in 1686 the Catholic Earl of Tyrconnel was made Lord Lieutenant of Ireland.

When the First Declaration of Indulgence, aimed at establishing complete religious tolerance, was followed by a second Declaration, in May 1688, to be read by the Anglican clergy to their congregations throughout the land, the Church of England leaders could take no more. The Archbishop of Canterbury and six bishops petitioned the King to have the order withdrawn; James's response was to have them put on trial for seditious libel. This time he had gone too far.

Public opinion was now mounting against the King. The bishops were acquitted, amid general rejoicing, and in the months that

followed events moved swiftly towards the deposition of the King. The final spur was the birth of a son to James's Queen, Mary of Modena, in June of that year. Hitherto, the two daughters of James's first marriage, the Protestant princesses Mary and Anne, had been next in line to the throne, but now there was a male, Catholic heir, to carry on the unpopular work of James II. The prospect had become intolerable. Rumours were spread that this child was not a true Stuart, but had been smuggled into the palace in a warming-pan; and an invitation was sent to James's son-in-law, William of Orange, to come and claim the throne on behalf of himself and his wife, the Princess Mary, to protect the people's 'liberties, religion and properties'. James began to offer concessions to his Protestant subjects, but it was too late. On November 5 1688, the Dutch Prince William of Orange landed at Torbay in Devon

The 'Venetian Ambassador's Bed, Knole, near Sevenoaks, Kent

(Left)
Despite its name, this ornate state bed was made for James II in 1688, probably by Thomas Roberts, and bears the King's cypher. It was originally in Whitehall Palace.

Pepys' Chess set, London Museum, London EC2
(Above)

Pepys was given this chess set by James while he was Duke of York and Lord High Admiral: Pepys was then Clerk of the Acts of the Navy.

Battlefield of Sedgemoor, near Bridgewater, Somerset

Charles II's popular illegitimate son, the Duke of Monmouth, attempted to seize the throne of the Catholic King James II in the summer of 1685. Monmouth led his men in a famous silent march by night from Bridgewater to the field of battle. In the bloody conflict the King's troops were victorious, on 6 July. It was the last battle fought on English soil.

Taunton Castle, Somerset

Now a partial ruin, the Great Hall of the castle was the setting for Judge Jeffries' 'Bloody Assize', where the survivors of Monmouth's rebel army were tried and sentenced.

IN JAMES II's ENGLAND

In April 1689, Jacobite troops, led by James II, besieged Londonderry (Derry), trying to starve it into submission. On 28 July two English relief ships cut through the blockade and the siege ended.

William III & Mary II
1688-1702 & 1688-94

WILLIAM AND MARY, the king and queen who gave their names jointly to an age, were the only husband and wife in English history to rule together as co-monarchs by right. Any suggestion that Mary, as the deposed King James II's elder daughter, should wear the crown alone was vetoed by her Dutch husband, who stated flatly that he was not prepared 'to become his wife's gentleman-usher'. As a grandson of Charles I William had a claim to the Stuart thrones in his own right; and as a great-grandson of the Dutch Protestant champion William the Silent, his religious credentials were impeccable. He agreed to the Declara-

with an army, and found himself faced with little opposition, even from those Catholics and dissenting Protestants on whom King James had thought to rely.

On the night of 10 December 1688, Mary of Modena and her baby son, named James Edward, were hurried secretly out of London, and James II soon followed. On his way he threw the Great Seal into the Thames, from where it was later recovered. The fleeing king was caught by a group of Kent fishermen and returned to London, but his successor, the new King William III, had no wish to keep him there as a political embarrassment, and so James was permitted to escape once more. On Christmas Day, 1688, James Stuart arrived in France, where he was to live out the rest of his life, an exile at St Germain.

tion of Rights, curbing the monarch's power over the law, the army and parliament and on 11 April 1689 the combined coronation of William III and Mary II took place in Westminster Abbey.

William of Orange had been 26 years old, already a seasoned politician and military campaigner, when he crossed to England to marry the Princess Mary, in the reign of Charles II. On 4 November 1677 they were married in St James's Palace. Mary was then a shy girl of 15, who wept at the prospect of marrying a stranger and leaving her own country, but she came to love Holland, and

William and Mary enthroned, a painting in the Royal Naval College by Sir John Thornhill.

128

also her husband, although he was often unfaithful to her, and may also have been homosexual. William was reserved and humourless, Mary shy and retiring; yet they had some shared interests, such as a love of architecture and gardens, and they were united in their devotion to the cause of Protestantism. Their marriage-alliance was itself a symbol of Anglo-Dutch unity in the face of the ambitions of King Louis XIV of France. Resisting French expansion in Europe was the central, driving aim of William's career, both as Prince of Orange and as King of England. In the Netherlands, he had successfully withstood the French king's territorial aggression, securing the Peace of Nijmegen in 1678. As King of England, in 1689, he proceeded to bring his new country into a treaty with the Spanish Empire and the United Provinces, to form a Grand Alliance against King Louis XIV's plans for French mastery in Europe. In the years that followed, Mary was often left to rule while William was campaigning abroad.

Early in the reign, in 1690, William was obliged to take the field close to home, against a French-backed attempt to restore King James to the Stuart thrones. In Ireland,

William of Orange landing at Torbay in 1688.

with its largely Roman Catholic population, the exiled James could still command fierce loyalty. He set up a court and Parliament in Dublin; and with the support of Louis XIV he set about reconquering his former possessions, beginning with the Protestant strongholds in the north of Ireland. In the spring of 1689, James personally conducted the siege of Londonderry, but despite sickness and near-starvation the Protestant inhabitants succeeded in holding out, until ships carrying supplies from England broke through the besiegers' coastal defences to relieve the city. A long and bitterly-fought campaign followed until finally, on 1 July 1690, King William and King James faced one another at the River Boyne, some 20 miles north of Dublin. James's army bore the French fleur-de-lys on their banners, as well as the Stuart insignia; William's army included soldiers from almost every Protestant nation. In the ensuing Battle of the Boyne, William was slightly wounded, but by the end of the day he had won a resounding victory. James escaped to exile in France once more, never to return; and the name of 'King Billy' has remained a potent symbol of the conflict between Catholic and Protestant in Ireland to the present day.

Though the wars against the French were

to occupy much of King William's energy and attention, the achievements of the reign of William and Mary were the constitutional changes which took place at home. The Triennial Act was passed, requiring Parliament to be summoned every three years; the Commons gained increased control over the army through the Mutiny Act, and over the king's expenditure through the Civil List Act, while a new Act of Indulgence brought a new degree of tolerance for non-conformist worship, though it precluded Roman Catholicism. In 1701, the Act of Settlement was passed, which, while settling the Stuart succession on James I's granddaughter, Sophia of Hanover and her children, debarred any monarch who was not a Protestant from succeeding to the throne, a provision still in force today. Though William and Parliament did not always see eye to eye, the power of Parliament increased during his reign, and a new balance between it and the monarchy was achieved.

The modest Queen Mary did not care for the responsibilities of power; except when William was away she preferred to leave matters of government in the hands of her husband and his ministers. She was, however, active in her role as Head of the Church of England, and it was she, rather than her

The Fountain Court, Hampton Court Palace,
Surrey
(*Below*)
Fortunately, William and Mary's plans to
demolish entirely the old palace of Henry
VIII were not completed. But parts of the
palace, such as the Fountain Court and
the Great Staircase, were rebuilt by Wren,
and Queen Mary's taste is evident in much
of the interior decoration, which reflects

her love of the Dutch style. She also had the
gardens laid out in the formal Dutch
fashion, by the gardener Henry Wise.

IN WILLIAM AND MARY'S ENGLAND

Kensington Palace, London W8
Because King William suffered from asthma,
he kept his court out at rural Kensington,
where the air was cleaner than in central
London. The former Nottingham House was
bought, and remodelled by Sir Christopher
Wren. Though it is still a royal residence,
parts of the palace are open to the public.

William and Mary's Funeral Effigies, the
Undercroft, Westminster Abbey, London
SW1
These contemporary figures of the King and
Queen are good likenesses, and were 'greatly
admired by every eye that beheld them'
when first put on display in the Abbey in
1725.

**Greenwich Hospital (now the Royal Naval
College),** London SE10
(*Below*)
Charles II had planned a new palace for
himself at Greenwich, where he could
indulge his love of sailing, but his money
ran out before it was completed. In 1694
William and Mary founded a hospital for
seamen on the site, and Wren's pupil,
Nicholas Hawksmoor, built the beautiful
Greenwich Hospital.

Calvinist husband, who made Church appointments. Her other notable sphere of
influence was in the building works carried
out on the royal palaces; under her direction,
much of Henry VIII's old river-palace of
Hampton Court was rebuilt by Wren, and its
gardens laid out in the formal Dutch style,
while Kensington Palace was created from
an earlier mansion, also by Christopher
Wren. William and Mary preferred to keep
their court out at rural Kensington, away
from the London air, because the King

suffered from asthma. A short man with a
habitual cough, he was never physically
strong, and many thought he would not
outlive his wife. But in the event she died
first, carried off by smallpox on 28 December
1694, aged only 32. For all his shortcomings
as a husband, William was overcome with
grief, and he wore a lock of her hair until the
day he died.

After the first enthusiasm of his arrival had
died down, William of Orange had not
enjoyed great personal popularity with his

subjects, and after Mary's death he seemed a
morose and isolated figure. His reign had
seen notable achievements, from the creat-
ion of the Bank of England, in 1694, to the
signing of the Treaty of Ryswick in 1697,
which curbed the power of France and
secured Louis XIV's recognition of the
invalidity of the Jacobite claim to the Stuart
throne. But the final defeat of Louis XIV's
France was yet to come; and when he died,
on 8 March 1702, William's chief regret was
that he had not lived to see it.

Anne 1702-14

THE YOUNGER of James II's two daughters was born on 6 February 1665 and named Anne after her mother, Lord Clarendon's daughter Anne Hyde. A sickly child, the Princess Anne was only six years old when her mother died; perhaps her deep emotional friendships with women, later in life, stemmed from a lack of maternal love in childhood. James's second wife, the Catholic Mary of Modena, was not unkind to her stepdaughters, but the princesses grew up with a deep distrust of their stepmother, and regarded her as a harmful influence over their father. Both Mary and Anne were jealously convinced that the baby boy produced by Mary of Modena in 1688 was not a true Stuart prince but the result of a shameful fraud.

Under the eye of Charles II, who was concerned at his brother's Catholicism, James's daughters were brought up to be staunch Anglicans. When the conflicts of King James's reign came to a head with the Glorious Revolution of 1688, Anne gave her tacit support to the cause of her sister and brother-in-law, William and Mary; and when William was victorious, and James in exile, she agreed to renounce her own right to the throne until after the death of King William, as well as Queen Mary – assuming their marriage was childless. Though the sisters sincerely believed the disinheritance of their father to be necessary, for religion's sake, both felt a sense of guilt over what had happened, and Anne's remorse was increased by the sorrows of her later life, which she believed were her punishment. Even the comfort of her sister's affection was lost to her; after Mary's accession the formerly warm friendship between the Stuart sisters cooled and, although Anne was voted an income of £50,000 a year by Parliament, and given lodgings in the part of Whitehall known as the Cockpit, she felt hard done by.

At the centre of the quarrel between the Queen and the Princess was Anne's infatuation with the young Churchills. Sarah Churchill, an energetic, domineering firebrand of a woman five years older than Anne, had been a member of Anne's household since the princess was a child, and despite the differences in their ages they

Queen Anne with her son the Duke of Gloucester.

formed an intense friendship. Though Anne was married in 1683, to the amiable, sottish Prince George of Denmark, and enjoyed a devoted relationship with her husband, her affection for Sarah was such that she even allowed her friend to dispense with royal formalities, and they addressed each other by nicknames – 'Mrs Morley' for the princess, 'Mrs Freeman' for Sarah. Anne's friendship extended to 'Mrs Freeman's' husband, the brilliant soldier John Churchill, later the 1st Duke of Marlborough and one of the greatest generals in history. John Churchill had served William of Orange well; but, believing himself to have been ill rewarded, he began to dabble in Jacobite intrigues on behalf of the exiled James II, with the result that he lost his offices and was briefly imprisoned in the Tower of London, in 1692. When Anne, the heir to the throne, continued to show great favour to the prisoner's wife Queen Mary was infuriated, and the Princess was eventually obliged to leave the court, taking her friend Sarah with her.

After Mary's death in 1694, King William took steps to mend the rift with his sister-in-law. Anne and Prince George were given St James's Palace as their London residence, and even the Churchills were shown favour by the King. The greatest sorrow of Anne's life remained unaltered, however; constantly, fruitlessly, she found herself pregnant with children who did not survive. One son, William, Duke of Gloucester, struggled through his infancy, to die just after his 11th birthday, and after some 17 pregnancies Anne was still childless, with her figure and health ruined. It was after the death of little Gloucester that the Act of Settlement of 1701 was passed, with Anne's agreement, putting the House of Hanover next to her in the line of succession.

When Anne became Queen at last, on 8 March 1702, she was a stout, florid woman, with a face 'rather round than majestic', a mind that had little intelligence or education, and a body that was prematurely aged at 47. Deeply pious, she took a close interest in Church affairs, and in 1704 she granted a portion of crown revenues to the relief of poor clergy, in a gift known as 'Queen Anne's Bounty'.

The Duke of Marlborough at Blenheim.

133

IN QUEEN ANNE'S ENGLAND

Blenheim Palace, Woodstock, Oxfordshire
The Queen gave the site to the Duke of
Marlborough, as a token of the nation's
gratitude for his victories in the Low
Countries. Built by Vanburgh in the gorgeous

Baroque style, the house took its name from
the Duke's most famous triumph, at the Battle
of Blenheim in 1704.

Sarah Churchill, Queen Anne's close friend, and wife of the Duke of Marlborough.

Apart from religion, hunting and horse-racing, Queen Anne had few interests in life. Yet she presided over one of the great eras of British achievement, when Swift, Pope and the satirists Addison and Steele were writing, when Isaac Newton was President of the Royal Society and Jeremiah Clarke Organist of the Chapel Royal, and Vanburgh was building gorgeous mansions in the new Baroque style. Above all, it was the age of Marlborough's victorious campaigns, when the most brilliant of all British generals took on the powerful French, in the War of the Spanish Succession, and made Europe ring to such names as Blenheim, Oudenarde and Ramillies. With the French inheritance of the Spanish empire, the balance of power in Europe had been dangerously tipped in France's favour; but, supported by his friend Lord Treasurer Godolphin at home and his Dutch and German allies in Europe, Marlborough destroyed Louis XIV's mastery. After routing the French at the Battle of Blenheim, on 13 August 1704, Marlborough was the hero of Queen and country. Queen Anne rewarded him with the gift of the royal manor of Woodstock, where Vanburgh was commissioned to build, at the Queen's expense, Blenheim Palace, as a fitting home for the Duke and Duchess.

Godolphin, the Marlboroughs' friend, served Anne well. It was he who negotiated the Act of Union with the Scots, so earnestly desired by James I a century earlier. The kingdoms were united at last in May 1707; the two Parliaments were united, and Great Britain was born. It was an achievement which Queen Anne valued highly.

Chronology

CHARLES II

1630	*29 May* Birth
1651	Crowned by Scots at Scone Battle of Worcester; Charles defeated, flees to France
1660	*Apr* Declaration of Breda; promises to pardon old enemies and submit to will of Parliament *29 May* Re-enters London; Restoration of monarchy
1662	Marriage to Catherine of Braganza
1665	Great Plague
1666	Great Fire of London
1668	Triple Alliance with Holland and Sweden
1670	Treaty of Dover
1673	Test Act; Catholics excluded from holding public office
1679	Exclusion crisis over Duke of York's Catholicism
1685	*6 Feb* Death of Charles II

JAMES II

1633	*14 Oct* Birth
1660	Marriage to Anne Hyde
1671	Death of Anne Hyde
1673	Marriage to Mary of Modena
1680	High Commissioner for Scotland
1685	Coronation *6 Jul* Battle of Sedgemoor; defeat of Duke of Monmouth *15 Jul* Monmouth beheaded
1688	Second Declaration of Indulgence; religious toleration *10 Jun* Son James born (the future 'Old Pretender') *5 Nov* William of Orange lands at Torbay

	10 Dec Queen Mary and Prince James escape *25 Dec* James II arrives in France
1701	*16 Sep* Death of James II in France

WILLIAM III AND MARY II

1650	*14 Nov* Birth of William
1662	*30 Apr* Birth of Mary
1677	Marriage of William and Mary
1689	*11 Apr* Combined coronation Declaration of Rights; established limited monarchy
1690	*1 Jul* Battle of the Boyne; James II defeated in Ireland
1694	Bank of England founded *28 Dec* Death of Mary II
1697	Treaty of Ryswick with France
1701	Act of Settlement; provided for succession to throne
1702	*8 Mar* Death of William III

ANNE

1665	*6 Feb* Birth
1683	Marriage to Prince George of Denmark
1702	Coronation
1702–13	War with France
1704	*13 Aug* Battle of Blenheim; French defeat by Allies under Marlborough
1706	Battle of Ramillies; Allied victory in Flanders
1707	*May 1* Union with Scotland
1708	Battle of Oudenarde
1709	Battle of Malplaquet
1710	Final breach between Anne and Sarah Churchill
1713	Treaty of Utrecht; peace with France
1714	*1 Aug* Death of Anne

In 1710, however, Godolphin was dismissed, and the Whigs were replaced by a Tory ministry. The nation was beginning to tire of the unending war, which the Tories loudly opposed, and the Queen found their views to be in sympathy with hers. She had grown disenchanted with the Marlboroughs. Sarah's fiery, temperamental nature no longer fascinated her; by 1708 – the year of her husband's death – the Queen had a new bosom-friend, the gentle Abigail Masham, whom she nicknamed 'Mrs Jenkins'. Abigail Masham was close to the prominent Tory, Robert Harley; and Harley acquired considerable influence over the Queen, often visiting her by the back stairs of the palace.

It was the Tories who obtained peace with the Treaty of Utrecht in 1713, securing most of Britain's gains and curbing French expansion. Yet the Tory supremacy did not last, even in the favour of the dying Queen Anne. An ultra-right-wing Tory group planned a Jacobite restoration, discrediting the rest of the party in the eyes of the Hanoverians who, under the provisions of the Act of Settlement, followed Queen Anne.

The Electress Sophia of Hanover, the last surviving child of the 13 born to James I's beautiful daughter Elizabeth, the Winter Queen, was named as Anne's heir in the Act. It was her cherished ambition to be Queen of Great Britain, but she was deprived of her wish by just two months. Sophia died in June 1714, Queen Anne on August 1. It was thus Sophia's elder son, George, who became the first Hanoverian to rule Great Britain.

Chapter nine
THE HOUSE OF HANOVER

George I
1714-27

THE FUTURE King George I was born, by a fortunate coincidence, almost in the hour of the Restoration – his birth took place in Hanover on 28 May 1660, the day before Charles II re-entered London in triumph. No one could then have foreseen that successive Stuart monarchs would die childless or in exile, and that half a century later this German great-grandson of James I would be the senior Protestant claimant to the British throne, under the Act of Settlement of 1701. But six weeks after the death of Queen Anne, on 18 September 1714, King George I was brought ashore at Greenwich, the first British king of the House of Hanover.

The English people's first impressions of their new King were not over-favourable. Unlike his grandmother and mother, the fascinating Winter Queen and her lively daughter Sophia, through whom he claimed his throne, George I had neither good looks nor charm. He was heavily built, with fair hair and prominent features, and in character he more resembled his stolid father's family than the colourful Stuarts. As Elector of Hanover he had ruled his small but prosperous state efficiently, and had shown himself to be courageous in battle, but he was a man of plodding intellect and small imagination. To the amusement of his new courtiers, he brought two very plain German mistresses over to England; as one was very fat and one very thin, they were given the nicknames of 'the Elephant' and 'the Maypole'. Mistresses apart, there was one

dark shadow over George's reputation when he landed in England: the celebrated 'Königsmark Affair'. Two decades earlier, his beautiful wife Sophia Dorothea of Celle had indiscreetly, if understandably, embarked on a romance with a Swedish adventurer, the glamorous soldier-of-fortune Count von Königsmark. In the summer of 1694, Königsmark suddenly vanished and was never seen again. Rumour had it that he had been butchered on George's orders and buried beneath the palace floorboards; what was certain was that the unfortunate Electress was not only divorced by her vengeful husband, but condemned to imprisonment in the castle at Ahlden for the rest of her life. For this, George I's son, George Augustus, never forgave him, and as King and Prince of Wales their relationship was to be one of open hostility.

As King of England, George I missed his old life in Hanover, and he found it hard to fit in with English ways. Accompanied by an entourage of 'German ministers and playfellows', waited on by two exotic Turkish servants, Mustapha and Mahomet, whom he had captured in battle, and hampered by a natural reserve, as well as the language difficulty, from conversing with his courtiers, the Hanoverian King seemed a remote figure to his new subjects. He showed little interest in the cultural life of the kingdom, though his was an age of great writers such as Defoe, Swift and Pope, who published such classics as *Robinson Crusoe*, *Gulliver's Travels* and *The Dunciad* during this era. 'I hate all boets and bainters', the King was heard to say flatly. Where George I did make a major artistic contribution was in the field of music, as patron of the composer Handel, who had been his Kappelmeister in Hanover. Handel came to live in London in 1715 and wrote some of his best-loved works, such as the 'Water Music', for English royal occasions.

LEFT *The South Sea Bubble* by E.M. Ward.

RIGHT George I and his grandson, Prince Frederick.

136

IN GEORGE I's ENGLAND

The King's Staircase, Kensington Palace, London SW1
William Kent designed the new King's Staircase for George I. Painted groups of his courtiers – including Kent himself – look down on it.

The Painted Hall, Royal Naval College, Greenwich, London SE10
(Below)
Beneath Sir James Thornhill's magnificent painted ceiling, the nobility of England assembled to greet their new king, George I, on his arrival from Hanover, in 1714.

With an unpopular foreign king holding court in London, the prospects for an attempt on the throne by the dispossessed Stuart claimant seemed bright, and in Scotland, at the beginning of September, 1715, the Jacobite standard was raised. The Jacobite Pretender, James II's son James Edward Stuart, had many of the qualities which his rival George I so conspicuously lacked – charming, handsome and cultured, he inspired intense personal loyalty in his followers. Major cities such as Edinburgh remained loyal to the Protestant crown, but the Highlanders rose against the 'wee, wee German lairdie', as James's followers called King George, and with good leadership the Jacobite rebels might have presented a serious threat to the House of Hanover. But in November 1715 they were effectively beaten at the Battle of Preston, before their leader, 'James VIII and III' had even landed, and by 1716 he had returned to exile in France, leaving the memory of 'the 15' (the 1715 rebellion) and 'the King over the Water' to be kept alive by Britain's Jacobites for the next 30 years.

The failure of the '15 rebellion had strengthened the position of the House of Hanover, and confirmed the Whigs – who had supported the Hanoverian succession, on the death of Queen Anne – in their political ascendancy. George I's reign saw the beginnings of the Cabinet as an instrument of government and the establishment of Sir Robert Walpole as the first British Prime Minister in the modern sense. King George's first loyalties were always to Hanover, and his absences from England, when he visited his Electorate, allowed Walpole to consolidate his power. He became an intimate of the rival 'Leicester House Set', led by the Prince of Wales and his lively Princess, Caroline of Anspach; and it was largely through Walpole's efforts that there was a somewhat stilted reconciliation between the King and the Prince, in 1720.

Walpole may not have been liked by King George I, but he was to become almost indispensable to him. With an alien and less than popular king on the throne, the bluff country gentleman Sir Robert Walpole was a figure whom the English people felt they could trust, and his reputation was to prove invaluable to the House of Hanover at the time of the 'South Sea Bubble'. This was the name given to the financial crisis of 1720, when speculation fever suddenly gripped court and country, and fortunes were lost. The South Sea Company had been given a contract to manage millions of pounds of the National Debt; its shares soared, then crashed in September 1720, bankrupting many over-eager investors. Some looked for scapegoats at court; and with the Jacobites only waiting for their opportunity to make another bid for the throne, the future of the House of Hanover looked decidedly uncertain. However, Walpole, unlike other prominent Whigs, had skilfully managed to remain untainted by the affair; by popular demand, he was brought back into office, and the nation's confidence in its monarchy and government was gradually restored. When Walpole's agents went on to uncover a series of Jacobite plots, the Whig minister's usefulness to his Hanoverian master was proved yet again.

As the reign progressed, George I increasingly left the affairs of his kingdom in Walpole's hands while he returned home to Hanover. He was on his way there when, in June 1727, he suffered a stroke, as his coach approached Osnabrück. He died in Osnabrück Castle, in the very room where he had been born, 67 years earlier, and he was buried as he would have wished, in Hanover.

George II
1727-60

THE INTENSE dislike which George II felt for his father – a precedent followed by later Hanoverian kings and their heirs – had begun during his boyhood years in Germany. Born on 30 October 1683, George Augustus was 11 years old when his mother was imprisoned in the Castle of Ahlden, following the tragic Königsmark affair. It was said that he tried to

break in to see her, but was prevented, and as Prince of Wales he looked forward to his father's death, so that he could give his mother her freedom. (From this, too, he was prevented, by Sophia Dorothea's death in captivity in 1726.) When, on 14 June 1727, Walpole broke the news to him that his father had died in Hanover, the new King George II could not, at first, believe it – 'Dat is one big lie!' he was said to have retorted, in his strong German accent.

George Augustus was 44 at the time of his accession. Having spent the first part of his adult life opposing George I, after coming to the throne he seemed to grow increasingly like him. In his youth, when he lived at Leicester House, he and his vivacious wife

George II at Dettingen. He was the last English monarch to lead his troops into battle.

Caroline of Anspach had surrounded themselves with a raffish set of lively-minded men and women; but as King, George II ran his court along lines of strict formality, insisting on rigid punctuality and etiquette, and constantly striving to keep down expenses. 'An obstinate, self-indulgent, miserly martinet', was Frederick, the Prince of Wales', uncompromising description of his father.

The dislike which George II had felt for his father was nothing compared to the loathing with which he regarded his eldest son and heir. 'Fretz', as the King contemptuously called Frederick, was sallow and sharp-

139

Horse Guards' Parade, Whitehall, London SW1
(Above)
George II, a military-minded king, became the last British sovereign to lead his troops into battle in person, at the Battle of Dettingen in June 1743. He laid out Horse Guards' Parade, and presided over the original Trooping the Colour ceremony.

Battlefield of Culloden, Inverness, Scotland
The scene of the bloody rout of the Jacobites, on 16 April 1745, by George II's second son, 'Butcher' Cumberland. Today, cairns and gravestones mark the resting-places of the fallen Highlanders.

IN GEORGE II'S BRITAIN

Prince Frederick's Barge, National Maritime Museum, Greenwich, London SE10
(Above)
George II's heir, Prince Frederick, used this exquisite barge; designed by William Kent in 1732, it has now been restored to its former elegance.

Traquair House, Peebles, Scotland
A tree-lined avenue ends in a pair of fine gates, known as the Bear Gates; according to tradition, Charles Edward Stuart (the 'Young Pretender') was the last person to pass through them, in 1745, and they have not been opened since.

featured, unlike his stout, fair, Hanoverian forebears, but he had done little else to merit the contempt which was heaped upon him. 'Our firstborn', George II once declared, 'is the greatest beast in the whole world, and we heartily wish he was out of it.' Where George II, as Prince of Wales, had had the 'Leicester House Set', Frederick acquired a following of his own which Walpole nicknamed 'The Patriot Boys'. In an attempt to curb the Prince's influence, George II kept him on a far smaller allowance than he himself had enjoyed, but this did not prevent 'Poor Fred' from making his political presence felt.

George II's acquisition of a new mistress, the heavily-German Madame von Walmoden, made him turn increasingly German in his speech and behaviour, and increased his mounting unpopularity in England; by contrast, Prince Frederick's standing with the politicians and the public grew. The King had a typically coarse comment – 'Popularity always makes me sick, but Fretz's popularity makes me vomit'. To Fretz's delight, and partly through his efforts, Walpole fell from power in 1742, while the country was at war with Spain and France. Walpole had been in favour of peace, but the war proved highly favourable to

George II's interests; at the age of 61 he was able to relive his early military triumphs, by leading an allied army of British, Hanoverians and Austrians, among others, to a splendid victory over the French at Dettingen on 15 June 1743. It was the last occasion when a British sovereign personally led his troops in battle, and it did a great deal to improve the King's image with his English subjects.

There was more fighting to be done on British soil, however, for in 1745 the Young Pretender, the Jacobites' 'Bonnie Prince Charlie', returned to try once more to reclaim the crown lost by his grandfather, James II. For a time, the Jacobite threat seemed grave. Edinburgh, Carlisle and Derby fell to the invader, but eventually the King's second son, the Duke of Cumberland, led the English to a bloody victory at Culloden, earning himself the name of 'Butcher Cumberland' for his brutality. The ''45' went down in history with the ''15', ballads were written and legends repeated about the 'Bonnie Prince', but after that defeat Charlie did not come again. A number of Scots noblemen were brought to London to die, and old Lord Lovat became the last peer to be beheaded in England.

The Battle of Culloden, on 16 April 1746, in which the English forces under the Duke of Cumberland defeated the Jacobite Scots.

The cost of such wars had to be found from taxes, voted by Parliament; George II constantly complained of Parliament's power, but he recognised that he could not curb it. He could, however, show his personal dislike for his ministers, and he made it plain that the Duke of Newcastle and his relations, the Pelhams, who rose to power in the 1740s, were not at all to his liking – and nor was William Pitt, who had been one of 'Fretz's' set. Pitt did, however, improve somewhat in his sovereign's eyes when he emerged as a great wartime leader, during the Seven Years' War. Military glory had always been George II's greatest desire.

It was his good fortune that his reign ended with a blaze of such glory: by 1759 Britain was supreme at sea, and a conquering power in Canada – where Wolfe had stormed Quebec – India and the West Indies. Before he died, aged 78, in 1760, George II had known another satisfaction – he had outlived his hated heir, 'Poor Fred', by 19 years. It was to his grandson, George III, that the crown now passed.

George III. Nicknamed 'Farmer George,' he was
one of Britain's most popular monarchs.

George III 1760-1820

EORGE III was the first British monarch since Queen Anne to be born in England and the first Hanoverian king to speak English without a foreign accent. At the time of his birth, on 4 June 1738, his father, Prince Frederick, had been obliged to take London lodgings in St James's Square since he was not welcome at court; and when 'Poor Fred' died, shortly before his son's 13th birthday, the traditional hostility between Hanoverian kings and their heirs was carried on between George II and the guardians of the boy who would one day succeed him to become George III.

Brought up by his mother, Augusta of Saxe-Gotha, and her close companion Lord Bute, who educated him for kingship, George developed into a shy, dutiful young man with a kindly nature and a strong sense of his royal responsibilities. He was better-looking than the previous Georges: in Horace Walpole's description, he was 'tall and full of dignity, his countenance florid and obliging'. In his youth, George more than once fell deeply in love, but was dissuaded from marrying by Bute, whom he looked on as his mentor. When, a year after coming to the throne, George III took a wife, his bride was his mother's choice, Charlotte of Mecklenburg-Strelitz. Though Queen Charlotte was no beauty and had little claim to wit or intellect, she suited King George; she shared his moral attitudes and fondness for domesticity, and theirs was to be an unusually happy royal marriage.

King George III was 22 years old when he ascended the throne, on the death of his grandfather. A conservative by instinct, he would have liked to see an end to party political divisions; he sought to break the long-standing Whig supremacy in government, and he re-asserted the constitutional power of the monarchy. 'Born and bred in this country, I glory in the name of Britain', he told his first Parliament proudly, and he saw it as his task to defend the British people's liberties, while exercising his royal authority in such vital matters as the appointment of Crown ministers. In an age of outstanding political figures, George III developed a sound judgement of men and in the 1780s, his protégé, the brilliant William Pitt the Younger, became Prime Minister at the uniquely early age of 24. He was to steer Britain through the troubled years which followed the French Revolution with the full backing of the King, who helped to maintain him in office.

The King's active opposition to political reform brought him the scathing abuse of radicals such as Charles James Fox and the

The Boston Massacre, one of the events which sparked off the American War of independence.

IN GEORGE III's ENGLAND

The Dutch House, Kew Gardens, Kew
(*Left*)
George III and his ever-growing family lived in this elegant little mansion while the now-demolished Kew Palace was under construction. King George and Queen Charlotte loved Kew, and the king – a knowledgeable horticulturalist – greatly enlarged the beautiful Botanical Gardens.

The Great Pagoda, Kew Gardens, Kew
(*Right*)
The fantastic Pagoda, which helped to introduce the fashion for Chinese art into Britain, was designed by the architect Sir William Chambers, to commemorate the wedding of King George III and Queen Charlotte.

The Gold State Coach, Royal Mews, Buckingham Palace, London SW1
(*Below*)
One of the most spectacular of all the royal coaches, the Golden State Coach was designed by Chambers, and first used by George III for the State opening of Parliament in November 1762. It can be seen by visitors to the Royal Mews, by previous arrangement with Buckingham Palace.

(*Above*)
King George III's Microscope, The Science Museum, London SW7
Science, as well as horticulture, interested George III; this microscope was part of his collection of scientific apparatus.

The Queen's Cottage, Kew Gardens, Kew
This ornamental cottage was designed for Queen Charlotte.

activist John Wilkes, but his genuine concern for what he saw as his subjects' welfare, coupled with his exemplary family life, won George III considerable personal popularity. In their palace at Kew, he and Queen Charlotte enjoyed a simple life by royal standards; she busied herself with their 15 children, he pottered about the gardens and sketched plants, earning himself the nickname 'Farmer George' for his interest in agriculture. Though scarcely a connoisseur, he liked painting, music and books of a suitable moral tone, and his patronage of the architect Sir William Chambers produced such diverse delights as the Pagoda in Kew Gardens and the gilded State Coach, still in use today. In an age of revolutionary fervour, when the tumbrils were rolling through Paris, the continuing stability in Britain owed at least something to the character and reputation of the monarch.

In his attitude to the growing demands for independence by the American colonists, George III displayed his characteristic conservatism. He was certainly no tyrant, but he was ardently paternalistic; he talked of the need for 'firmness', referred to 'the parent's heart', and supported the government's refusal to countenance any form of concessions to the patriots. The upshot was the American War of Independence, which ended in 1781 with the defeat of the British and the surrender of General Cornwallis at Yorktown. It was a terrible loss of face, as well as territory, for Britain, and for George III himself the American secession marked the beginning of a bleak period, during which three Whig ministries sought to reduce the political influence of the monarch. By the end of 1783, however, William Pitt was in power, and king and nation alike began to recover their morale.

Sadly, the later years of George III's long life were to be marred by a mysterious illness. From a healthy, upright, middle-aged man, he turned into a ranting creature who foamed at the mouth, rolled bloodshot eyes and bellowed obscenities amid a constant stream of gibberish. The symptoms came on in earnest in November 1788, and the King was generally thought to have 'gone mad'; after a cruel and outlandish course of treatment, which included burning his skin with poultices and strapping him to a chair, he seemed to recover in the spring of 1789, but he suffered further attacks over the next twelve years. The true cause of George III's violent symptoms can only be surmised, but modern medical opinion suggests that he suffered from porphyria, a rare disease affecting the red pigmentation of the blood which, without proper treatment, could

poison the nervous system and even the brain. Whatever its true origin, the King's illness brought him a wave of public sympathy. A bill was drawn up empowering his eldest son to act as Regent if necessary, but public opinion was generally against the pleasure-loving Prince of Wales, who was believed to have made fun of the King's sickness. George III's long periods of lucidity enabled him to continue as effective ruler, however, until the last decade of his life.

It was, unfortunately, during one of King George's phases of good health that the troubled question of Catholic Emancipation arose, with the passing of the 1801 Act of Union between England and Ireland. Pitt believed that concessions should be made to the Irish, and that Catholics should be permitted to hold public office and sit in Parliament. But the King was implacably opposed to this; like many of his subjects, he believed it would be a betrayal of his Anglican coronation oath, and the upshot was that Pitt was forced to resign. It was another sorry moment in the history of Anglo-Irish political relations.

In 1810, George III's illness finally overcame him completely, and for the last ten years of his life, while his son acted as Regent, the old King was a pitiful figure, ambling about his apartments in Windsor Castle with a flowing white beard and staring eyes. As a tragic token of his former greatness, he kept the Order of the Garter pinned to his purple gown. The events of the Regency years, even the defeat of Napoleon at Waterloo, passed him by; and his death on 29 January 1820, when he was almost 82, truly came as a release for the spectral monarch of Windsor.

George IV
1820-30

FEW BRITISH monarchs have been so strongly criticised and caricatured in their own time as the king who came to the throne in 1820 as King George IV. As Prince Regent, during the years of his father's illness, the pleasure-loving 'Prinney' was thought by many to compare disfavourably with the dutiful, responsible and highly moral George III; and when he was king, *The Times* once summed him up as 'a hard-drinking, swearing man who at all times would prefer a girl and a bottle to politics and a sermon'. The great cartoonists of the time, such as Gillray and Rowlandson, added their own scathing attacks, depicting Prinney in the midst of his extravagant debaucheries. Yet the truth was, as the Duke of Wellington commented after George IV's death, that he was 'a medley of the most opposite qualities, with a great preponderance of good'.

George Augustus Frederick, first child of King George III and Queen Charlotte, was born on 12 August 1762. He grew into an attractive and promising boy, but despite – or perhaps because of – a heavily moral upbringing, he showed early signs of an excessive fondness for food and pretty women. By the time he was 20 years old he was tall, golden-haired and plumply charming, and in education and artistic tastes he was to be one of the most sophisticated kings in British history. Though no poet or politician himself, he admired ability in others, and in his youth he counted among his closest friends the radical Charles James Fox and the great arbiter of style, George 'Beau' Brummell. It was Brummel who persuaded the prince to abandon his favourite gaudy satins for a severely elegant style of dress, thereby setting a fashion for masculine society.

Prinney's natural taste ran to exuberance, however, and he gave it free reign when creating his palaces – whether redesigning Royal Lodge, Windsor, in a riot of rustic charm, or building a unique Oriental pavilion for himself in the newly-fashionable seaside resort of Brighthelmstone, or Brighton. At the Brighton Pavilion, 'Prinney''s fancy for the exotic was translated by the architect John Nash into a magical palace of domes, minarets and cupolas, with furnishings to match the eastern theme and dragons in profusion. It was a startling but successful concept, and the Brighton Pavilion remains one of the oddest and most delightful examples of early 19th-century English architecture.

Love-letters found after George IV's death bear witness to 'the most furious passion' which he had felt for numerous ladies. He tended to fall overwhelmingly in love, only to end the affair curtly once he had tired of the mistress, but in 1784, when he was 22 years old, one of his relationships had had a very different outcome. The object of his desires was a Roman Catholic widow named Maria Fitzherbert, who refused to yield to him; the upshot was a secret marriage. Though valid in canon law, the marriage had been contracted without the King's consent and was null and void under the Royal Marriages

Act of 1772. However, it remained a serious source of potential embarrassment for the Prince – and particularly after he was officially married, in 1795, to his cousin Caroline of Brunswick.

This suitable royal alliance was contracted by the Prince as a means of writing off his enormous debts, but he was to pay a high price for the financial relief. His bride turned out to be a foolish, charmless, badly-behaved young woman who did not wash enough; she was entirely unsuited to be a future Queen of England. For her part, Caroline was most disappointed in her husband, who made no secret of his distaste for her, and flaunted his current mistress, Lady Jersey, before her. The marriage was a failure from the beginning, and after the birth of an 'immense girl,' their daughter Charlotte, on 7 January 1796, the couple lived apart.

Princess Caroline went abroad for some time, and followed her husband's example of openly committing adultery; but in 1820, on the death of George III, she returned to

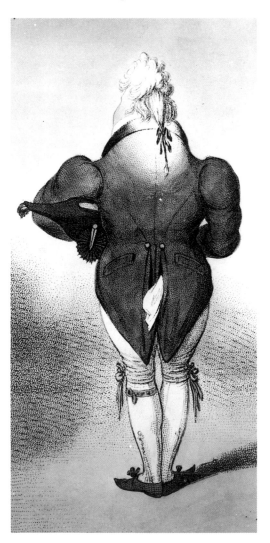

The contemporary caricaturist's view of the Prince Regent.

England to claim her rights as queen. The scandal that followed rocked the kingdom. George IV sought to have a Bill passed by Parliament which would deprive Caroline of her rank and rights and 'dissolve the marriage between His Majesty and the said Queen'. But Caroline vigorously contested the action, and though she was becoming a stout, rouged figure of fun, the press and the public championed her cause against the unpopular King. Much of the evidence concerning the Queen was extremely salacious, and for a time nothing else seemed to be talked of. Eventually the Bill was dropped, but Caroline proceeded to make a scene at the King's Coronation by turning up at Westminster Abbey and demanding admission, and it was an inexpressible relief to George IV when, on 8 August 1821, she became ill and died. Her last wish, to have 'Caroline of Brunswick, the injured Queen of England', inscribed on her coffin, was not granted.

Politically, George IV steered a changeable course. His youthful friendship with Charles James Fox, and support for the Whigs, had served the satisfying purpose of baiting his father, but as he grew older he became increasingly Tory in his views. On coming to the throne he announced that he intended to leave his father's Tory ministers in office, to the disappointment of his Whig friends; and he seemed to undergo a similar change of heart on the subject of Catholic Emancipation. Having appeared to accept it, he was later to change his mind. The truth was that George IV could not think deeply on any subject for very long.

Where George was undoubtedly successful as a monarch was in the exercise of his talent for the spectacular, and sense of royal pomp. 'There was something about him', the novelist Sir Walter Scott observed, 'which, independently of the prestige, the divinity, which hedges a king, marked him as standing by himself.' His coronation – possibly the most lavish in British history – was a dazzlingly theatrical occasion. According to Beau Brummell, Prinney was a clever mimic, and there was undoubtedly something of the actor in his personality. On a state visit to Scotland in 1821 he won the hearts of the crowds, in spite of making an appearance dressed in a kilt and flesh-coloured tights; and even in Ireland, which he visited in the previous year, he was received with joy by those who had usually little love for the British crown. 'I was a rebel to old King George in '98', one old Irishman

George IV as Prince of Wales, in a uniform which he designed himself.

146

IN GEORGE IV's ENGLAND

The Royal Pavilion, Brighton, Sussex
(Top right and below)
As Prince Regent, George IV helped to turn the little seaside town of Brighton into a fashionable resort. There he built himself one of Europe's most elaborate palaces – the Pavilion, designed by John Nash.
(Below) The Music Room.

Windsor Castle, Berkshire
(Bottom right)
By George IV's reign, the mediaeval castle at Windsor was falling into an uncomfortable state of disrepair. During the 1820s, the King commissioned the architect Jeffry Wyatt to make extensive (and expensive) alterations to the structure of the castle. The central Round Tower was raised by 33 feet, the private apartments were moved, and the imposing, battlemented exterior of the Gothic fortress was restored.

Princess Charlotte's Memorial, St George's Chapel, Windsor, Berkshire
King George IV's only child, the Princess Charlotte, died in childbirth in 1817 and was greatly mourned. The loss of this heir to the throne paved the way for the accession of George IV's niece, Queen Victoria, in 1837.

was heard to say, 'but by God I would die a thousand deaths for his son!'

Although King George III and Queen Charlotte had produced 15 children, among their sons and daughters there was a marked lack of legitimate offspring. With the death of the only child of George IV's disastrous marriage, his daughter Charlotte, in November 1817, the succession to the throne began to look precarious. The eldest of George IV's brothers, the Duke of York, was already married, but childless; on the Princess Charlotte's death, the next two brothers hastily found themselves suitable wives. The sole surviving offspring of their marriages was a daughter, Alexandrina Victoria, born to the Duke and Duchess of Kent in 1819. As George IV's reign drew towards its close, it became apparent that this little princess would one day be queen; and one of Victoria's earliest memories was of meeting her uncle, the King – a vast bulk, with a shining, grease-painted face, who told her kindly, 'Give me your little paw'.

There was no sign of great public grief when George IV died, on 26 June 1830. *The Times*, always his bitter opponent, declared, 'There never was an individual less regretted by his fellow-creatures than this deceased king'. Yet there were many friends who mourned Prinney; and when Mrs Fitzherbert was informed that he had been buried with her picture about his neck, 'some large tears fell from her eyes.'

William IV
1830-37

WILLIAM IV had not been educated for kingship. Born on 21 August 1765, he was the third son of George III and Queen Charlotte, and with two elder brothers in the succession before him there seemed little likelihood that he would ever be called upon to rule. Accordingly a career was found for him: at the age of 13, William Henry, Duke of Clarence, joined the Royal Navy as a midshipman.

It was a life which 'Sailor Billy' came to enjoy. Though he was no Nelson, he did well at sea, and he kept a nautical air and a liking for salty language even after he became King, at the age of 64. At the time of his

accession, *The Times* commented on 'the blunt and unaffected – even should it be grotesque – cordiality of his demeanour', and in the first few days of his reign the new King could be seen moving informally about the streets of London, waving to the crowds and allowing himself to be kissed by street-women. William's delight in his new role was obvious; he had been practising his royal signature, 'William R', for several months before his brother's death. Yet he heartily disliked pomp and ostentation, and he insisted that his coronation should take place with the minimum of expense and fuss.

In this, as in many decisions, he seemed eager to show how different he was from the late king. Whereas Prinney had 'put on a dramatic, royal, distant dignity to all', William IV was bluff, informal, and occasionally slightly embarrassing, as in his habit of cheerfully spitting in public. The extravagant innovations of the previous reign were, where possible, done away with: William had much of the Royal Lodge demolished, sent away the French cooks and the German band which his brother had enjoyed, and had the animals from the royal menagerie sent to form the nucleus of the new Zoological Garden in Regent's Park. Many of Prinney's cherished works of art were similarly made available to the nation; William IV could see little merit in them himself, as he jovially admitted.

An old nickname for William had been 'Silly Billy', and he was certainly not a man of great intellect; yet he did not lack courage, or, on occasion, common sense. Politically he was naïve, and he had come out with some startling statements when making speeches in the House of Lords in his younger days; on one occasion, having declared himself firmly opposed to the abolition of the Slave Trade, he accused the great William Wilberforce of being either a fanatic or a hypocrite. Yet William IV was not always so reactionary. Against the advice of the Duke of Wellington, he took a liking to his first Prime Minister, Lord Grey, whose Whig government sought to undertake major Parliamentary reforms. In the spring of 1831, Grey required a general election to be called, so that his government could be returned to power with a large enough majority to permit them to carry out their extensive reforms. At short notice, Grey requested the King to dissolve Parliament. When officials demurred that there would be no time for proper ceremonial to be observed, no time even to prepare the royal coach, the king declared to Grey, 'My lord, I'll go if I go in a hackney coach!' Parliament was promptly dissolved, William was cheered in the streets, and in 1832 the

The Waterloo Chamber, Windsor Castle, Berkshire
William IV, by his own admission, was not interested in art: he was a bluff, sailor king. It was in his reign that the Waterloo Chamber begun by George IV as Prince Regent was completed. This was constructed to house a series of portraits by Sir Thomas Lawrence of the allied soldiers and statesmen who had taken part in the defeat of Napoleon at Waterloo.

IN WILLIAM IV's ENGLAND

historic Parliamentary Reform Act was passed. Though William's cordial relationship with the Whigs did not last, it had had important results.

In one unfortunate respect, William IV resembled his brother George IV: neither had a legitimate child who survived him. William's most famous liaison, with the blowsy but amiable actress Mrs Jordan, had produced a number of royal bastards, who took the surname Fitzclarence, but his marriage to Adelaide of Saxe-Coburg-Meiningen was not so blessed. Adelaide, a pious woman with no claims to beauty, had several pregnancies which ended unhappily, in children who did not live, and as King William's childless old age approached it became certain that the next British ruler would be a girl – his niece, Alexandrina Victoria, daughter of his brother the Duke of

Kent. Even in this relationship the Hanoverian tradition of conflict between king and heir was continued: between the widowed Duchess of Kent and King William there was a cordial dislike, and each spread gossip about the other. According to the Duchess, William IV's court was a den of vice, where she would not permit her young daughter to be seen; the King countered with offensive accusations about the nature of the relationship between the sanctimonious Duchess and her mentor Sir John Conroy. For William, this enmity had one beneficial side-effect – it gave him the willpower to live until his niece should be 18 years old and of age to rule, so that her mother would not have the satisfaction of acting as Regent. When on 20 June 1837, 'Sailor Billy' died, at the age of 73, it was just one month after Victoria's 18th birthday.

Victoria
1837–1901

Q UEEN VICTORIA was a girl of 18 when her uncle William IV died, in June 1837, and she succeeded to the throne. An only child with a widowed mother, she knew singularly little of the world; she had been educated alone, at home, by a possessive German governess, Baroness Lehzen, and until her accession she was dominated by her mother, the Duchess of Kent, and the Duchess's reputed lover, Sir John Conroy. Yet as soon as she became queen, Victoria acquired an air of authority which was both charming and impressive, and she proved her new-found independence by barring Conroy from her court, to her mother's chagrin.

During her early years as monarch, Queen Victoria relied heavily on her Prime Minister, Lord Melbourne, as her mentor. An attractive man in his late fifties, Melbourne became both a father-figure and the object of a half-acknowledged crush for the young Queen, and she followed his opinions slavishly. It was an unfortunate bias. Though a Whig, Melbourne had a reactionary distrust of all kinds of reform; and under his influence the new Queen became extremely unpopular for a time.

In 1839 Queen Victoria was obliged, by Melbourne's resignation, to invite the Conservative Sir Robert Peel to form a

A painting by Landseer of Queen Victoria and Prince Albert at Windsor.

The Great Exhibition of 1851.

Lithographed, Printed & Published by VINCENT BROOKS, 421 Oxford St. London.

government. Peel asked that the Queen's Whig Ladies of the Bedchamber should be replaced by Conservatives, in the usual way; when the Queen refused, causing the 'Bedchamber Crisis', Peel refused to govern, and Melbourne, to his satisfaction, returned to office. An equally damaging incident, in the same year, was the Lady Flora Hastings scandal, which arose when a lady-in-waiting began to swell suspiciously about the stomach. Queen Victoria, censoriously believing the worst, pursued the matter relentlessly, and when Lady Flora died of the cancer which had caused her swelling, the Queen was hissed in public, and mocked as 'Mrs Melbourne'.

It was the young Queen's marriage, in 1840, which began to turn the tide of public opinion in her favour. The husband selected for her, with her ardent approval, was her cousin, Prince Albert of Saxe-Coburg Gotha, Victoria was charmed by his good looks and graceful manners; she proposed to him and was accepted, and on 10 February, the couple, both aged 20, were married.

At the time, there was some mockery of Albert; the smallness of his father's German state, and his own relative poverty, were laughed at, and Parliament quibbled over his allowance and future status. But the Prince emerged as a man of intelligence and taste, and he did much to widen the outlook of his adoring, if not always easy-tempered, wife.

Their first child, the Princess Royal, was born within a year of their marriage, to be followed by 'Bertie', the heir to the throne, and seven more babies, all of whom survived infancy. Queen Victoria hated the indignities of pregnancy and childbirth, but she and Prince Albert believed devoutly in the importance of family life, and their example of virtuous domesticity set the tone for Victorian Britain. In 1845 they acquired a new home, Osborne, in the Isle of Wight, which Albert helped to design; and in their castle of Balmoral, in Scotland, they enjoyed regular Highland holidays, setting a fashion for all things Scottish back in England.

Albert had a liking for new ideas. Not only did he introduce Christmas trees into Britain, and take a hand in redesigning the nation's military uniforms and ceremonial, he achieved a spectacular success with his Great Exhibition, in 1851. This remarkable venture, aimed at encouraging industry and trade of all kinds, was housed in a vast Crystal Palace erected in Hyde Park; a showcase for British ingenuity, it drew visitors from all over the world, and greatly

The marriage of the Prince of Wales to Princess Alexandra of Denmark in 1863.

IN QUEEN VICTORIA's BRITAIN

The Royal Mausoleum, Frogmore, Berkshire
(Right)
Queen Victoria and Prince Albert planned their mausoleum together; the Prince's remains were placed here on its completion in 1868. The presence here of the memorial to John Brown, Queen Victoria's 'faithful and devoted Personal Attendant and friend' indicates the closeness of their friendship. The Mausoleum is open to the public three days a year.

Osborne House, near Cowes, Isle of Wight
(Below)
Rebuilt for Victoria and Albert by Thomas Cubitt, Osborne became one of their favourite residences. The Queen retired here for a time after the Prince's death in 1861, and she died here. The State Apartments are open to the public.

Balmoral Castle, near Ballater, Grampian, Scotland
(Far right)
The original Scottish manor house was completely reconstructed between 1852 and 1855 under Prince Albert's direction. It became Queen Victoria's favourite retreat, and after Albert's death she spent a good part of each year here.

The Dairy, Windsor Castle, Berkshire
(Bottom right)
Prince Albert's many innovations ranged from Christmas trees – which he introduced into Britain – to the Great Exhibition of 1851, which he conceived and organised. His Dairy at Windsor is a charming example of a Victorian model dairy, built to the highest standards of efficiency and hygiene.

Queen Victoria's Dolls, Kensington Palace, London SW1
As an only child, the future Queen Victoria attached great importance to her pets and dolls. Some examples of her dolls are displayed here.

The Ivory Throne and Footstool, Kensington Palace, London SW1
Created Empress of India in 1876, Queen Victoria was keenly interested in her Indian subjects. This ivory throne, presented to her by the Maharajah of Tavancore, was displayed in the Great Exhibition of 1851.

ABOVE   The Albert Memorial in South Kensington, built in memory of the Prince Consort.

RIGHT   Queen Victoria was the first British monarch to be photographed. Here she is seen with two Indian attendants in 1896.

enhanced the Prince's reputation.

The Crimean War, which broke out in 1854, brought some unpopularity for Albert, as he was known to be in favour of peace, and in some quarters he was hysterically rumoured to be a Russian agent. In 1857, however, he was created Prince Consort, in accordance with his wife's wishes, and just before his death, in 1861, he made his most valuable contribution to British affairs, by intervening in an explosive situation which might have brought Britain into the American Civil War. A US warship had boarded a British merchantman, the Trent, to remove two Southern envoys on board her; when President Lincoln refused a request from Queen Victoria's government to release the envoys, a major crisis flared up. Albert, though already ill, worked tirelessly to prepare a carefully-worded despatch which would enable the Americans to step down without losing face. The threatened war was averted – but the Prince Consort died of typhoid shortly afterwards, on 14 December 1861, at the age of only 42.

Queen Victoria was devastated. She shut herself away with her grief, hiding from her subjects' eyes and carrying out her administrative duties from the seclusion of Osborne or Balmoral. Her refusal either to play a full part in state affairs or to hand over to her

heir, the Prince of Wales, was much criticised, as was her growing reliance on a bluff Highland servant, John Brown, whom she allowed to treat her with rare familiarity. Yet Brown's masterful care helped her to regain some interest in life. In 1868, with the encouragement of a very different servant, Benjamin Disraeli, she published a book of memoirs, *Leaves from the Journal of Our Life in the Highlands*, which was a great popular success, and helped to restore her standing with her people. Disraeli, himself an acclaimed novelist, flattered her with the phrase, 'we authors, Ma'am . . .!'

Of the two great political figures who dominated the later, widowed, years of her reign, Queen Victoria hated the reforming Liberal, Gladstone, but was immensely taken with Disraeli. While the admirable but

pompous Gladstone addressed her, in her own phrase, as if she were a public meeting, Disraeli had the right blend of charm and flattery, and his Conservative politics were far more to her liking. He encouraged her to make public appearances, from opening Parliament to unveiling the lavish Albert Memorial in Kensington Gardens, and it was he who, in 1876, secured for her the title of Empress of India, to her delight.

While Queen Victoria, in common with many of her subjects, held views which would be called imperialist and reactionary today, her attitudes were sometimes surprisingly un-hidebound. She did not, for example, share in the general outcry for reprisals against the Indian people after the massacres of English women and children had taken place in the Indian Mutiny of

1857. During the tragic Irish potato famine of 1845–9, she had been shocked by the plight of the starving, and sent aid from her own purse, while many of the Establishment did nothing; and she deplored colour prejudice, whether displayed by the British in India or by the Boers in South Africa. Her own most familiar servant, after John Brown, was an Indian known as 'the Munshi' – and in 1898, writing about the next Viceroy of India, she insisted that he must '*hear* for *himself* what the *feelings* of the natives really are, and not be guided by the *snobbish* and vulgar and overbearing and offensive behaviour of many of our Civil and Political agents.' In both style and content, it was a characteristic passage.

Writing was one of Queen Victoria's passions; she wrote endlessly and copiously to her children and descendants throughout Europe, whose marriages into foreign royal houses earned her the title of 'the Grandmother of Europe'. She took a close interest in foreign affairs, giving every encouragement to Disraeli's foreign policy, which included supporting Turkey against Russia during their war of 1876–7, and then in 1878 propping up the Balkan regime of the Ottoman Sultan. Her opposition to Gladstone increased; in 1885, when Britain's General Gordon was killed in the Sudan, attempting to hold the city of Khartoum against nationalist forces, the Queen administered a public dressing-down by sending Gladstone an uncoded telegram which rebuked his government for not aiding Gordon in time. The contents of the telegram became common knowledge, adding to the public outcry over Gordon's death.

By 1887 Queen Victoria had been on the throne for 50 years, and few of her subjects could remember another monarch. At her Diamond Jubilee, on 20 June 1897, there were scenes of wild public rejoicing; the Queen had become a revered symbol of Britain's stability and prestige, and when she drove to St Paul's Cathedral for the thanksgiving ceremony in her usual simple black dress and bonnet, shunning robes and jewels, it was a successfully dramatic touch. Amidst the splendours of prosperous, Imperial Britain, the Queen herself stood out as a small, unostentatious figure, still mourning her dead husband.

She died, appropriately perhaps, at the beginning of the 20th century, on 22 January 1901, aged 81, and was buried beside her beloved Albert in their mausoleum at Frogmore. Several of her descendants were with her when she died, but the arm which supported her was that of her grandson Kaiser Wilhelm II of Germany.

Chronology
THE HOUSE OF HANOVER

GEORGE I

1660 *28 May* Birth
1682 Marriage to Sophia Dorothea of Celle
1694 Divorce over Königsmark affair
1714 *18 Sep* George arrived in England
       Coronation
1715 Jacobite rebellion, crushed at Battle of Preston
1720 *Sep* South Sea Bubble
1727 *11 Jun* Death of George I

GEORGE II

1683 *30 Oct* Birth
1705 Marriage to Caroline of Anspach
1727 Coronation
1739 War of Jenkins' Ear with Spain
1741 War of Austrian Succession begins
1743 *Jun* Battle of Dettingen; victory against French
1745 Second Jacobite rebellion
1746 Battle of Culloden; Jacobites crushed
1748 Treaty of Aix-la-Chapelle; inconclusive peace with France
1756 Seven Years' War begins
1757 Battle of Plassey; Robert Clive secures India for Britain
1760 Battle of Montreal; conquest of Canada
     25 Oct Death of George II

GEORGE III

1738 *4 Jun* Birth
1751 Death of Prince Frederick
1761 Marriage to Charlotte of Mecklenburg-Strelitz
     Coronation
1769 James Watt patents steam engine
1770 Captain Cook discovers Australia
1775–83 American War of Independence
1776 American Declaration of Independence
1788 *Nov* Onset of George's illness
1789 French Revolution
1793 Napoleonic Wars begin
1798 Battle of the Nile; British victory
1801 Act of Union with Ireland
1802 Treaty of Amiens; temporary truce with France
1805 Battle of Trafalgar; British victory
1805 Battle of Austerlitz; Napoleonic victory in Eastern Europe
1809–14 Peninsular War
1810 Prince George appointed Regent
1815 *18 Jun* Battle of Waterloo; defeat of Napoleon by allies under Wellington
1815 Congress of Vienna; peace in Europe

1819 'Peterloo' riots
1820 *29 Jan* Death of George III

GEORGE IV

1762 *12 Aug* Birth
1795 Marriage to Caroline of Brunswick
1796 *7 Jan* Birth of Princess Charlotte
1815 Publication of Jane Austen's *Emma*, dedicated to Prince Regent
1820 Brighton Pavilion completed
1821 Coronation
     Death of Caroline of Brunswick
1829 Catholic emancipation
1830 *26 Jun* Death of George IV

WILLIAM IV

1765 *21 Aug* Birth
1818 Marriage to Adelaide of Saxe-Coburg-Meiningen
1831 Coronation
1832 Parliamentary Reform Act
1833 Abolition of slavery throughout British Empire
1837 *20 Jun* Death of William IV

VICTORIA

1819 *24 May* Birth
1838 Coronation
1840 *10 Feb* Marriage to Albert of Saxe-Coburg Gotha
     Introduction of Penny Post
1845–9 Great Famine in Ireland
1851 Great Exhibition
1854–6 Crimean War
1856–7 Indian Mutiny
1857 Albert created Prince Consort
1859 Publication of Darwin's *Origin of Species*
1861 *14 Dec* Death of Albert
1861–5 American Civil War
1868 Publication of Victoria's memoirs
1876 Victoria created Empress of India
1884 Siege of Khartoum
1897 Diamond Jubilee
1899–1902 Boer War
1901 *22 Jan* Death of Victoria

Chapter ten
THE HOUSE OF SAXE-COBURG

Edward VII 1901-10

THE FUTURE Edward VII was born on 9 November 1841, the second child and eldest son of Queen Victoria. He was christened Albert Edward, after his father, but to Queen Victoria's undisguised disappointment, 'Bertie' showed from his earliest years that he had little in common with the high-minded Prince Consort.

As a child, Bertie showed more interest in sports and amusements than in books, and his parents feared for his moral character. Prince Albert drew up a rigorous programme of education, intended to equip him for his future role as king, which even his tutors thought too severe. The result of his strict upbringing was to make forbidden pleasures seem the more attractive to the young Prince, and he grew up to be all that Prince Albert and Queen Victoria most deplored – easy-going, self-indulgent and promiscuous.

Yet, in spite of his faults, Bertie had qualities which his parents failed to appreciate. At the age of 18 he was sent on his first state visit, to Canada and the United States; Queen Victoria was most apprehensive about sending so irresponsible a young man, as she thought, to represent Britain overseas, but the Prince's trip was a great success. His charm and informality delighted his hosts; in America he tactfully visited George Washington's grave, and his friendly manners were much remarked on. So was his interest in the pretty girls who were introduced to him.

It was this interest which brought him most painfully into conflict with his strait-laced parents, on his return. Bertie was the first heir to the throne to go to university,

becoming first an Oxford undergraduate, in 1859, and then going up to Trinity, Cambridge, in 1861. Though to his regret he was not allowed to share in the ordinary college routine by 'living in', he enjoyed his taste of normal life, and he was popular with those of his fellow-students who knew him. In the summer of 1861 a further experiment was tried, and the Prince of Wales went to serve with the Grenadier Guards, on manoeuvres in southern Ireland. A group of his brother-

officers arranged for a pretty actress to be brought to him, as a surprise; but the joke misfired badly when it came to the notice of the Queen and Prince Albert. They were outraged, and when Prince Albert became ill and died soon after, the Queen harshly laid the blame on her son's misconduct. Her bad opinion of her heir had been confirmed. In spite of her widowhood, and her grief-stricken semi-retirement, she wanted Bertie to have as little part in government affairs as

GOTHA

possible, and for the next 37 years he patiently fulfilled the role of an ageing, powerless heir to an empire.

His marriage, in 1863, did much to increase his existing popularity with his mother's subjects. His bride was the 19-year-old Danish Princess Alexandra; she was later to suffer from deafness, but she was beautiful, fashionable and warm-hearted, and their marriage was a notable success, despite the Prince's constant infidelities with a series of

A still from an early film showing Edward VII at Queen Victoria's funeral.

Edward VII and Queen Alexandra.

IN EDWARD VII's ENGLAND

The Imperial State Crown, the Jewel House, Tower of London, London E1
The crown, originally made for Queen Victoria's Coronation, incorporates the 'Second Star of Africa' diamond, given to Edward VII by the Transvaal government.

Edward VII's Railway Carriage, The Railway Museum, York
The splendid railway carriage fitted up for Edward VII can be seen here.

Sandringham House, near King's Lynn, Norfolk
(*Below*)
Edward VII acquired Sandringham as his country retreat, when he was Prince of Wales; since then it has been a much-loved home for each generation of British royalty. The present house dates from 1870, and retains the stamp of Edward VII's taste. Parts of the house are open to the public, when the royal family are not in residence.

162

mistresses. One of their favourite homes was Sandringham, in Norfolk, where the Prince could indulge his passion for shooting, but they were also leading figures in London society. Apart from his enthusiasm for beautiful women, such as Lily Langtry, the Countess of Warwick and Mrs Keppel, Bertie liked the company of rich, amusing men-friends, with whom he could gamble, dine and go racing. It was a way of life which allowed him to move freely among certain groups of his future subjects, but it took its toll of his constitution and his character: he became vastly fat, and was twice involved in major scandals.

The Mordaunt affair, in 1870, was an unsavoury divorce case, in which the Prince of Wales appeared as a witness. His firm denial of Lady Mordaunt's damaging al-legation that he had been one of her lovers was accepted in court, but his association with such a case was highly undesirable. Still worse was the scandal twenty years later, when he was proved both to have taken part in the illegal gambling game of baccarat, and then – as a Field-Marshal – to have breached army Regulations by suppressing accusat-ions that one of his fellow-players, a serving officer, had cheated. The newspapers re-flected public opinion in roundly condemn-ing the future king's behaviour.

In other fields, however, the Prince earned widespread approval, both at home and abroad. His gregariousness was one of his most attractive qualities; he liked to meet people of all types and backgrounds, from the Italian guerrilla leader Garibaldi, who visited London in 1864, to the early Trades Union leader Joseph Arch. On a state visit to India in 1875 he was critical of the attitude displayed towards the Indian people by certain colonial officials (though he disapproved of the suggestion that Indians should be allowed to join the ruling Council). As an unofficial roving diplomat, with unique access to the crowned heads and government ministers of the world, he tried sincerely to work for peace, at a time of mounting tensions in Europe.

In 1901 Queen Victoria died, and Bertie became King at last, at the advanced age of 59. His stout, bearded, cigar-smoking figure was often lampooned, but he and Queen Alexandra achieved great popularity, not least through the King's peacemaking efforts. His state visit to France, in 1903, marked the beginning of a new chapter in Anglo-French relations – a situation which did not endear him to his nephew the Kaiser of Germany, though Edward VII frequently visited Berlin too. A meeting with another of his numerous ruling relations, the Tsar of

The Delhi Durbar of 1903 – the state entry of the Viceroy, Lord Curzon.

Russia, was strongly citicised by the left wing in Britain; it was a time of political op-pression in Russia, and several MPs spoke out against the visit. But in general the King's own political views were relatively liberal; he had always liked Gladstone, and he far preferred the Liberal Sir Henry Campbell-Bannerman, to the Conservative Prime Minister Arthur Balfour – though the more radical views of the young Winston Churchill and David Lloyd George were not to his liking. In the grave political crisis which arose in the last year of his life, with the rejection of a Liberal budget by the strongly Conservative House of Lords, Edward VII was not in sympathy with either side, but did all he could to bring the opponents together, by arranging dis-cussions between the party leaders.

Over-indulgence in life's pleasures, such as eating and smoking, had weakened the King's constitution, and the strain of this Parliamentary crisis finally proved too much for him. On 6 May 1910, aged 68, he died; and the colourful, high-spirited era to which he had given his name gave way to a grimmer chapter in Britain's history.

Chapter eleven
THE HOUSE OF WINDSOR

George V 1910-36

FROM THE time of his birth, on 3 June 1865, until the summer of 1917, the first monarch of the House of Windsor bore the names George Frederick Ernest Albert of Saxe-Coburg Gotha. As the younger son of the Prince and Princess of Wales, with an elder brother to inherit the throne, he grew up free from the knowledge of his future responsibilities, and his boyhood was unusually happy for a royal child.

With his elder brother and three sisters Prince George was brought up chiefly at Sandringham, in Norfolk, with trips to the royal residences in London and Scotland. Princess Alexandra, whom he called 'Motherdear' all his life, was an intensely affectionate mother, and Prince George and his brother Albert Victor, known as 'Eddy', were close boyhood friends, despite great differences of character. They shared a tutor, the Reverend John Dalton, and in 1877 they were both sent to Dartmouth as naval cadets. It was an unusual step, and one which Queen Victoria thought unsuitable, but Prince George in particular benefited from it. Once the early problems of shyness and teasing had been overcome he became popular with the other cadets, and he found that he had a real love of the naval life.

Prince Eddy later went into the army, but Prince George stayed on in the Royal Navy, and by 1891 he had been promoted Commander. But a year later his promising career was dramatically cut short – in January 1892 Eddy caught pneumonia, and died.

It was a terrible family tragedy, yet in the long term it may have been a blessing for Britain and the Empire. Instead of Eddy, who had been a somewhat shadowy character, with a reputation for loose living, the sober, responsible and dutiful Prince George now prepared to inherit the throne. With Eddy's role he also took on his fiancée; shortly before the elder prince died he had been betrothed to Princess 'May' of Teck, a steady girl chosen for her character and good influence. It was now agreed that she should marry the new heir instead, and their wedding took place in July 1893. The bride, the future Queen Mary, was not given to

A detail from a painting of the coronation of George V in 1910.

displaying her emotions, but she was the ideal consort for the rather reserved Prince George, and they found much happiness together. Their first child, Prince Edward – afterwards Edward VIII – was born within the year, and four more sons and a daughter followed.

Edward VII was determined that his heir should not be excluded from the affairs of government as he had been. He made sure that the Prince saw state papers, did plenty of public speaking and undertook royal tours throughout the Empire. Nevertheless, when King Edward died in 1910, the new King George V was left with an acute sense of loss,

heightened by the knowledge that he was ascending the throne at a particularly tense moment in history.

He inherited the political crisis which had begun with the Lords' veto of the Liberal budget. The Commons had introduced the Parliament Bill, aimed at limiting the power of the Lords, and the result was a dangerous confrontation between the two Houses. Caught between the two sides, the King became unwillingly involved in a political issue; he had little choice but to agree to a

An unusually light-hearted photograph of George, Duke of York, aged about 27.

request from the Liberal Prime Minister, Asquith, that if necessary he would create dozens of new peers, to produce a Liberal majority in the Lords.

From this difficult situation the King and Queen set off for India at the end of 1911, to preside over a Coronation Durbar, or public audience; and they returned in 1912 to a deeply troubled Britain. There were industrial relations problems, with widespread strikes, and the pioneers of women's rights, the Suffragettes, were facing great public hostility in their struggle to win the vote for women; King George himself, though no supporter of their cause, disapproved of their harsh prison treatment. But from 1912 onwards two dangerous and potentially tragic situations came to overshadow all others – the question of Irish Home Rule, and the looming conflict in Europe.

RIGHT   George V with the Prince of Wales in France during World War I.

The royal family entering St Paul's Cathedral for the Silver Jubilee service of thanksgiving, 1935.

In the struggle between demands for Irish independence and Conservative and Unionist fears for Ulster's Loyalist Protestant population, King George tried to keep a balance. He feared that there would be civil war in Ireland, and was deeply troubled; he arranged for an all-party conference at Buckingham Palace, in July 1914, between representatives of the different factions involved. It was a constructive, if unsuccessful, move. Within two months, however, Europe was at war, and the problems of Ireland were temporarily overwhelmed.

George v worked tirelessly for Britain's war effort, inspecting troops and awarding medals, visiting hospitals, encouraging people at home and visiting his armies in Flanders. In 1917, when anti-German feeling in England was at fever-pitch, he took the step of giving up his family name of Saxe-Coburg Gotha, which Prince Albert had brought to Britain's royal line. Despite his

The Delhi Durbar of 1911 – George v and Queen Mary show themselves to the people of India.

IN GEORGE V's ENGLAND

King George V's and Queen Mary's Tomb,
St George's Chapel, Windsor, Berkshire
On a sarcophagus designed by Lutyens, the pale stone effigies of King George V and Queen Mary lie side by side, modelled by Sir William Reid Dick.

Queen Mary's Dolls' House, Windsor Castle, Berkshire
(*Below*)
This remarkable work of art and craftsmanship was presented to Queen Mary by the nation, to be used on her behalf to collect funds for charity. Designed by Sir Edwin Lutyens, its contents – made precisely to scale – include a gunroom with tiny shotguns, and a library with real miniature books commissioned from famous authors of the time.

Chronology

EDWARD VII

1841	*9 Nov* Birth
1859	Undergraduate at Oxford University
1860	State visit to Canada and United States of America
1861	Undergraduate at Cambridge University
1863	Marriage to Princess Alexandra of Denmark
1875	State visit to India
1902	Coronation
1903	State visit to France; Anglo-French entente
1910	*6 May* Death of Edward VII

GEORGE V

1865	*3 Jun* Birth
1877	Cadet at Dartmouth
1892	*Jan* Death of brother, Prince Albert Victor
1893	*Jul* Marriage to Princess Mary (May) of Teck
1911	Coronation Coronation Durbar in India Parliament Act limiting power of House of Lords
1914	Home Rule Bill for Ireland
1914–18	World War I
1916	Easter Rising in Dublin Battle of Jutland; severe British and German naval losses Somme; British offensive Conscription introduced
1917	Royal family name changed to Windsor United States of America enters war October Revolution in Russia
1919	Treaty of Versailles
1926	General Strike
1932	First royal Christmas broadcast
1935	Silver Jubilee
1936	*20 Jan* Death of George V

German ancestry, King George was entirely British in his outlook; he had had little affection for his cousin the Kaiser, even before the war, and he even disliked the German language when he had to learn it as a schoolboy. He now changed his name without great regret, and took instead the name of the ancient royal residence of Windsor, which the British monarchy still bears.

In the victorious, but battered, Britain which emerged from the devastation of the Great War to face the 20th century, the King remained a reassuring symbol of stability. George V constantly advocated conciliation, whether he was addressing the Parliament of the newly-formed Ulster or attempting to restrain Baldwin from over-reacting to the General Strike of 1926.

Undoubtedly the king's sympathies were not with the strikers (though he had no time for exploitative bosses either); he was more of a diehard Conservative than his father had been. Yet he faced the prospect of Britain's first Labour government with equanimity. On 22 January 1924 he wrote, 'Today 23 years ago dear Grandmama [Queen Victoria] died. I wonder what she would have thought of a Labour government!' In the depressed Thirties he chose to give up part of his Civil List income, and in 1931 he encouraged the formation of a coalition, the National Government.

King George V and Queen Mary never courted popularity; they were not glamorous or fashionable figures, and the King – whose personal tastes were for stamp-collecting and sailing – often felt out of step with the Jazz Age Britain of the Thirties. Yet to many of their subjects they represented stability and solid virtues in a changing world, and they were greatly loved. At the celebrations for their Silver Jubilee, in 1935, the King was surprised by the warmth with which the crowds received them. 'I had no idea I was so popular', he remarked.

He was the first monarch to make Christmas broadcasts to the nation; and it was over the wireless that his approaching death was announced early in 1936, with the words, 'The King's life is moving peacefully to its close'. He died on 20 January 1936, at Sandringham, greatly mourned.

Edward VIII 1936

IN HIS ELDEST son, Edward Albert Christian George Andrew Patrick David, King George V seemed to have the ideal successor. The Prince, who was 'David' to his family, was handsome, charming and refreshingly modern in his outlook; yet he also seemed genuinely concerned with the social problems of post-war Britain. As Prince of Wales, David was an unqualified success; as King Edward VIII he was to be a near-disaster.

He was born on 23 June 1894 at White Lodge in Richmond Park, and spent much of his childhood at his parents' favourite home, York Cottage, in the grounds of Sandringham. He had a strict upbringing; his father was a disciplinarian, and his mother, Queen Mary, did not express her feelings easily. In 1907 the prince began his naval training at Osborne, and he then moved on to Dartmouth, but the death of his grandfather in 1910 temporarily interrupted his Dartmouth studies. He was now the heir to the throne, and in July 1911 he was invested as Prince of Wales in Caernarvon Castle.

After two years at Magdalen College, Oxford, where he enjoyed the sports and social life but achieved little academically, the Prince went into the Grenadier Guards on the outbreak of World War I. A lack of physical courage was never one of his faults; he was desperately keen to be allowed to serve at the Front, and resented being restricted to staff appointments, even though these took him to France, Suez and the Italian front.

In peacetime, the Prince still found himself subjected to restraints, not least where dangerous activities were concerned; he took up the breakneck sport of steeplechasing, but was pressured into giving it up by his father, and his interest in flying was also discouraged. However, he was kept busy with a full programme of royal duties. An official visit to Canada in HMS Renown, in the company of his friend and second cousin Lord Louis Mountbatten, was highly successful, and tours to Australia, New Zealand and India followed. But the country where he felt most at home was the United States of America. The luxurious yet informal American way of life, and the warmth of the people, appealed to him as they had to his grandfather Edward VII, and after his second visit, in 1924, it was noticed that he had even adopted Americanisms in his speech. The gulf between the Prince and his more conventional father and brothers was widening.

The King made no secret of his disapproval of his son's circle of friends, who were mostly sophisticated and fun-loving. The Prince liked nightclubs, such as the fashionable Embassy, in Berkeley Street; he liked smart clothes, and set a few fashions of his own, notably for Prince of Wales checks, and ties with the new 'Windsor knot'; he liked elegant, mature women, and his affairs with Lady Furness and Mrs Freda Dudley Ward were no secret in London society. Unfortunately for the future of the House of Windsor, the Prince of Wales seemed only

A watercolour of Edward VIII by Sickert.

Edward as Prince of Wales talking to miners in South Wales in 1936.

169

interested in women with previous marriages; suitable young girls did not attract him.

Just as King George V and Queen Mary's favourite home was the relatively small and simple York Cottage, at Sandringham, so the Prince's preferred retreat was the 18th-century Fort Belvedere, near Sunningdale in Berkshire, which his father gave him in 1930. Looking somewhat like a miniature mock-castle outside, but luxuriously modernised inside, the Fort, as he called it, was the setting for some of the Prince's happiest hours. There he could relax with gardening and golf; there he could enjoy his friends' company in privacy; and there, from 1931 onwards, he frequently entertained the woman whom he had come to adore – Mrs Wallis Warfield Simpson.

Mrs Simpson, a chic, charming, twice-married American in her mid-thirties, was already becoming estranged from her second husband when she entered the Prince's life. Ernest Simpson, an American who had taken British nationality, proved complaisant about his wife's affair with the heir to the throne, but others, as the Prince knew, would not be. For a time it was kept out of the British press, though foreign newspapers discussed it excitedly, printing photographs of the couple together whenever possible; gradually, however, the British public came to hear of it. By 1934 the Prince was determined to marry Mrs Simpson, divorcee or not, and once he had become King, in 1936, the issue almost provoked a constitutional crisis.

'King's Moll Reno'd in Wolsey's Home Town!' one American newspaper blared, when Mrs Simpson's divorce from Ernest Simpson was granted at Ipswich, in 1936. In Britain, the new King continued to receive glowing publicity for visiting the unemployed of South Wales, and for his evident concern at the state of the poor in the depressed areas. But his passion for Mrs Simpson was distracting him from his duties; behind the ever-charming, popular façade, the selfish and headstrong side of the King's character was causing alarm to the Prime Minister and the Cabinet. Though an American queen might have been welcome, a woman with two husbands living could not be the consort of the Head of the English Church. In November, the King told his Prime Minister, Stanley Baldwin, that if he could not marry her, he was 'prepared to go'.

He still had considerable sympathy among his subjects; and Lord Beaverbrook, the powerful newspaper magnate, believed that a morganatic marriage, by which Mrs Simpson would become the King's legal wife, but not his Queen, might be possible. Mrs Simpson herself stated that she was willing to retire altogether from the situation; this, however, the King could not contemplate. By 4 December the newspapers were talking of abdication; on 10 December the king announced to Parliament that he had that morning signed an Instrument of Abdication; on the morning of December 11 it was passed by Parliament. An Independent MP's proposed amendment that the monarchy should be done away with altogether was massively defeated.

That evening the former King broadcast to the nation, explaining his reasons for quitting public affairs, with the historic phrase, 'I have found it impossible to carry the heavy burden of responsibility ... without the help and support of the woman I love'. His brother the Duke of York now became King George VI; as such he created the former Edward VIII Duke of Windsor. To the former king's anger,

the title of 'Royal Highness' was not granted to his wife, though he insisted that it should be used at all times, despite the ban.

On 3 June 1937 the Duke of Windsor and Mrs Simpson were married in France, at the Château de Candé. They made their home for most of their lives in France, with regular trips abroad. One of these, to Berlin, in 1937, included a meeting with Hitler, which added to disquieting speculation that the Duke's politics were far too favourable to the Nazi ideology. After war broke out, in 1939, he was anxious to serve his native country, and was appointed Governor of the Bahamas.

The rest of the former king's life became a somewhat purposeless round of golf, travel and entertaining, and he never fulfilled the promise of his golden youth. During his last illness, in 1972, his niece, Queen Elizabeth II, demonstrated the continuing family ties by visiting him in France. For his funeral the Duchess of Windsor came over to England, and stayed as a guest in Buckingham Palace, where she might have presided as Queen. In death, the Duke was reunited with his royal forbears; he lies by Queen Victoria's mausoleum at Frogmore.

LEFT The Duke and Duchess of Windsor on their wedding day at the Château de Candé.

RIGHT The Windsors in their Paris home.

171

George VI 1936-52

IN DECEMBER 1936, for the second time in two generations, a younger son succeeded to the British throne. But there was little resemblance between the situations of the two Georges; whereas King George V had 18 years of preparation for his future role, his son King George VI had kingship thrust upon him. Yet, in marked contrast to his abdicated elder brother, he was inspired by a strong sense of duty, and he had the support and encouragement of an exceptional consort.

Albert Frederick Arthur George, as he was christened, was born on 14 December 1895, at Sandringham. He had a traumatic childhood; not only did he suffer from gastric illnesses and weak legs, for which he was made to wear splints, but he stuttered badly, possibly as a result of his father's insistence that he should be forced to write with his right hand, though naturally left-handed. At the naval training colleges of Osborne and Dartmouth he showed little academic ability; he proved a courageous and conscientious young officer, however, and in 1916 he took part in the Battle of Jutland, as a sub-lieutenant in HMS Collingwood. In 1917 his poor health obliged him to leave the navy, and he served in the Royal Naval Air Service for a spell before joining the newly-created Royal Air Force and qualifying as a pilot.

After a year at Trinity College, Cambridge, he began to play a part in public life. 'Bertie', as he was known to his family, was always overshadowed by his handsome, extrovert brother David, the heir to the throne, yet he acquired his own popularity among his father's subjects. As Duke of York he showed an interest in welfare projects and industrial conditions, and he set up the Duke of York's camps, which aimed to bring the different social classes together for outdoor activities such as hiking, camping and fireside singsongs. But the Duke's role in life seemed to take on a new meaning when he married a daughter of the Earl of Strathmore, Lady Elizabeth Bowes-Lyon, in April 1923 in Westminster Abbey.

The new Duchess of York won all hearts, from the severe old king's downwards. Her warm, outgoing personality – the result of a happy and informal childhood in Scotland – was allied to great strength of character, which enabled her to help her more diffident husband to overcome many of his problems,

most notably the stammer which had always dogged him, making public speaking of any kind an ordeal. The Duchess helped to bring her husband closer to King George V and Queen Mary; and the family bonds were sealed by the birth of the Duke and Duchess's two children, the Princess Elizabeth in 1926 and the Princess Margaret Rose in 1930.

In 1936 the tranquillity of their family life was disrupted for ever by the abdication of Edward VIII. The Duke of York told his cousin, Lord Louis Mountbatten, 'This is absolutely terrible … I'm quite unprepared for it', but added, 'I will do my best to clear up the inevitable mess'. He was crowned on the day set for his brother's coronation, 12 May

1937, and to emphasise the continuity of the royal line, took the name, not of Albert I, but of George VI.

George VI, like many of his subjects, at first shared Neville Chamberlain's hopes that war with Germany might be avoided. But as it became clear that there could be no peaceful settlement, the King dedicated himself to the war effort, and in the spring of 1939 he and Queen Elizabeth went on an official visit to the United States, to ensure American friendship in the coming conflict.

'Today we are at war again, and I am no longer a midshipman in the Royal Navy', the King wrote in his diary on 3 September 1939. But though he could not take part in

Queen Elizabeth with the Princesses Elizabeth and Margaret, 1937.

RIGHT   King George VI.

172

IN GEORGE VI's BRITAIN

George VI's Shooting Brake, Sandringham Museum, near King's Lynn, Norfolk
(*Right*)

This custom-made Daimler, built in 1937, was used by George VI while out shooting.

Glamis Castle, Angus, Scotland
(*Below*)

In this historic and beautiful castle, already old when the Old Pretender stayed there in 1716, King George VI's consort Queen Elizabeth (now the Queen Mother) was brought up. Princess Margaret was born there. Still the seat of the Queen Mother's family, the Earls of Strathmore, the castle is open to the public.

King George VI Memorial Chapel, St George's Chapel, Windsor, Berkshire

This Chapel, in the north choir aisle, was dedicated in 1969. King George VI's body lies here under a simple black stone.

the action, as he had in the First World War, at Jutland, he had a still more valuable role to play. He and the Queen worked tirelessly and bravely; they stayed in London despite the Blitz, and when Buckingham Palace was bombed, the Queen commented cheerfully that she was glad, as 'it makes me feel I can look the East End in the face'. As well as visiting bomb victims, factories and countless Home Guard units in Britain, the King flew to North Africa, and went to Malta; he wished to sail with his forces on D-Day, but was overridden. When the war in Europe came to an end at last, on 8 May 1945, the crowds in London flocked to Buckingham Palace, where the King and royal family came out again and again onto the balcony, to share in the nation's joy. The Princesses were allowed to go down and mingle,

unrecognised, with the cheering, singing throng.

In the early days of the war, George VI had been cool towards Winston Churchill, but he had soon forged a deep bond with the great Prime Minister. It was the same with the post-war Labour leader, Clement Attlee; after a slow start, the King came to like Attlee, though no socialist himself.

However well King George VI fulfilled his unlooked-for role as King and Emperor, there was no doubt that it took its toll of his health. In 1947 he undertook a royal tour of South Africa and Rhodesia, saw his daughter and heir the Princess Elizabeth married to Lieutenant Philip Mountbatten, and presided over a momentous event, the granting of Independence to India and the newly-created Pakistan. The appearance of norm-

The royal family and Winston Churchill wave to the crowds from the balcony at Buckingham Palace on VE Day, 1945.

ality was kept up, but in the following year, after celebrating his Silver Wedding anniversary with the Queen, he became very ill with arterio-sclerosis, which was undoubtedly worsened by strain.

The last Emperor of India lived to open the Festival of Britain, in 1951, and see the birth of his daughter's heir Prince Charles and his granddaughter Princess Anne, but by the beginning of 1952 he was fatally ill with cancer, and he died in his sleep, at Sandringham, early on 6 February. He had, magnificently, 'cleared up the mess' created by his elder brother's abdication, and re-created a stable, secure monarchy.

Elizabeth II
1952–

WHEN THE Princess Elizabeth, first child of the Duke and Duchess of York, was born on 21 April 1926, there seemed little prospect that she would become Queen. In 1936, however, her uncle King Edward VIII abdicated, to be succeeded by her father as King George VI, and the 10-year-old princess became the heir presumptive to the British throne.

The Princess had a happy, if sheltered, upbringing. With her sister Margaret Rose, four years her junior, she was educated at home, first by governesses, later by the Provost of Eton. Though her opportunities to mix with other children were somewhat

limited, she and her sister had a great deal of fun together; they had a miniature house of their own to play in, given by the people of Wales, and they put on Christmas pantomimes at Windsor, in which Princess Elizabeth took the part of the Principal Boy. Country sports and riding were among Princess Elizabeth's favourite occupations, and she is reputed to have said that if she were not a future queen, she would have liked to be 'a lady living in the country, with lots of horses and dogs'.

During the war years the Princesses were sent away from the bombing, like many London children, and Windsor Castle became their base. At the beginning of 1945, when she was 19, Princess Elizabeth persuaded her father to let her do National Service, like other girls, and as Second

LEFT   Princess Elizabeth at the age of 16, shortly after becoming Colonel of the Grenadier Guards.

BELOW   The coronation of Queen Elizabeth II in 1953.

RIGHT   The famous portrait of Queen Elizabeth by Pietro Annigoni.

176

IN ELIZABETH II's BRITAIN

Broadlands House, near Romsey, Hampshire (*Below*)
The home of Earl Mountbatten of Burma, Prince Philip's uncle, until his death in 1979. Here the Queen and Prince Philip spent part of their honeymoon, and here too Prince Charles brought his bride for the first few days of their honeymoon, in 1981. Broadlands is open to the public.

The Queen's Gallery, Buckingham Palace, London SW1
The only part of Buckingham Palace which the general public may visit, the Queen's Gallery houses regular exhibitions of works of art from the royal collections. The present Queen instituted the Gallery in 1965.

The Royal Mews, Buckingham Palace, London SW1
The Mews is home to the Queen's horses in London; here also can be seen the spectacular state coaches and landaus, including the Glass Coach used at Prince Charles's wedding, and the Gold State Coach in which the Queen drives to the State opening of Parliament. The Mews can be visited by previous arrangement with Buckingham Palace.

Castle of Mey, near John O'Groats, Sutherland, Scotland
Queen Elizabeth the Queen Mother bought this castle when it was badly dilapidated; since then she has restored it, and stays here regularly. A skilful gardener, the Queen Mother has created beautiful gardens below the Castle, which the public may visit.

Lieutenant Elizabeth Windsor she became a useful driver in the ATS. With the end of the war came a still greater change in her life: she had fallen in love.

The young man was her third cousin, Prince Philip of Greece. His mother was a sister of Lord Louis Mountbatten, his father the deposed Prince Andrew of Greece. Prince Philip, who had been born in Corfu in 1921, was educated at the Scottish public school of Gordonstoun, and largely brought up by his uncle Lord Louis; he looked on Britain as his home. During the war he had served with the Royal Navy, being mentioned in dispatches, and he planned to make his career at sea. He

and the Princess had first met as children, but during the war their paths crossed again, and friendship turned to attraction and love. The King was anxious that his daughter should not make a hasty decision, when she had met so few young men; he persuaded her to wait until after her 21st birthday. But the couple's feelings did not change, and with the blessing of the King and Queen, their engagement was announced on 10 July 1947. The wedding of the heir to the throne took place in Westminster Abbey on 20 November, and just a year later their first son, Prince Charles, was born. Before King George VI died in 1952, he had seen his

ABOVE Prince Philip, the Duke of Edinburgh, driving a team of bays in the Royal Windsor Horse Show, 1976.

Queen Elizabeth, the Duke of Edinburgh, the Queen Mother, Prince Charles and other Knights of the Garter leaving St. George's Chapel, Windsor Castle after the Garter Ceremony.

daughter happily and securely established, with a supportive, yet strong-minded consort beside her, and a son and daughter of her own to secure the succession.

The princess was visiting Kenya when her father died, and she at once flew home to take up her new duties. She was then 25, the same age as her namesake Elizabeth I had been at her accession. Though there were few outward resemblances between the two queens, they shared a willingness to make themselves personally accessible to their subjects – Elizabeth I by constant royal progresses throughout her kingdom, Elizabeth II through the modern means of television, film and radio, as well as constant visits all over Britain, at which the innovation of 'walkabouts', during which the Sovereign would stop and speak to members of the crowds, was introduced. At Buckingham Palace, the archaic presentation of debutantes to the sovereign was discontinued, and large summer garden-parties, to which people from all walks of life were invited, were held. Without ever compromising the dignity of the monarchy, Elizabeth II brought it up to date.

Chronology

EDWARD VIII

1894	*23 Jun* Birth
1911	*Jul* Investiture as Prince of Wales
1936	Accession
1936	*11 Dec* Abdication Created Duke of Windsor
1937	*3 Jun* Marriage to Mrs Simpson
1939	Appointment as Governor of Bahamas
1972	Death of Edward

GEORGE VI

1895	*14 Dec* Birth
1916	Fights in Battle of Jutland
1923	*Apr* Marriage to Lady Elizabeth Bowes-Lyon
1926	Birth of Princess Elizabeth
1930	Birth of Princess Margaret
1936	Spanish Civil War
1937	*12 May* Coronation
1938	German annexation of Austria
1939	Hitler attacks Poland
1939–45	World War II
1941	Japanese attack Pearl Harbour Entry of United States of America into war
1944	Allied landing in Normandy
1945	Atomic bombs on Hiroshima and Nagasaki; surrender of Japan United Nations charter
1947	Independence of India and Pakistan
1949	North Atlantic Treaty Proclamation of Republic of Eire
1951	Festival of Britain
1952	*6 Feb* Death of George VI

ELIZABETH II

1926	*21 Apr* Birth
1945	Serves in ATS
1947	*20 Nov* Marriage to Prince Philip of Greece
1948	Birth of Prince Charles
1950	Birth of Princess Anne
1952	Accession to the throne
1953	Coronation
1956	Suez crisis
1960	Birth of Prince Andrew
1964	Birth of Prince Edward
1965	Rhodesian Unilateral Declaration of Independence
1971	Britain agreed to enter European Economic Community
1973	Marriage of Princess Anne to Captain Mark Phillips
1978	Silver Jubilee
1979	*27 Aug* Assassination of Earl Mountbatten of Burma
1981	*29 Jul* Marriage of Prince Charles to Lady Diana Spencer
1982	Falklands crisis *21 Jun* Birth of Prince William of Wales

For the first time, an heir to the British throne was sent away to school; at Gordonstoun, his father's old school in Scotland, Prince Charles mixed normally with other boys, and he went on to experience ordinary undergraduate life at Trinity College, Cambridge, before following royal tradition and entering the Royal Navy. The experiment was a success, and both his younger brothers – Prince Andrew, born in 1960, and Prince Edward, born in 1964 – followed him to Gordonstoun, while Princess Anne was sent to the girls' public school Benenden.

The young Queen took her function as Head of the Commonwealth intensely seriously; whether hosting conferences for the Commonwealth leaders, or travelling extensively among the various countries, she gave the role an identity and an importance which helped to maintain the ties between an increasingly separate group of independent nations. As Britain's monarch she retained considerable political powers – such as the right, if necessary, to appoint a Prime Minister if a General Election should result in stalemate – but these, by mutual consent, would only be used in consultation with others, never as the expression of a private preference. Its political neutrality is one of the modern monarchy's greatest strengths.

Public opinion polls taken during the reign of Queen Elizabeth II show a remarkable rise in the popularity of the monarchy. The voices of the critics, such as the Labour MP Willie Hamilton, have tended to be drowned by the cheering of the crowds: as the celebrations for Elizabeth II's Silver Jubilee in 1977, and the wedding of Prince Charles and Lady Diana Spencer in 1981, demonstrated, the British monarchy has the overwhelming support of the nation. In an unstable world the continuing presence of a responsible, dutiful, politically neutral Head of State undoubtedly fulfils an important need.

In Britain, the monarchy has a long and eventful past, but it also has a future. With the birth of the Prince and Princess of Wales's first child, Prince William of Wales, on 21 June 1982, that future seems happily assured.

TOP The royal family on the balcony at Buckingham Palace after Prince Charles's wedding on 29 July 1981.

BOTTOM The royal yacht *Britannia*, used by the royal family for their voyages throughout the world.

THE NORMANS AND ANGEVINS

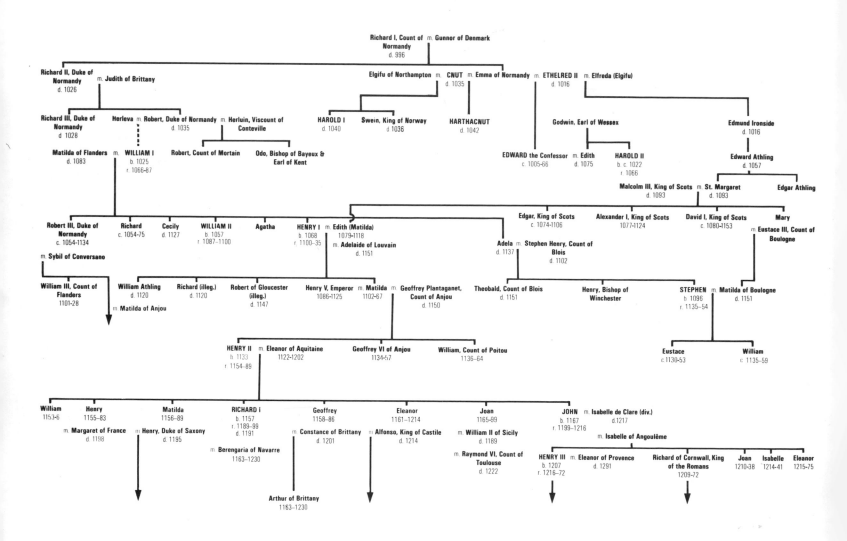

THE PLANTAGENETS

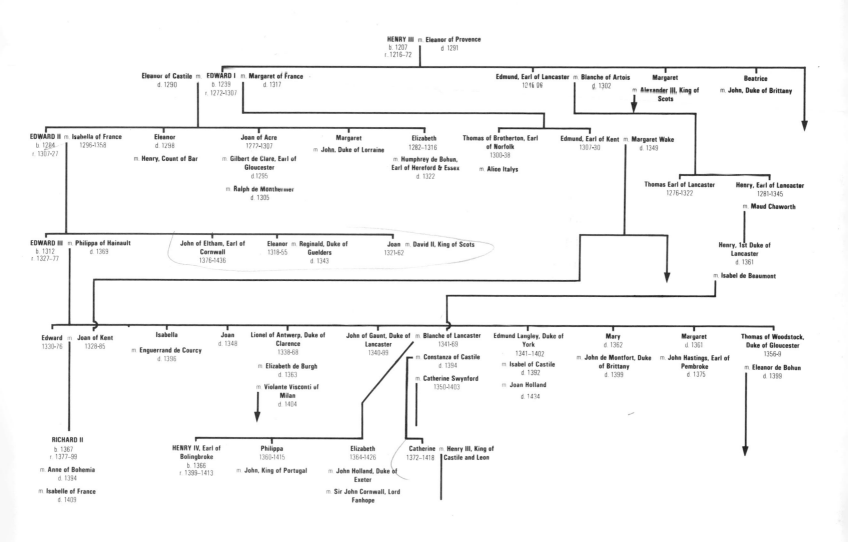

HENRY III m. **Eleanor of Provence**
b. 1207   d. 1291
r. 1216–72

Eleanor of Castile m. **EDWARD I** m. **Margaret of France**
d. 1290   b. 1239   d. 1317
r. 1272–1307

Edmund, Earl of Lancaster m. **Blanche of Artois**   **Margaret**   **Beatrice**
1246–96   d. 1302   m. **Alexander III, King of**   m. **John, Duke of Brittany**
                                    Scots

EDWARD II m. **Isabella of France**   **Eleanor**   **Joan of Acre**   **Margaret**   **Elizabeth**
b. 1284   1296–1358   d. 1298   1272–1307   m. **John, Duke of Lorraine**   1282–1316
r. 1307–27

m. **Henry, Count of Bar**   m. **Gilbert de Clare, Earl of**   m. **Humphrey de Bohun,**
                                 Gloucester   Earl of Hereford & Essex
                                 d.1295   d. 1322

                         m. **Ralph de Monthermer**
                            d. 1305

Thomas of Brotherton, Earl   **Edmund, Earl of Kent** m. **Margaret Wake**
of Norfolk   1307–30   d. 1349
1300–38

m. **Alice Italys**

Thomas Earl of Lancaster   **Henry, Earl of Lancaster**
1276-1322   1281-1345

                                 m. **Maud Chaworth**

EDWARD III m. **Philippa of Hainault**   **John of Eltham, Earl of**   **Eleanor** m. **Reginald, Duke of**   **Joan** m. **David II, King of Scots**
b. 1312   d. 1369   Cornwall   1318-55   Guelders   1321-62
r. 1327–77   1376-1436   d. 1343

Henry, 1st Duke of
Lancaster
d. 1361

m. **Isabel de Beaumont**

Edward m. **Joan of Kent**   **Isabella**   **Joan** **Lionel of Antwerp, Duke of**   **John of Gaunt, Duke of** m. **Blanche of Lancaster**   **Edmund Langley, Duke of**   **Mary**   **Margaret**   **Thomas of Woodstock,**
1330-76   1328-85   m. **Enguerrand de Courcy**   d. 1348   Clarence   Lancaster   1341-69   York   d. 1362   d. 1361   Duke of Gloucester
                         d. 1396   1338-68   1340-99   1341–1402   1356-9

                                           m. **Elizabeth de Burgh**   m. **Constanza of Castile**   m. **Isabel of Castile**   m. **John de Montfort, Duke**   m. **John Hastings, Earl of**   m. **Eleanor de Bohun**
                                              d. 1363   d. 1394   d. 1392   of Brittany   Pembroke   d. 1399
                                                                                                                             d. 1399   d. 1375
                                           m. **Violante Visconti of**   m. **Catherine Swynford**
                                              Milan   1350-1403   m. **Joan Holland**
                                              d. 1404   d. 1434

RICHARD II
b. 1367
r. 1377–99

m. **Anne of Bohemia**
d. 1394

m. **Isabelle of France**
d. 1409

HENRY IV, Earl of   **Philippa**   **Elizabeth**   **Catherine** m. **Henry III, King of**
Bolingbroke   1360-1415   1364-1426   1372–1418   Castile and Leon
b. 1366
r. 1399–1413   m. **John, King of Portugal**   m. **John Holland, Duke of**
                                           Exeter

                                        m. **Sir John Cornwall, Lord**
                                           Fanhope

183

THE HOUSE OF LANCASTER AND YORK

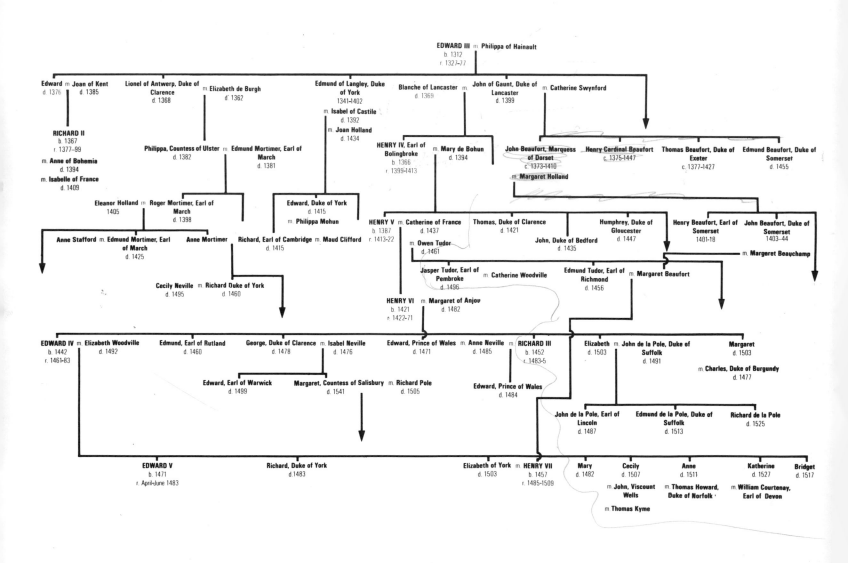

EDWARD III m Philippa of Hainault
b. 1312
r. 1327-77

Edward m Joan of Kent — d. 1376 / d. 1385

Lionel of Antwerp, Duke of Clarence d. 1368 — m Elizabeth de Burgh d. 1362

Edmund of Langley, Duke of York 1341-1402 — m. Isabel of Castile d. 1392 — m. Joan Holland d. 1434

Blanche of Lancaster d. 1369 — m — John of Gaunt, Duke of Lancaster d. 1399 — m Catherine Swynford

RICHARD II b. 1367 r. 1377-99 — m. Anne of Bohemia d. 1394 — m. Isabelle of France d. 1409

Philippa, Countess of Ulster d. 1382 — m Edmund Mortimer, Earl of March d. 1381

HENRY IV, Earl of Bolingbroke b. 1366 r. 1399-1413 — m. Mary de Bohun d. 1394

John Beaufort, Marquess of Dorset c. 1373-1410 — m. Margaret Holland

Henry Cardinal Beaufort c. 1375-1447

Thomas Beaufort, Duke of Exeter c. 1377-1427

Edmund Beaufort, Duke of Somerset d. 1455

Eleanor Holland 1405 — m Roger Mortimer, Earl of March d. 1398

Edward, Duke of York d. 1415 — m. Philippa Mohun

Anne Stafford m Edmund Mortimer, Earl of March d. 1425

Anne Mortimer

Richard, Earl of Cambridge m Maud Clifford d. 1415

HENRY V b. 1387 r. 1413-22 — m. Catherine of France d. 1437 — m. Owen Tudor d. 1461

Thomas, Duke of Clarence d. 1421

Humphrey, Duke of Gloucester d. 1447

John, Duke of Bedford d. 1435

Henry Beaufort, Earl of Somerset 1401-18

John Beaufort, Duke of Somerset 1403-44 — m. Margaret Beauchamp

Cecily Neville d. 1495 — m Richard Duke of York d. 1460

Jasper Tudor, Earl of Pembroke d. 1496 — m Catherine Woodville

Edmund Tudor, Earl of Richmond d. 1456 — m Margaret Beaufort

HENRY VI b. 1421 r. 1422-71 — m. Margaret of Anjou d. 1482

EDWARD IV b. 1442 r. 1461-83 — m. Elizabeth Woodville d. 1492

Edmund, Earl of Rutland d. 1460

George, Duke of Clarence d. 1478 — m. Isabel Neville d. 1476

Edward, Prince of Wales d. 1471 — m. Anne Neville d. 1485 — m RICHARD III b. 1452 r. 1483-5

Elizabeth d. 1503 — m. John de la Pole, Duke of Suffolk d. 1491

Margaret d. 1503 — m. Charles, Duke of Burgundy d. 1477

Edward, Earl of Warwick d. 1499

Margaret, Countess of Salisbury d. 1541 — m. Richard Pole d. 1505

Edward, Prince of Wales d. 1484

John de la Pole, Earl of Lincoln d. 1487

Edmund de la Pole, Duke of Suffolk d. 1513

Richard de la Pole d. 1525

EDWARD V b. 1471 r. April-June 1483

Richard, Duke of York d. 1483

Elizabeth of York d. 1503 — m. HENRY VII b. 1457 r. 1485-1509

Mary d. 1482

Cecily d. 1507 — m. John, Viscount Wells — m. Thomas Kyme

Anne d. 1511 — m. Thomas Howard, Duke of Norfolk

Katherine d. 1527 — m. William Courtenay, Earl of Devon

Bridget d. 1517

184

THE TUDORS AND STUARTS

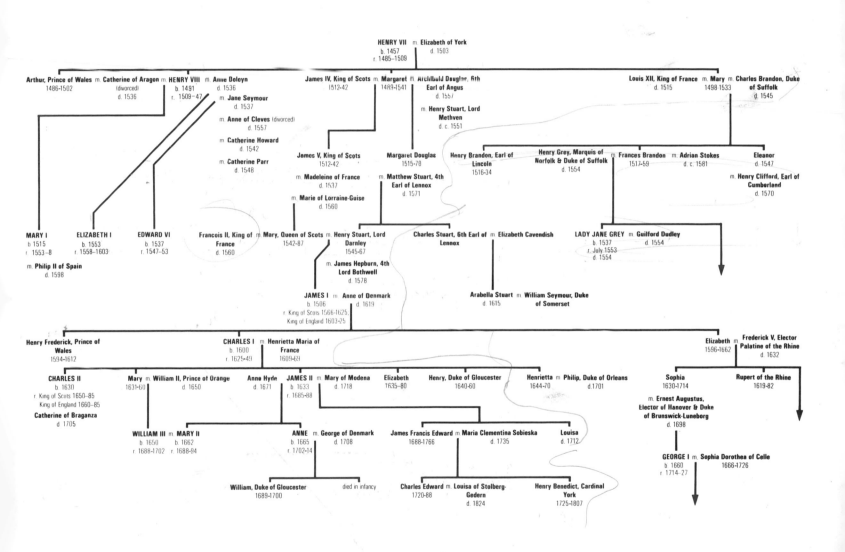

HENRY VII m. Elizabeth of York
b. 1457   d. 1503
r. 1485–1509

Arthur, Prince of Wales m. Catherine of Aragon m. HENRY VIII m. Anne Boleyn
1486-1502   (divorced)   b. 1491   d. 1536
d. 1536   r. 1509–47

James IV, King of Scots m. Margaret m. Archibald Douglas, 6th
1512-42   1489-1541   Earl of Angus
d. 1557

Louis XII, King of France m. Mary m. Charles Brandon, Duke
d. 1515   1498-1533   of Suffolk
d. 1545

m. Jane Seymour
d. 1537

m. Anne of Cleves (divorced)
d. 1557

m. Catherine Howard
d. 1542

m. Catherine Parr
d. 1548

m. Henry Stuart, Lord
Methven
d. c. 1551

James V, King of Scots   Margaret Douglas   Henry Brandon, Earl of   Henry Grey, Marquis of   m. Frances Brandon m. Adrian Stokes   Eleanor
1512-42   1515-78   Lincoln   Norfolk & Duke of Suffolk   1517-59   d. c. 1581   d. 1547
1516-34   d. 1554

m. Madeleine of France   Matthew Stuart, 4th
d. 1537   Earl of Lennox
d. 1571

m. Henry Clifford, Earl of
Cumberland
d. 1570

m. Marie of Lorraine-Guise
d. 1560

MARY I   ELIZABETH I   EDWARD VI   Francois II, King of m. Mary, Queen of Scots m. Henry Stuart, Lord   Charles Stuart, 6th Earl of m. Elizabeth Cavendish   LADY JANE GREY m. Guilford Dudley
b. 1515   b. 1553   b. 1537   France   1542-87   Darnley   Lennox   b. 1537   d. 1554
r. 1553–8   r. 1558–1603   r. 1547–53   d. 1560   1545-67   r. July 1553
d. 1554

m. Philip II of Spain
d. 1598

m. James Hepburn, 4th
Lord Bothwell
d. 1578

JAMES I m. Anne of Denmark   Arabella Stuart m. William Seymour, Duke
b. 1506   d. 1619   d. 1615   of Somerset
r. King of Scots 1566-1625,
King of England 1603-25

Henry Frederick, Prince of   CHARLES I m. Henrietta Maria of   Elizabeth m. Frederick V, Elector
Wales   b. 1600   France   1596-1662   Palatine of the Rhine
1594-1612   r. 1625-49   1609-69   d. 1632

CHARLES II   Mary m. William II, Prince of Orange   Anne Hyde   JAMES II m. Mary of Modena   Elizabeth   Henry, Duke of Gloucester   Henrietta m. Philip, Duke of Orleans   Sophia   Rupert of the Rhine
b. 1630   1631-60   d. 1650   d. 1671   b. 1633   d. 1718   1635–80   1640-60   1644-70   d.1701   1630-1714   1619-82
r. King of Scots 1650–85   r. 1685-88
King of England 1660-85

Catherine of Braganza
d. 1705

m. Ernest Augustus,
Elector of Hanover & Duke
of Brunswick-Luneborg
d. 1698

WILLIAM III m. MARY II   ANNE m. George of Denmark   James Francis Edward m. Maria Clementina Sobieska   Louisa
b. 1650   b. 1662   b. 1665   d. 1708   1688-1766   d. 1735   d. 1712
r. 1688-1702   r. 1688-94   r. 1702-14

GEORGE I m. Sophia Dorothea of Celle
b. 1660   1666-1726
r. 1714-27

William, Duke of Gloucester   died in infancy   Charles Edward m. Louisa of Stolberg-   Henry Benedict, Cardinal
1689-1700   Gedern   York
1720-88   d. 1824   1725-1807

185

THE HOUSE OF HANOVER

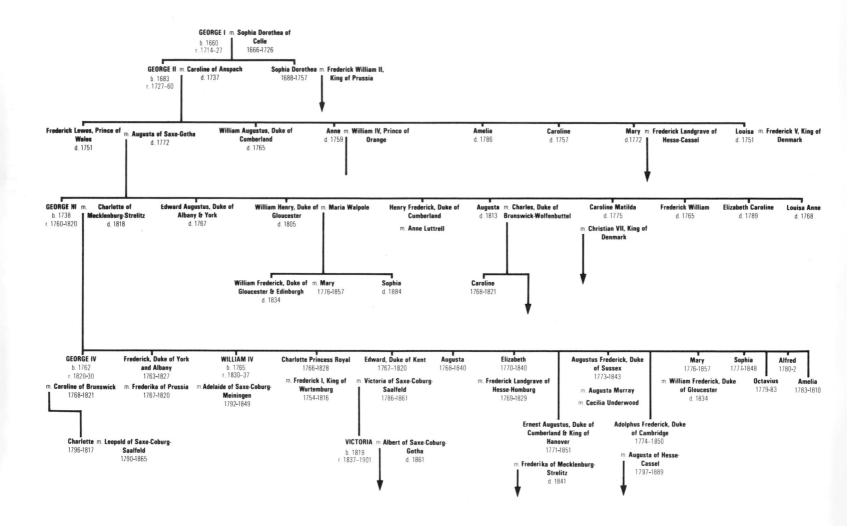

THE HOUSES OF SAXE-COBURG-GOTHA AND WINDSOR

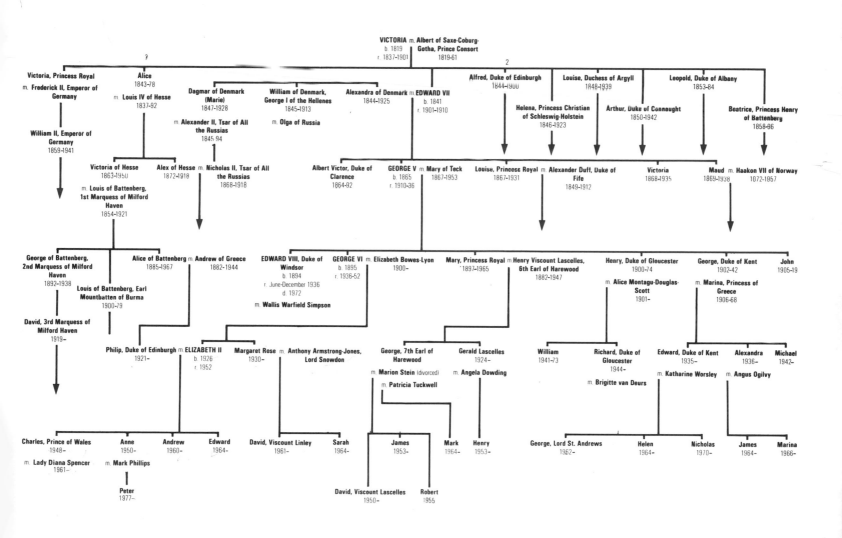

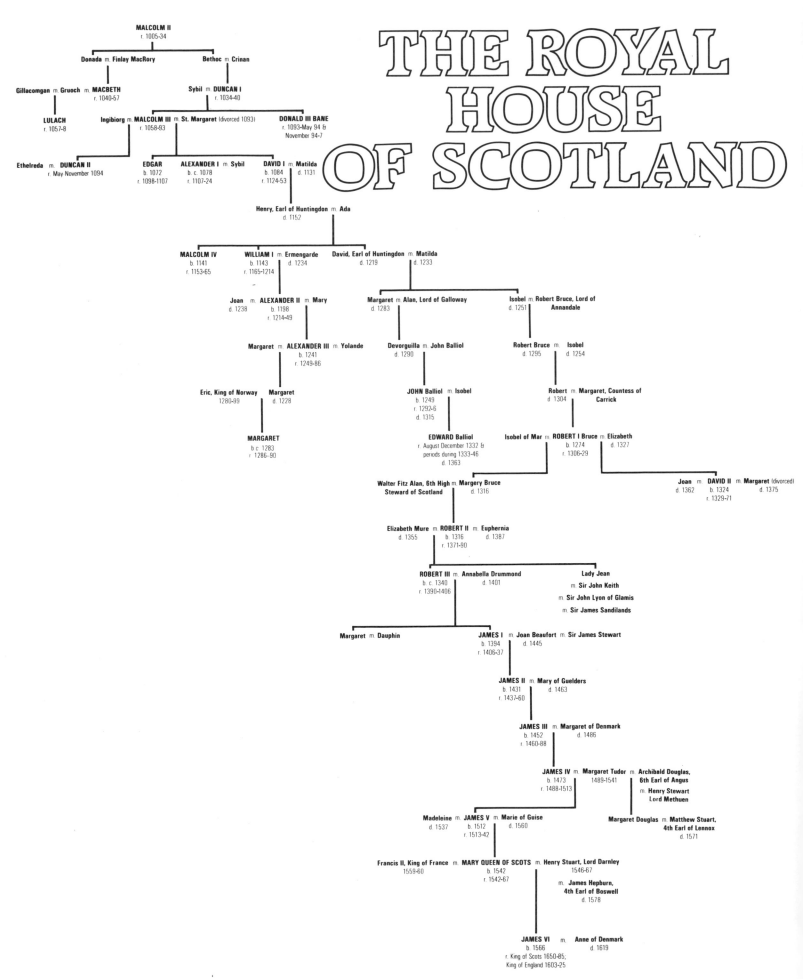

THE ROYAL HOUSE OF SCOTLAND

INDEX